"A gem of a book! Flip to any page and you'll find practical, well-researched examples of how to reach the public where they're at right now and steer them toward more compassionate, sustainable behaviors. Changing hearts and minds just got a whole lot easier!"

—**Judy Wicks**, co-founder,
Business Alliance for Local Living Economies (BALLE)

"*Change of Heart* has helped my understanding not only of how the public reacts to the labor movement and workers' rights, but how our own members will be motivated and empowered to take action as well. A concise and complete handbook for anyone looking to get their message to the masses effectively."

—**Dena Fleno**, Council 4 AFSCME Union

"If we want to create a more compassionate world, we need to understand what motivates people to make compassionate choices. *Change of Heart* provides fresh, research-based insight into how non-profits and individuals can more effectively create social change through a better understanding of the human mind."

—**Gene Baur**, Director, Farm Sanctuary

"Social justice advocates often lack the research needed to support successful campaigns. Cooney helps fill in this gap by culling the social-psychology research and teaching non-profits and grassroots organizations how to develop more effective campaigns."

—**Carol Glasser**, Humane Research Council

"Finally, an effective grassroots activist tells us directly and simply how to win a campaign and the hearts and minds of the public. Read this book and act!"

—**Anthony J. Nocella, II**, co-editor of
Igniting a Revolution: Voices in Defense of the Earth

"One thing is clear about this century. We have to fast-track changes in our relations with, and practices toward, other species. Nick Cooney has provided us with important food for thought in examining how we might intensify the process."

—**Richard Twine PhD.**, author of *Animals as Biotechnology:
Ethics, Sustainability and Critical Animal Studies*

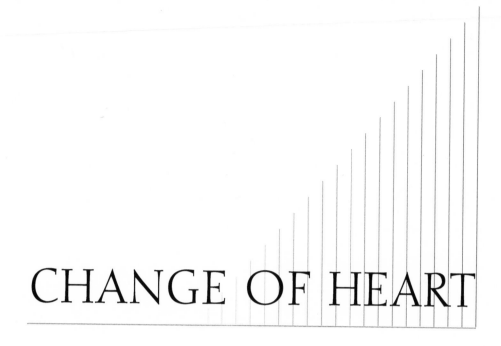

CHANGE OF HEART

WHAT PSYCHOLOGY CAN TEACH US ABOUT SPREADING SOCIAL CHANGE

NICK COONEY

Lantern Books ● New York
A Division of Booklight, Inc.

2011
Lantern Books
128 Second Place
Brooklyn, NY 11231
www.lanternbooks.com

Printed in the United States of America
Library of Congress Cataloging-in-Publication Data

Cooney, Nick.
Change of heart : what psychology can teach us about creating social change / Nick Cooney.
p. cm.
ISBN-13: 978-1-59056-233-8 (alk. paper)
ISBN-10: 1-59056-233-X (alk. paper)
1. Social change—Psychological aspects. 2. Social action—Psychological aspects. 3. Influence (Psychology) 4. Persuasion (Psychology) I. Title.
HM831.C67 2010
303.4—dc22
2010029718

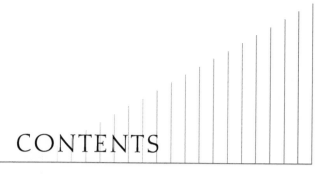

CONTENTS

INTRODUCTION

THIS IS A BOOK ABOUT CREATING SOCIAL CHANGE. PEOPLE who work to change society are often called *activists*, though they may not think of themselves in that way. They may call themselves community organizers, volunteers, or nonprofit employees, or they may not call themselves anything at all. What they all have in common is that they want a change: they want people to change their behavior, institutions to change their policies, and governments to change their laws. This book is about how to create change, particularly in individuals. If you're seeking a more compassionate world, consider this a psychological road map.

Over the past decade, my advocacy work has taken me from the woods of Oregon to the villages of Mexico, from the streets of San Francisco to jail cells in Washington D.C. While the vast majority of my time is now spent on animal protection work as director of The Humane League, this book was written for progressive activists of all stripes. It won't give solutions to every problem, but it will examine why people are so resistant to change and discuss tools of influence that can be used to help people adopt more compassionate behaviors.

SHOULD ACTIVISTS USE graphic images to get public support for their cause, or will such images turn the public off?

In encouraging people to adopt sustainable behaviors, should environmental organizations ask for small changes like using fluorescent light bulbs or big changes like giving up cars?

Why do most Americans say they oppose the cruel practices of factory farms and sweatshops yet still buy products from these places?

And how can non-profits get more people to say "yes" to requests that they volunteer, donate, recycle, write a letter to a political prisoner, support gay rights, go vegetarian, conserve energy, or make other positive changes?

Questions like these are debated by activists all the time, sometimes causing serious divisions among organizations that have similar goals but different viewpoints on how to get there. Typically such debates are viewed as opinion questions, with anecdotal evidence to support both sides but no definitive answers. But is that really the case? If experimental research was done that found answers to these questions and dozens more like them, would you want to know the results? If research proved certain techniques to be effective at changing people's behaviors, would you want to know what those techniques were?

In his bestselling book *The Tipping Point*, sociologist Malcolm Gladwell notes that "We have an innate belief that a dogged and indiscriminate application of effort is best and will work—it is not, and will not, and often is not even possible" (Gladwell). While his statement is directed toward the general public, it holds particularly true for those who are trying to create social change. Lawyers, teachers, and other professionals study for years to learn the bodies of knowledge needed to succeed in their fields, yet activists and many advocacy organizations (especially smaller grassroots groups) often assume that passion, sweat, and a few tried-and-true campaign methods are all they need to be effective.

Attention is sometimes paid to the how to's of activism: books, websites, and workshops provide guides on how to stage protests, pass out flyers, circulate petitions, recruit volunteers, build coalitions, and contact the media. But what's really at the heart of social change is an entire field of knowledge largely ignored by the activist community: the area of human psychology.

If we want to change society, the only way we can do so is by changing the attitudes and behaviors of human beings. To do that, we need to know how to work with (and sometimes work around) the human mind and all of its eccentricities. The more we understand how people's minds work, the more influential we will be in changing behaviors and the more successful we will be at winning campaigns. A truly effective activist is a psychologist at heart.

Most of us assume we know enough about how the brain works to get by. After all, we all have one. But much of our common-sense knowledge in this area is "naïve psychology," misperceptions about how the mind works. These misperceptions reduce our effectiveness in creating change, and in some cases they will prevent us from creating any change whatsoever. In the worst scenarios, they'll cause us to bring about the exact opposite of what we're trying to achieve.

Fortunately, a wealth of scientific research exists that gives insight into how the human mind works. This research can tell us where attitudes and behaviors come from, how they spread through society, why people are resistant to change, and how we can influence people to adopt more compassionate behaviors. It can provide clear answers to the questions presented earlier, as well as many others.

In the following chapters we'll discuss the highlights of a hundred years of peer-reviewed experimental research in areas including social psychology, behavioral science, personality psychology, persuasion science, network science, diffusion science, and social marketing. While scientific research is fallible, and future research will surely provide corrections to some of the results reported here, using the research currently available will get us a lot further than relying on our own assumptions and so-called common sense.

If you want to be as influential an activist as possible, read on. The research has been done and the lessons are clear. It's up to us to learn them and to put them into practice so that we can more successfully create the world we wish to see.

chapter one

LOOKING INWARD

IF WE WANT TO INFLUENCE OTHER PEOPLE, WE NEED TO KNOW how they operate. We wouldn't get in a car and drive to an unfamiliar town without first getting directions, and likewise we can't expect to switch people from one behavior to another without understanding how the human mind works. But even before discussing that, there's a first and perhaps more important step: understanding ourselves. Why are we activists in the first place? What motivates us to pick the particular cause we focus on? And how do we judge whether we've succeeded in our work? The answers are not nearly as simple—or logical—as we'd like to believe.

SELF-IDENTITY AND ACTIVISM

In 2008, the Philadelphia Phillies baseball team won the World Series, becoming the first Philadelphia sports team to win a national championship in twenty-five years. Fans filled the streets, shouting, cheering, setting off fireworks, and giving high fives to total strangers into the early morning hours. In a few spots around the city, cars were overturned and lightposts came crashing down after revelers climbed up them to wave Phillies flags and chant "Phillies, Phillies!" (As a matter of fact, this happened so much that when the Phillies went back to the World Series in 2009, the Philadelphia police department greased all the polls on one major street to prevent fans from climbing up them.)

A few days later, a victory parade made its way through Philadelphia, with onlookers shouting to one another and to TV cameras that it was the greatest day of their lives. That the fans themselves had accomplished nothing and that their personal lives had not changed one bit didn't reduce the euphoria they felt. For many fans, the Phillies were such an important part of their self-identity that the team's victory felt like their own.

Self-identity plays a crucial role in the actions of all people, including those of us who consider ourselves activists. The work we do as advocates for a particular cause often makes up a significant part of our self-identity. If we were asked to describe ourselves, we'd say we're anti-war or animal rights activists, environmentalists, anarchists, pacifists, or labor organizers. This intertwining of activism and our self-identity can have beneficial effects. For example, it provides a strong internal motivation for us to keep going even in the face of disillusionment, just as die-hard Phillies fans remained true to the team despite years of failure (Pilliavin, Grube, and Callero 2002). Unfortunately, it can also have a negative impact on the effectiveness of our activism.

Eight years ago, as a college senior at Hofstra University, I had a little game I used to play with an unfortunate sales rep from CitiBank who would set up a table in the school's student center each week to promote student bank accounts. At the time, the environmental organization Rainforest Action Network had a campaign in full swing to get CitiGroup (the parent company of CitiBank) to commit to no longer investing in environmentally disastrous development projects around the world. Our campus social justice group was involved with the campaign, in part because CitiBank had a contract with Hofstra wherein they were the only bank whose representatives, ATMs, or services were allowed on campus. Our hope was to kick CitiBank off campus, or at least shame them for their involvement in environmental destruction and make enough of a ruckus that word traveled up the corporate ladder.

Whenever the sales rep would come to campus and set up a table I would don a ratty old shirt on which I'd scrawled, in permanent marker, the words "Fuck CitiBank." I would then grab a stack of photocopied flyers and stand directly in front of the woman's table, passing out flyers and telling other students not to open CitiBank accounts. While I certainly had an effect on this woman (she eventually stopped coming back to campus) and perhaps by extension a very small impact on CitiBank, I doubt I provided much more than comic relief to most of the students who saw me standing in front of the table.

Why? Because I looked like the stereotypical hippie college activist (not to mention being a jerk for standing right in front of the woman's table). If the ratty shirt with permanent marker scrawled across it wasn't enough, the equally tattered pants, beard, and unwashed shoulder-length hair certainly completed the package. At the time, I didn't think about how my appearance might impact the persuasiveness of my message. But that year Dan Firger, a campaigner from the Rainforest Action Network who'd come to campus to speak about the CitiGroup campaign, shared a story that's stuck with me ever since:

A long-time environmental activist was speaking to an enthusiastic group of young environmentalists at a rally. He warned of the precarious situation the environment was in, the toll that corporate greed had taken on forests, and the dire consequences that lay ahead if serious changes were not made.

He then shouted out to the crowd, "Are you ready to get out there and fight for the environment?"

To which they answered an enthusiastic, "Yeah!"

"Are you ready to get arrested and go to jail for the environment?"

"Yeah!!"

"Are you ready to give your life for the environment?"

"Yeah!!!"

"Are you willing to cut your hair and put on a suit for the environment?"

The crowd fell silent.

Whether this is a true story or just a colorful fable, the lesson is one we should all take to heart. How we look and dress is intimately tied up with our self-identity. How we look and dress also has a significant impact on how persuasive we will be and therefore how effective we will be at creating change. Abandoning an aspect of self-identity in order to be more effective at protecting the environment (or animals or people) can be a lot harder than it seems for those who've never had to make such a decision.

Doing so can be particularly hard when you're a member of a subculture that has its own style of dress and appearance. Here, making a change in appearance doesn't just mean abandoning part of your self-identity; it also means abandoning the social signifiers of a group identity. An anarchist who cuts off their dreadlocks and discards their patched black clothing in favor of khaki pants and a sweater vest is going to be more effective at persuading the public and winning campaigns, but they're also going to feel a bit disconnected from their fellow anarchists. They may no longer "feel" like an anarchist—and may feel that a part of who they are has been lost. It took me a year and a half to shave off my beard and wear more conventional clothes, and a few more years to finally cut my hair short.

It seems unfair that we should have to alter our tastes in fashion, hairstyle, and the like just because people have biases against others who look different from them. After all, isn't judging people based on their appearance (some call it "lookism") a social problem in and of itself? Whether or not the situation is fair, the reality is that those biases exist and will continue to exist for many years to come. If we don't alter our appearance to be as persuasive as possible with those we're seeking to influence on our main issue, we won't be fighting one battle, we'll be fighting two at the same time—and chances are we'll lose both. The psychologically difficult but practically simple action of altering our appearance won't lessen our quality of life by any significant measure, but it really can (and if we're doing thoughtful outreach and campaigning, it really will) mean a life-or-death difference for other people, for animals, and for portions of the ecosystem.

In addition to considering the consequences our appearance has on our advocacy, we also need to consider the consequences our emotions have. Just as wearing whatever we like may seem justifiable but won't lead to the best results for our cause, saying whatever we feel and acting out our emotions may seem justifiable but will usually not lead to the best results.

Being competent at something makes us feel good, and can be a powerful motivator for us to continue moving forward with our work. But the more negative aspects of self-identity—egos, jealousies, and other insecurities—need to be checked at the door when making decisions and interacting with others. Letting ourselves be steered by old emotional scars, by insecurities we have about our self-worth, or by egoistic desires to be praised for our work will have very negative consequences for our effectiveness.

You may have already encountered activists living out these negative aspects of self-identity: the woman who constantly criticizes other organizations in order to feel better about her own efforts; the man intent on appearing more in-the-know than those around him; the woman whose hatred of something (capitalism, animal abusers, logging companies, etc.) is fueled by childhood abuse that makes her lash out at whoever she perceives to be the bad guy; the man who joins an activist group or subculture in order to find social acceptance; the woman whose activism is driven more by personal problems like depression or alienation than by compassion.

Paying close attention to our motivations can be upsetting because we're steered by these insecurities more often than we'd like to admit. Remembering that lives really are on the line should give us the push we need to work toward the self-understanding and self-control needed to be effective advocates.

Emotional self-control is particularly important when deciding how to go about our activism. For example, it's tempting to choose tactics that are the most personally satisfying for us: holding a noisy protest so we can vent our anger and frustration on an issue, or writing letters to congresspersons because it's an easy way to announce our opinions. We also have an instinctive response to snap back at those who argue with our viewpoint. Doing so feels good because we get to express ourselves and garner a sense of power; absorbing the insult without lashing back doesn't feel good at all.

In these types of situations, the question we need to ask ourselves is not "What do I want to do?" or "What does this person deserve?" but "What will be most effective for helping those whom I'm trying to help?" Are we as activists willing to keep our anger and passion in check so that we're directing them rather than they directing us? Are we willing to put those we hope to help ahead of our own desires for self-expression, for standing up for ourselves, and for loudly proclaiming what we believe regardless of how others will respond? Are we willing to go beyond the comfortable boundaries of our current self-identity in order to be as effective as possible?

A substantial amount of activism is reactionary in nature: an event occurs that upsets us and makes us want to protest, write angry letters to the editor, and otherwise voice our disapproval. Once our cause has become a part of our self-identity, our instincts tell us to lash out when that which we oppose pops up in the headlines or in our neighborhood.

In August of 2009, the Philadelphia Eagles football team hired Michael Vick to fill the slot of backup quarterback. Vick was a standout player with his former team, the Atlanta Falcons, so his acquisition would normally have been seen as a great move by Eagles fans. Yet there was one notable difference between Vick and the other new players hired that year: Vick had just been released from federal prison after spending nearly two years behind bars for running an interstate dog-fighting ring called the Bad Newz Kennels. He'd financed the operations himself, and had directly participated in the fighting and execution of dogs.

While some in Philadelphia supported the hiring of Michael Vick, the majority lashed out in angry protest at the Eagles management. Protests were held outside the Eagles stadium during pre-season games. Pet supply stores began carrying shirts that said "Lock up your hounds, Vick's in town," and selling chew toys shaped like a Michael Vick jersey. Letters criticizing the team filled local newspapers and calls poured in to radio talk shows. In a bid to stave off some of the bad publicity, the Eagles launched a new program offering hundreds of thousands of dollars in grants to area animal protection agencies.

Public outcry against the arrival of a loathed person or group is nothing new. When Ku Klux Klan or neo-Nazi groups visit a city to hold a rally they're often met with angry counter-protests. Unpopular politicians, religious leaders, and executives are sometimes given the same treatment. Reactionary activism such as this has some benefit in that it displays social disapproval for a policy, and it may keep an issue in the public's mind. But it typically fails in regards to the issue it's directly addressing (for example, getting the Eagles to fire Vick, or forcing the KKK to stay out of one's town), because the undesirable event has already occurred and little has been done to prevent it from happening again.

In the case of Michael Vick, the outcry didn't change the Eagles' decision (in 2010 the organization renewed Vick's contract). Nor did it bring back the dogs who'd suffered and died at Vick's hands. Vick's prison term and post-conviction financial collapse had already sent a clear message to other professional athletes that it was in their own best interest to have no part in dog fighting; the threat of public scorn was not likely to provide much additional incentive. In fact, Vick's teammates unanimously selected him for the 2009 Ed Block Courage Award, an honor given to players who show a commitment to sportsmanship and courage.

Reactionary campaigning, such as what happened when Michael Vick was hired by the Eagles, is motivated largely by our own instinctual emotional reactions to situations and often fails to produce change. The better alternative for achieving specific changes is proactive campaigning, where we calmly examine the lay of the land in regard to a particular issue, figure out where and when we will be able to have the greatest impact, and then move forward accordingly.

Philadelphians who are really opposed to dog-fighting could take some time to learn how, where, and why dog fighting occurs, and then figure out how they can best intervene. They might work with the SPCA to help identify dog-fighting rings more quickly, provide a tip line offering financial incentives for people who report such rings, or work to develop a foster network so rescued pit bulls can be saved instead of euthanized. Any of these actions would have done more good for dogs than simply venting anger at Vick and the Eagles. Similarly, those protesting a Klan rally could do much more to advance racial equality by focusing on issues where racial disparity still exists, such as differing pay scales for equal work, or by laying the educational groundwork to prevent children from developing the same racist views as Klan members.

Proactive campaigning takes a lot more thought and effort than reactionary campaigning. It also takes emotional self-control. Instead of instinctively lashing out to condemn the most visible symbols of that which we oppose, we need to restrain ourselves and focus on how we can best address the root causes of the problem.

Thinking critically about how effective we're being and whether we can find ways to be more effective also requires us to face another challenge. Once our activist work has become tied to our self-identity, how are we going to respond if faced with evidence that our work is not achieving very much?

The more we've emotionally invested in something, the more highly we value it and believe it to be right. This makes it very difficult to abandon campaigns and strategies even when (as would be obvious to an impartial outsider) they're deeply flawed. If we are strongly invested in a cause, as many activists are, it becomes tied up with our identity to such an extent that any criticism of our advocacy methods feels like a criticism of us; any thought that the campaign we're working on is flawed carries the implication that we ourselves are flawed.

Researcher Daniel Batson of the University of Kansas wanted to test how people would respond when confronted with evidence that an important element of their self-identity was flawed. To do this, he approached a Presbyterian church in New Jersey with an interesting request: allow him and his research team to visit the church to test how religious beliefs might withstand evidence that contradicted those beliefs. In order to stimulate discussion on the issue of faith and doubt, the church agreed and fifty teenagers in the church's youth group volunteered to take part in Batson's study.

Participants were brought into the research room and asked to sit down in one of two distinctly marked areas: one area for those who believed that Jesus was God, and one area for those who didn't. After the participants were seated, they were given questionnaires to determine how strongly they believed that Jesus was God (I'm using the capital G here because it's the common spelling, not because I hold a religious belief). After the questionnaires were collected, Batson dropped a bombshell on the church-group members: the *New York Times* was sitting on a story that threatened the very foundations of Christianity. Scrolls had been discovered in the Jordanian desert that turned out to be letters from Jesus' disciples to one another discussing how Jesus did not rise from the dead. The letters read in part:

> *Since our great teacher, Jesus of Nazareth, was killed by the Romans, I am sure we were justified in stealing away his body and claiming that he rose from the dead. For, although his death clearly proves he was not the Son of God as we had hoped, if we did not claim that he was, both his great teaching and our lives as his disciples would be wasted!*

Radiocarbon dating and close examination of the dialect used revealed the letters to be authentic, said Batson. The *New York Times* was holding back on printing the article at the request of the World Council of Churches, and was surveying the public to see what impact this information would have if it were released. Having revealed this shocking information, Batson then polled participants a second time to see if they believed the article to be a true story and to see if the article had shifted their beliefs about the divinity of Jesus.

As you probably guessed, Batson's story was a fraud. There was no such discovery and no such article. Batson's goal was to see how church-group members would respond when their lifelong belief that Jesus was God was confronted with hard evidence that this was not the case. If humans were perfectly logical creatures, then belief should have declined. The results, however, told a very different story.

For participants who were non-believers or weak believers (and who believed the *New York Times* story to be authentic), there was indeed a slight reduction in the belief that Jesus was God. But for those who were strong believers (and who also believed the *Times* article was authentic), their belief that Jesus was God actually grew stronger! Why would this be the case?

Put yourself inside the subconscious minds of the believing church-group members as they hear the story indicating that Jesus was not God. Now they they've received this information, what should they do? It would seem irrational for them to change beliefs that they've held so deeply for so many years after a mere five-minute conversation with a researcher. Furthermore, if Jesus was not God then many of their prayers, efforts, and beliefs up until that time had been misguided and perhaps meaningless. "Publicly committed to an apparently untenable belief, subjects seemed more concerned with defending and justifying themselves than with dispassionately reading off the logical implications of their statements," wrote Batson. In order to defend themselves against this new and threatening information, church-group members who already believed that Jesus was God had to become even more positive that this was true (Batson 1975).

The same phenomenon has been observed a number of times with doomsday cults. Common sense would suggest that when doomsday prophecies fail to materialize, most members would realize their beliefs were faulty and leave the cult. Conversely, on many occasions cult members have experienced even stronger belief and renewed fervor in spreading their message to others after their doomsday predictions failed to materialize.

The increased faith experienced by church members and cult members in these situations was probably not consciously chosen—it was the automatic process of cognitive dissonance. Cognitive dissonance is the feeling that arises when we perceive a disjunction between our beliefs and our behaviors. Most of us feel a strong need for self-consistency, for our behaviors to match up with our stated beliefs. When they don't—when our beliefs seem out of line with our behaviors—we'll often respond in irrational ways.

Some parents, when confronted with evidence that their teenage child is having sex or using drugs, will respond by clinging even more firmly to the belief that their child would never do things like that. They may lash out at teachers who raise the issue or blame one of their child's friends for any perceived wrongdoing that might have happened. Parents like these will often fail to speak to their children about sex or drug use, since doing so would be admitting their child might possibly be involved with these things—a thought too frightening to accept.

Cognitive dissonance plays a significant role in many of the decisions people make throughout their lives. When we as activists are confronted with evidence that our hard work is not paying off, or that the methods we're using may not be the most effective ones, it takes serious mental discipline to make sure we don't respond in the way that our mind instinctively wants to: clinging even more firmly to our failed methods. I myself have been in this position in the past, holding on too long to a campaign that wasn't worth waging because I'd already invested so much of myself in it.

The activist community is filled with organizers who've learned one or two methods of campaigning and one or two issues that can be campaigned about, and who stick with those methods and issues for countless years regardless of their level of success. Such decisions may be due in part to limited experience, and in part to the human tendency to fall into comfortable routines. But cognitive dissonance plays a role as well. Faced with evidence that we aren't being as effective as possible, or that we could do more good by working on another issue or using another tactic, we inevitably find justifications for why we should continue down our current path: "This is what I know how to do," "This is what's right for me," "This really will succeed soon," "Someone has to do this work," etc.

The intertwining of our activist work and our self-identity can have both positive and negative consequences. On the one hand, helping others can become part of who we are, which can provide a strong motivation to keep going in our valuable work. On the other hand, we need to pay careful attention to whether aspects of our identities are getting in the way of our being as effective as possible. Specifically, we should watch whether our personal styles of dress and appearance, emotional reactions, or desires to express our beliefs are preventing us from being as influential as possible. We also need to carefully consider whether we're judging the effectiveness of our work logically or whether we've become so personally invested in it that we've lost the ability to think critically and switch directions (sometimes dramatically) when doing so would lead to better results.

MORE STUMBLING BLOCKS

Self-identity isn't the only psychological stumbling block that can make us less effective in our activism. Consider for a moment how you came to be doing the type of activist work you're doing now. Which of the following better describes what led you down this path?

(a) One day, or perhaps over a period of time, you thought to yourself: "I don't like suffering and injustice. I don't like unnecessary death and destruction. How can I reduce as much suffering and destruction of life as possible?"

(b) Personal or circumstantial reasons led you to do the type of work you do: the issue is interesting to you, the issue affects you and your loved ones personally, your friends are involved in this type of work, you had been hearing about it a lot in the media, etc.

Chances are that most of us came to be involved in the work we're doing for personal or circumstantial reasons. It's much rarer that someone will make a dispassionate decision to try to create as much change as possible, as described in scenario (a).

The causes that people work for often have an element of self-interest. For example, most gay rights activists are gay, most civil-rights activists are African-American or Latino, and most people participating in breast-cancer walks know someone with breast cancer. Even when causes don't directly relate to self-interest, people are much more likely to embrace issues that affect those similar to them. Ninety-eight percent of donations made in the U.S. go toward human issues (health, social services, arts, religious, and educational organizations) with only two percent going to environmental and animal protection organizations, despite the catastrophic state of our ecosystem and the fact that animals experience pain and suffering and have virtually no legal protection (Charity Navigator 2010). Furthermore, of the donations that do go to animal protection organizations, the overwhelming majority go to groups working to help the types of animals that people are most familiar with (cats and dogs), even though other animals (farmed, laboratory, and fur-bearing) suffer much more and in vastly higher numbers. Similarly, Americans give significantly more money to U.S.-based charities than they do to international ones, even though the suffering of people in developing countries is exponentially greater than that of most people in the U.S. Studies have shown that people are more likely to help those similar to them in dress, attitude, nationality, and other related attributes (Dovidio 1984).

This *bias of concern* likely stems in part from evolutionary biology: caring about those similar to us helps pass our genetic material along to future generations, while caring for those very different from us does not. The bias of concern also reflects cultural values. Americans have some concern for domestic animals like cats and dogs but little concern for farm animals, placing these types of animals in two different ethical boxes. People view human causes as inherently valuable, while they view environmental issues as only marginally important, quickly ignoring them when they interfere with short-term human benefit.

People also gravitate toward flashpoint issues that either receive a significant amount of media coverage or are hot-button concerns in that person's social group. As a general psychological principle—called the *availability bias*—people perceive something as more valuable the more they've heard of it (Schwarz *et al.* 2007). This is as true for the activist cause we choose to work on as it is for the brands of soda we buy and the artists that we choose to admire. As a result, societal issues that already get a lot of attention tend to stay popular, and often serve as a point of entry for new activists. Current hot-button issues include the Israel–Palestine conflict, whatever war the U.S. is currently engaged in, the prisoner Mumia Abu-Jamal, anti-globalization activism, and pro-life and pro-choice activism.

Issues that are confrontational are more likely to be covered by the media, and therefore be seen as more important by budding activists. Many issues that cause a vast amount of suffering get little attention because they are systemic problems and there are no dramatic events occurring to thrust them into the spotlight. Activists are therefore likely to ignore some of the most serious problems and focus instead on the most confrontational.

Those of us who are activists probably consider ourselves altruistic people because we hope to make the world a better place, but our decisions about what issues to work on are strongly mediated by perceptual biases. These biases lead us to prioritize issues that have an element of self-interest, issues that involve others who are similar to us (probably people), and issues that are popular either in general society or in our social group. It is personal and circumstantial factors that have most likely led us to the social cause we're engaged in.

Is that a problem? After all, what's important is that we're activists and that we're doing good work, right? Since there's so much work that needs to be done, doesn't it make sense to focus on the issues that matter most to us?

Working on issues that affect us, that our friends work on, or that captivate our attention form good starting points for realizing the importance of working to create social change. It is to effective activism what recycling is to an environmentally sustainable lifestyle: it's the place that pretty much everyone starts out at. But it shouldn't be an endpoint. Once we've developed the spirit of social concern, once we've seen the value in working to create a better world, we need to move forward in becoming more thoughtful about how we spend the limited amount of time and energy we have. We need to begin choosing our activist work from a utilitarian perspective: How can I do the most good? How can I reduce the most suffering and destruction of life?

Slogans like "practice random acts of kindness" feel good and are easy to put into practice. But if we don't take our activism more seriously than that, our motive is probably a desire to feel good about ourselves, to help ourselves or those close to us, or to act out our self-identity. The endpoint of authentic compassion is a desire to do the most good that one can, to be as effective as possible in creating a world with less suffering and destruction and more joy. Figuring out how we can do the most good takes careful thought over a long period of time, and it means moving into new and possibly uncomfortable areas of advocacy. But the importance of taking our activism seriously and approaching it from this utilitarian perspective cannot be overstated. It will mean a difference between life and death, between happiness and suffering, for thousands of people, for thousands of acres of the ecosystem, and for tens of thousands of animals.

As we move toward this more thoughtful approach to activism, the question becomes: How can we do the most good?

THE BOTTOM LINE

Once we as activists have decided that we want to do the most good we can, the next step is figuring out how to quantify the amount of good we're doing now and compare it to the amount of good we could be doing by using other tactics, engaging in other campaigns, or working on other issues entirely. Quantifying the results of our work is incredibly important for every activist and non-profit; without it, our decisions will be guided by the powerful perceptual biases discussed earlier, making us dramatically less effective than we could be.

When I give talks about the Humane League, the non-profit organization I run, I like to point out that, just like a for-profit corporation, we have a bottom line. Only our bottom line is not dollars and cents; it's not shareholder dividends. Our bottom line is measured by two things: the number of animals whose lives we've saved and the amount of animal suffering we've eliminated. We try to make every decision—be it financial, organizational, or campaign-oriented—with an eye toward that bottom line. What is going to do the most good? What is going to give us the greatest return for the limited amount of time, money, and energy that we and our volunteers have?

We closely track the result of each of our programs to determine the number of animals whose lives we've impacted by rescuing them from euthanasia or by reducing or preventing their suffering. While it's not possible to achieve the same precision that a financial bottom line provides to for-profit companies, it's possible to get a very good working estimate of how much we've accomplished. For example, we know that for each person who goes vegetarian or vegan, over forty animals per year will be spared a lifetime of suffering on factory farms (Friedrich and Ball). We can also get a decent estimate of the number of new vegetarians and vegans our different outreach methods have created through follow-up surveys and data collection. By multiplying the two figures together, we get a good estimate of the number of animals who've been spared a great deal of suffering as a result of our work.

At the moment, one of our other main campaigns is getting universities to switch to using cage-free eggs in their dining halls. While cage-free does not mean cruelty-free, when an institution switches to cage-free eggs it does significantly reduce the suffering of hundreds or thousands of egg-laying hens. With each campaign victory, we can use dining services' data to calculate exactly how many hens will benefit from the switch to cage-free.

With both of these activities we can also take the number of animals affected and divide it by the money we spent, and so find out how much we're spending for each life we've been able to impact. While we don't keep formal track of how much time is spent on each activity, that could be factored in as well. With just a little work, we now have a fairly clear picture of what real-world results we've been able to accomplish for animals. More importantly though, we can compare the results of different campaigns and out-reach methods to see which have the biggest payoff for our bottom line of saving lives and reducing suffering.

It's impossible to overstate the importance of creating a bottom line for our activ-ism. Large for-profit corporations, including those that we often find ourselves fighting pitched battles against, spend millions of dollars each year gathering data to compare the success of different approaches in advertising, audience targeting, and product offerings. Imagine what would happen to businesses if, instead of using a financial bottom line to analyze their success, they used the type of information commonly cited by non-profits: anecdotal evidence, raw output, and how much they cared:

Dear Pepsi Shareholders,

This has been a very successful year for us, indeed. We know Pepsi is the best cola out there and this year we spoke truth to power and really told the public that Pepsi was the superior cola. We passed out a lot of flyers that detailed the many reasons that Pepsi is better than Coke: our higher sugar content (yum!), snazzier bottle, and our Pepsi Generation street cred. We also held bi-weekly protests outside the World of Coca Cola Museum in Atlanta, GA. Plus we spent lots of money on advertising, and that means people probably bought more Pepsi. Consider the inspiring story of 58-year-old Mary Clarence of Butte, AZ. She'd been a Coca-Cola drinker her whole life, but thanks to our work she realized that Pepsi really was a better product and now she buys a 12-pack of Pepsi every week from the grocery store! As you can see, we're really moving toward a world where everyone's favorite cola is Pepsi. We've also

got some exciting street theater planned for next year that is really going to stick it to
the Coke drinkers of the world—you're going to love it!

Yours truly,
The Pepsi Collective

As laughable as this sounds coming from the mouth of a large corporation, for most grassroots advocacy organizations this sort of analysis represents the farthest they've gone in measuring their impact. Anecdotes and reports of what was done can't tell us much about how effective we've been and they provide no guidance for how to be more successful in the future. How many people we've gotten to make a lifestyle change (for example, reducing consumption) is harder to track than the number of Pepsis that have been sold—but it is trackable. For small volunteer grassroots groups, a lack of data gathering is somewhat understandable; but even large non-profits often fail to measure their results in any quantifiable way.

A study of 155 foundations with more than one hundred million dollars in assets found that only eight percent could describe the specific types of information or data that led them to believe they were likely to achieve some of their goals. The study, conducted by the Center for Effective Philanthropy, found that instead of hard data most foundations used anecdotal evidence to demonstrate the effectiveness of their programs. Only thirty-nine percent used any tools or indicators whatsoever in assessing even a portion of their work, with even less (twenty-six percent) using indicators or tools to assess all of their work (Mass Nonprofit 2010).

It's true that some non-profit work and some activist campaigns lack the sort of easily identifiable metrics that could be used to define a bottom line. For example, those seeking wide-reaching changes on the political level (such as the anti-war or the pro-Palestine movements) have little to measure other than perhaps whether or not they changed public attitudes on these issues. But because attitudinal change often doesn't lead to behavioral or policy changes (especially on major political issues like these), attitudinal change isn't a good metric to use in analyzing how successful you've been. Of course, as activists we'd like to change people's attitudes; but if attitudinal change doesn't carry over into behavioral or policy change, it means that, at least in the short term, we're not accomplishing anything. This should be factored into our decisions of what campaigns to work on and what tactics to use.

I'm not trying to minimize anyone's efforts at creating a better world. I've been involved in plenty of anti-war activism myself. When the Iraq war began in 2003, myself and a few friends at Hofstra held the biggest protest rallies on campus since the early 1970s, when a campus radical named Norm Coleman shimmied up a flag pole to protest the Vietnam War. (Coleman later went on to become a conservative, pro-war senator from Minnesota, and happened to give the commencement speech at my graduation. In 2009, he was ousted from his senate seat by comedian-turned-politician Al Franken). But in honestly assessing how effective our work is, we need to note that campaigns focused on major political issues sometimes have little or no payoff. We need to keep this in mind when figuring out how to analyze our success, and in deciding what issues to work on. We'll be much more effective by focusing on issues where we can actually change behaviors and policies.

Effective activism starts with a specific goal and ends with measurable results. The animal advocacy projects mentioned earlier offer results that are fairly easy to define, as do others animal advocacy efforts like promoting spaying and neutering, encouraging people not to wear fur, or working to end specific laboratory experiments. Environmental campaigns also usually have definable bottom lines: we can estimate the pounds of recycling diverted from a landfill and the resources that saves; the number of trees that won't be cut down because an institution switched to using recycled paper; and the carbon-dioxide savings of mass transit and bicycling. These measurements can be used whether the focus is on influencing the behaviors of individuals, institutions, or governments.

For social justice issues, campaigns that succeed by changing individual or institutional behaviors can also be easily be measured: for example, how many employers began paying their employees a living wage or how many African children were fed by hunger-relief efforts. An even more thoughtful measurement of hunger-relief efforts would examine whether systemic change has been created to prevent hunger in the first place, as opposed to simply the short-term impact of mouths fed.

The Jameel Poverty Action Lab at the Massachusetts Institute of Technology has applied a bottom-line focus to analyzing poverty-reduction and public-health efforts around the world. Founded by M.I.T. economist Esther Duflo, J-PAL's mission is to conduct randomized trials of aid projects to see which are successful and which aren't. Much like clinical drug testing, J-PAL researchers create both a test group and a control group for a particular project and then analyze what impact the project had.

For example, in trying to prevent the spread of malaria, is it more effective to give away bed nets (which protect people from malaria-carrying mosquitoes) or to sell them at a low price under the assumption that a person is more likely to use a net if they had to purchase it themselves? To find out, researchers divided a segment of Kenya's population into two groups, giving away free nets to the first group and selling the nets at low cost to the second group. Researchers then tracked how many of the nets were put to use and how they impacted the spread of malaria in each of the two groups. The result: Free nets did more to combat the spread of malaria than low-cost nets, at least in Kenya (Parker 2010). J-PAL's scientific analysis on the effectiveness of different aid programs should serve as a model for advocacy organizations. Any non-profit serious about creating social change should be collecting data on how effective their programs are (and whether they're effective at all).

As a side point, in measuring our impact we should compare it against a baseline of what would have happened had we *not* been involved. Even without our work, some people will begin using recycled paper, biking to work, or boycotting sweatshop clothing. Finding out the baseline rate of change is essential for determining what our actual impact was.

If we're focused on our bottom line, then as a general principle we should look for the low-hanging fruit. That doesn't mean working for small changes that only do a marginal amount of good; it means finding the most cost- and time-effective ways of doing good—situations where it's easiest to make significant change. Some people and institutions are going to be more receptive to our message and more likely to change than others, so it makes sense to target them with our efforts. Certain types of behavioral change will do more good than others, and those are the ones we should be emphasizing. Doing so is consistent with focusing on our bottom line.

Likewise, creating systemic change will almost always do more good than caring for individuals who are in need. I mentioned earlier how the Humane League is able to calculate a working number of the animals we've been able to impact. By taking the number of animals impacted and dividing it by our expenditures, we found that in 2009 we spent about fifty-five cents for each animal whose life we impacted by reducing or eliminating their suffering (and for a small portion of those animals by rescuing them). In examining a similar cost-per-animal result for a Pennsylvania animal shelter, we found that they spent about $280 per animal impacted. Granted there's a difference between saving a shelter dog from euthanasia and reducing an animal's suffering or preventing it from being born into a life of misery; one could make the claim that either of those does more good than the other. But no one can make the claim that rescuing a shelter dog does five hundred times more good than sparing a pig from a lifetime of daily misery.

Nevertheless, shelter work dominates the animal protection field in comparison to farm animal–protection issues, even though the former costs (in this comparison) five hundred times more per animal. While this example comes from the animal advocacy movement, similarly vast disparities are apparent if you examine the comparative outputs of different environmental protection and human rights/social justice organizations. As was mentioned earlier, creating systemic change so that fewer people are facing hunger can do far more good than feeding a certain number of hungry people each day. Increasing the use of recycled paper products by major corporations is likely to prevent more deforestation than trying to prevent a specific area of land from being clear-cut.

These facts aren't presented to glorify some organizations over others, but simply to demonstrate that choosing campaigns based on the impact they have on our bottom line can make us exponentially more effective. If each one of us really wants to do the most good possible during the short time we have to live, we need always to be mindful of the alternative routes of activism available to us and whether those alternative routes would produce more good than what we're doing now. Some environmental campaigners have switched over to population-control work because they realized that they might be able to have more of an impact for the planet by reducing birth rates (and subsequently reducing resource use) than through traditional environmental advocacy methods. PETA Vice-President Bruce Friedrich worked in a homeless soup kitchen for many years until he realized he had the ability to reduce much more pain and suffering and save many more lives by focusing on animal protection issues.

Attitudes such as "do something, do anything," or "do what is right and let the ripples fall where they may" may sound nice and may make us feel good about ourselves, and they're better than nothing. But when it comes to our activism, lives really hang in the balance. If we truly care about others, then we need to be responsible and put in the mental effort necessary to figure out how we can do the most good. A good parent doesn't just perform "random acts of kindness" for their child. Nor does a good parent just show up once a week to hold a sign for two hours letting the child know they're loved. A good parent takes time to read up on child psychology, learns the different developmental stages and the best ways to raise a happy child, and puts that knowledge into practice every day. We need to be just as thoughtful in our activism, for not just one but many lives hang in the balance.

As Bruce Friedrich and Matt Ball put it in *The Animal Activist's Handbook*:

> Given our limited time and resources, as well as our inherent biases, we should make our choices based on reducing as much suffering and increasing as much happiness as possible, remembering that when we choose to do one thing we're choosing to not do another. Simply making the "right" choice for ourself isn't enough. By influencing others, we can make the impact of our lives exponentially greater.

chapter two

THE UPHILL BATTLE

IF YOU LIVE IN OR HAVE EVER VISITED A MAJOR CITY, YOU'VE certainly encountered the homeless. Many people react to their presence with a mixture of curiosity from afar and, when they get close, a desire to avoid making eye-contact so they don't get asked for change. The impact of making eye-contact is twofold: acknowledging the homeless person makes them more likely to talk to you, and looking at them makes you more likely to pity them and hand over a few bills. In order to avoid that feeling and its consequences, many people will stare straight ahead and try to ignore the presence of the homeless. The same situation occurs when we encounter people collecting money for a charity on the street: we'll often do our best to avoid them (sometimes even crossing the street) or at least avoid eye-contact, for fear that if we stop to talk we'll end up giving money to children in Africa, environmental conservation efforts, or the local fire brigade. This experience encapsulates one of the many human tendencies that prevent people from making more compassionate decisions: *empathy avoidance.*

A major frustration of doing advocacy work is that we know how much is at stake, and in a lot of cases a small change in behavior from the people we're trying to influence would lead to so much good for others, sometimes even saving lives. Yet when we try to communicate that to the public, we're often met with resistance or apathy. Even when people do express support for our cause, many times that support is just verbal and they're not willing to actually make the change that's needed. For example, the vast majority of Americans disagree with the cruel conditions that child laborers have to endure in sweatshops, and if someone handed them a pamphlet on the subject, most would express sympathy for those being exploited. Yet very few Americans avoid buying clothing or other products made in sweatshops. Human beings are typically slow to accept new ideas and even slower to make changes to their lifestyle.

Because of how frustrating advocacy work can be, it's tempting to write off much of society as greedy, apathetic, and willfully ignorant. Conclusions like these can be a good way to let off steam, and may have some truth to them, but they fail to get us any closer to understanding why people don't care about our issue, and they fail to teach us how we can get more people to care. The unfortunate reality is that many aspects of the human mind make people resistant to adopting new attitudes and behaviors. The more we understand this resistance, the more we'll able to work around it and succeed at creating change.

THE DANGERS OF EMPATHY

According to researcher Daniel Batson, people commonly respond in two ways when they see or hear about someone suffering. One response is to empathize, the core of which is perspective-taking—seeing the world through the eyes of another. The second common response is a self-oriented one, focused mostly on one's own upset feelings (Batson, Early, and Salvarani 1997).

You've probably seen this second response in action. When animal activists pass out flyers about the cruelties of factory farming, one response they'll often get is, "Oh I don't want to look at that, it's going to make me sad." Similarly, the reason why many people dislike the Sally Struthers–style TV advertisements, where viewers are asked to make a donation to help the starving African children flashed across the screen, is that the commercials make people feel bad. While that bad feeling may be caused in part by guilt, some of it is a self-oriented reaction of feeling upset by others' suffering. Because of the bad feeling they get, many people will change the channel when those appeals air, yet sit happily through commercials for a new Clorox® mop or any other product, since those ads don't cause the same feelings of distress.

According to Batson, if you see someone in need and imagine yourself in their shoes, you're likely to be motivated to help. On the other hand, if you focus on your own upset feelings, you'll be motivated to reduce that distress by turning away and ignoring the problem (Batson, Early, and Salvarani 1997; Stotland 1969). This observation pro-vides several insights into why our outreach work often fails. First, it means that when we tell people about the issue we're working on, many of them will ignore us in order to avoid the negative feelings that might come from thinking about an upsetting situation. Secondly, it means that when people do express concern and do agree with us that a situation is unjust, they may only be agreeing with us because the situation makes them feel upset—not because they're putting themselves in the shoes of those who are suffer-ing. When this is the case, people are rarely going to change their behavior to help ease the suffering. They'll simply express their support and then move on, happy to no longer be thinking about the issue.

While it's easy for people to say they care about a problem, caring enough to take action requires a higher level of empathy. Daniel Batson conducted a series of experi-ments in which participants were placed in situations where they could choose to help or not help a homeless person who appeared to be in great need. Batson's experiments showed that participants with high levels of empathy often helped, whether or not it was easy to avoid helping. On the other hand, those with lower levels of empathy rarely helped when it was easy for them to avoid doing so (Batson 2002; Batson 1997; Batson *The Altruism Question*; Batson and Weeks 1996).

In addition to avoiding personal feelings of distress, there's another motivation for the public to avoid helping or even thinking about distressing situations: helping could be costly (Shaw, Batson, and Todd 1994). Costs could include physical demands, anxi-ety or emotional distress, money, time, opportunities missed, and lifestyle changes. As a result, people will often try to avoid empathy-inducing experiences. Psychologists use the term *empathy avoidance* to refer to the tendency people have to avoid feelings of empathy in order to escape the consequences those feelings could have on their own behavior (Shaw, Batson, and Todd 1994).

In order to examine empathy avoidance, researcher Laura Shaw and her colleagues set up a study in which student participants were told about the Friend-in-Need pro-gram, a university organization pairing students with homeless people. Students were informed about Harold Mitchell, a Friend-in-Need client who had become homeless three years prior, after losing his job due to illness. Some students were told that at the end of the research study they would be asked to make a significant time donation to help the Friend-in-Need program, working five to six hours directly with Harold. Oth-ers were told they'd be asked to volunteer one hour of their time stuffing envelopes for the program, and still other students weren't told that any request would be made of them. All of the students were then asked to choose which appeal they'd rather read: a calm, information-only appeal about Harold and his needs, or an emotional appeal that detailed what Harold was going through and the suffering it had caused him.

Students who were aware that they'd soon be given a high-cost opportunity to help Harold preferred to hear a low-empathy version of his appeal for help rather than a high-empathy version. Those who were unaware they'd soon be given the opportunity to help, and those who thought the cost of helping would be low, didn't show the same strong preference for hearing the low-empathy appeal. In other words, participants wanted to avoid feeling empathy for the homeless man when they knew that empathy might lead them to donate a significant amount of time to help him (Shaw, Batson, and Todd 1994).

The process of empathy avoidance can take many forms. In their publication *Meeting Environmental Challenges: The Role of Human Identity*, the World Wildlife Fund's U.K. office describes the typical ways people ignore societal problems. The first type of response is to use diversion strategies: individuals limit their exposure to information that discusses the problems; they keep their minds in the present moment or present surroundings; they do something small to theoretically help the situation so that they can continue to ignore it again; and they seek pleasure. One study found that seeking pleasure was the most popular diversion strategy among adults in coping with the looming environmental problems the world faces (Homburg, Stolberg, and Wagner 2007).

A second way that people ignore societal problems is to adopt an attitude of apathy (pretending they don't care) or resignation (pretending that what they do won't make a difference anyway, so why bother caring?). Adopting one of these attitudes helps a person to justify their decision to ignore the problem, and enables them to avoid the anxiety and costs that might come from responding to it. Lastly, people can deny the presence of a societal problem by reinterpreting the situation through relativism (claiming the problem really wasn't that big), refusal of guilt (it's not my fault) or projection (blaming others).

Survey research shows that all these methods of ignoring environmental problems are correlated to environmentally destructive behaviors. People who respond to environmental problems in these ways are more likely to engage in environmentally destructive behaviors than those who don't (Crompton and Kasser).

The techniques people use to avoid empathy need to be considered by activists deciding how to go about their work. The distinction between those who feel actual empathy and those with a self-oriented reaction to learning about suffering should also be considered.

Instead of just making people feel bad by exposing them to images of suffering, we need to get them to empathize with those affected. That doesn't mean that including graphic images or vivid descriptions of suffering is not useful; as we'll discuss later on, these things *can* be helpful in changing behavior. But the tone of our communication should be one that helps people put themselves in the shoes of others, not just cringe at their suffering.

Since we know the public will try to avoid empathy when the potential costs of empathy are high, it would be helpful to present our high-empathy appeal before making a specific request of our audience. The effective animal protection group Vegan Outreach distributes booklets on factory farming and the benefits of veganism on college campuses across America. While the booklets are virtually identical on the inside, the cover comes in several different versions. One older version stated on the cover "Try Vegetarian." A newer version is titled "Compassionate Choices." Batson's research on empathy appeals would suggest that the latter booklet will be read by (and therefore affect) more people than the former.

With the first booklet, recipients know as soon as they look at the cover that a seemingly large request will be made of them: to go vegetarian. If they read through the booklet, they may feel motivated to go vegetarian—a decision that seems like it would have a high cost (they could no longer eat some foods they currently enjoy). Therefore, as Batson found in his research, many will intentionally avoid the empathy-inducing booklet by refusing to read through it. In fact, vegetarian leafleters always encounter people who take a pamphlet and then remark, "Oh no, I can't read this; it will make me want to go vegetarian." On the other hand, with the "Compassionate Choices" booklet, recipients aren't sure what it's about at first, because the title is intentionally vague. People are more likely to start reading through the booklet and its high-empathy appeal before getting to the actual encouragement to go vegetarian or vegan.

This same principle applies to other activist causes as well. An environmentalist giving a talk encouraging people to take public transportation to work instead of driving shouldn't title their talk: "Give Up That Car! The Impacts Your Transportation Choices Have on the Environment." A number of people will avoid the lecture because they don't want to hear information that might motivate them to stop driving. Taking a lesson directly from Batson's experiment, a homeless advocacy group looking for volunteers shouldn't air television ads that begin by stating, "Weekly volunteers needed for the Men's Drop-In Center," and that then introduce viewers to some of the center's clients. The empathy-inducing appeal should come first, followed by the request.

Activist fliers, advertisements, talks, and other communications can also try to prevent empathy avoidance by: emphasizing how action on the recipient's part has a real impact on those in need; showing how the cause is in line with what the recipient already believes; noting that there's always more that can be done; and making clear how serious the problem is.

BLAMING THE VICTIM

"Protect the innocent" is a well-worn phrase in American culture. Everyone from the Marines to anti-abortion activists to the fictional character RoboCop have incorporated that line into their personal credo (Statement of Commander's Intent, Vision and Philosophy; Abortion Information You Can Use; RoboCop). The concept is so familiar that it needs no explanation: those who are innocent are the ones most deserving of our love and protection.

Researchers Melvin Lerner and Carolyn Simmons of the University of Kentucky weren't so sure that Americans value innocence as much as they claim. Earlier, we discussed how people will avoid dealing with societal problems through responses like deciding that the situation really isn't that bad or saying that it's not their own fault. Lerner and Simmons believed that another way people cope with discomforting information about how the world works is by blaming and denigrating victims. Like other coping mechanisms, this type of response could reduce people's feelings of discomfort when faced with the suffering of others.

On the day of Lerner and Simmons' experiment, groups of female college students gathered in a waiting room along with a confederate—a member of the research team posing as a student participant, who'd play the victim in the experiment. Each group was then taken to the research room and provided with a fictitious story for what the experiment was about. They were told that employers were interested in learning more about how people with different personality traits operate under stressful situations. To find out, the victim would be given a series of questions to answer and would be punished with electrical shocks for incorrect answers. The student participants were told that their role was to watch the victim's face closely for cues as to how emotionally aroused she was. The testing would be shown to the participants via a live closed-circuit TV camera.

The testing began, and the participants watched as the victim (who had previously been in the waiting room with them) was strapped to a shock apparatus, questioned, and shocked for her numerous incorrect answers. Doing a fine job of acting, the "victim" reacted to the seemingly painful shocks with shouts and expressions of pain.

After watching the first ten minutes of the shock experiment, one group of participants was allowed to choose whether they wanted the shocks to the second test-subject halted, and all of them did. A second group of participants wasn't given the ability to have the shocks to the second test-subject halted, and were told the experiment would continue shortly. A third group of participants was unable to have the shocks to the second test-subject halted, and were also made to feel that they were partly responsible for the second test-subject being shocked. (Before the shock tests began for this group, the victim complained that she didn't want to be shocked and so didn't want to take part in the experiment. She only agreed to go forward with it after the researcher repeatedly pointed out to her that she needed to take part in the experiment for the sake of the other participants, who wouldn't get the lab credits they needed if the experiment didn't take place. This verbal exchange was acted out in front of the real participants.) Other groups of participants were told either that the experiment was now over or that it had actually been filmed in the past and just re-broadcast over the TV.

Participants in all groups were then asked to fill out a survey on how highly they thought of the victim and how similar she was to them. The survey included ratings on how likable or unlikable she was, how mature or immature, whether they thought other people would respect and admire her, whether she would fit in with their friends, whether she had a good sense of humor, whether she was insecure or selfish, etc.

The group of students who were able to end the shocks had the most favorable perceptions of the victim. Those who were told that the experiment was over, or that it had been filmed in the past, had a slightly lower opinion of the victim. Those who believed that the experiment was going to continue, and that the victim may continue to be shocked, had a much lower opinion of the victim. And those who felt that the victim was a martyr—allowing herself to be shocked in order to get them their

lab credits—had the lowest opinion of her. In other words, the more the victim suffered, the more participants denigrated her (thought less of her in terms of likeability,
similarity, etc.). In the most innocent condition—when the test-subject was allowing
herself to be shocked just to help the participants—their denigration of her reached
its peak (Lerner and Simmons 1966).

Studies that added variations to the shock experiment found a couple of ways to
prevent or remove the denigration effect. One study found that asking participants to
imagine themselves in the victim's shoes (in other words, creating empathy) led to a
removal of denigration (Aderman, Brehm, and Katz 1974). The denigration effect was
also removed when participants were led to believe they might share the same fate of
being shocked (Chaiken and Darley 1973). Another study found that even when denigration occurred, participants who were then given the chance to help the victim were
no less likely to provide help, even if they'd just denigrated the victim (Kenrick, Reich,
and Cialdini 1976). However, researchers analyzing this last study indicate that denigration might not have impacted helping because there was virtually no cost to helping.
Denigration is probably correlated to helping when the costs of helping are high (Lerner
and Miller 1978). In other words, when we denigrate a victim we find it easier to avoid
helping them because we feel they don't deserve our help.

Common sense would suggest that the more innocent and helpless a victim is, the
more we'd be willing to help them, and the more highly we'd think of them. Yet research
suggests that our judgments often work in the opposite way; that seeing an innocent
person suffer without any control over their situation (especially if we've caused it) leads
us to denigrate that person.

As Lerner and Miller note in their review of victim-denigration research: "The sight
of an innocent person suffering without the possibility of reward or compensation
motivated people to devalue the attractiveness of the victim in order to bring about a
more appropriate fit between her fate and her character" (Lerner and Miller 1978). This
general phenomenon has been repeated numerous times in a variety of studies (Simons
and Piliavin 1972; Sorrentino and Hardy 2006).

Research subjects who heard reports about a stabbing victim valued the victim less
when there was no way he could have avoided the stabbing. Victims who were more
responsible for their fate, for example, by engaging in risky behaviors like walking alone
late at night down dark alleys, were valued more highly by research subjects (MacDonald 1972). In a simulated jury situation where the victim was a woman who'd been

raped and was said to be either a virgin, married, or a divorcee, the victim was seen as more at fault if she was a virgin or a married woman (and therefore by the conventional standards of the time more innocent and pure) than if she was a divorcee (Jones and Aronson 1973). Another study presented participants with reports of innocent victims attacked by police officers. Participants viewed victims who were unable to file complaints against the police more negatively than those victims who could file complaints (Lincoln and Levenger 1972).

Why do people denigrate victims more when the victims seem most deserving of sympathy? Melvin Lerner, the Canadian researcher who conducted the shock experiments and several other similar studies, explains the phenomenon through what he calls the Just World hypothesis. People, he argues, want to believe that they live in a world where individuals generally get what they deserve. This belief helps the world appear stable and orderly, which is comforting. People are reluctant to give up this belief and are troubled by evidence that it isn't true. When people do see injustice, they can either try to help the victim or they can decide that the fate was deserved because the victim was a bad or flawed person (Lerner and Miller 1978). People denigrate victims of misfortune in order to try to make sense of otherwise senseless and undeserved suffering (Jones and Aronson 1973; Lerner and Miller 1978).

In the study that examined peoples' reactions to the stabbing victim, the more power the victim had over their fate (he could have avoided walking down the dark alley late at night) the less unjust the situation was. The stabbing didn't happen because the world was unjust; it happened because the man made a foolish choice. Therefore, study participants' belief in a just world wasn't threatened, so they had no need to denigrate the victim.

On the other hand, if the victim had no way to avoid the stabbing, that would mean the world is unjust and chaotic, and a similar fate could happen to anyone. In order to avoid this frightening realization, study participants had to denigrate the victim so the fault lay with him: he somehow deserved what he got, or his life mattered less. In the simulated rape trial, because the women who were virgins or married were perceived as more innocent, the idea that they could be raped was more of a threat to the "just world" belief than the idea that a divorcee could meet the same fate. Therefore, when the rape victim was a virgin or married woman, fault had to be found with her in order to keep the world seeming just.

Even outside of situations involving clear victims, people tend to believe in a consistency between virtue and outcome: those who are good will be happy, and those who are bad will suffer. Study participants who found out that a student had won a lottery drawing thought that the student had worked harder than most, even though they knew the outcome was completely random (Lerner 1965). A study published in the *Journal of Personality and Social Psychology* found that the more damage done to an automobile during an accident, the greater study participants blamed the driver—irrespective of the driver's actual responsibility for the crash (Walster 1966).

Now that we know about the human tendency to denigrate victims—a tendency that's particularly strong when the victims are completely innocent or when we're partly responsible—what implications does this have for our advocacy work? For one thing, it helps explain the lack of concern the public has for groups that are particularly innocent and particularly exploited, such as farm and laboratory animals, migrant laborers, and people starving in other countries. Secondly, it suggests that when we're advocating on behalf of others, stressing the innocence of the victims might be counterproductive.

The impact of denigration on helping is unclear, and there are some situations where people seem to provide more help when the victim appears more innocent (for example, pictures of children are particularly effective in fundraising efforts). The tendency to denigrate innocent victims doesn't mean people won't ever provide help to them, but it probably makes helping less likely in many situations. When help is forthcoming, it will probably be fairly minimal, such as a small donation to a charity, as opposed to lifestyle changes that would have a far greater impact. Furthermore, for issues where people are partly responsible for the suffering and destruction (through eating chicken, buying clothing made in sweatshops, wasting paper, etc.), there's a strong tendency to denigrate the victim. People decide that farm animals, foreign laborers, and trees don't have much value in order to prevent themselves from feeling guilty or from having to alter their behavior. Doing so also allows individuals to continue holding the comforting belief that the world is just.

A common reaction of those who see migrant Hispanic workers picking crops beneath the hot sun is to note how oppressive the work seems and then try to find a mental justification as to why the situation is not as bad as it seems. "They're used to this sort of work," people may tell themselves, or "They're lucky just to be in the United States in the first place." People search for reasons to believe these workers deserve less consideration than American workers would, that they matter less. This allows people to no longer be upset about the workers' conditions or feel guilty for buying produce from farms that treat their workers this way and pay very low wages.

The tendency to denigrate victims should be carefully considered when deciding what messages to use in promoting our cause. Emphasizing the innocence of those we're seeking to help seems like a good way to garner sympathy, but research suggests that it could backfire—especially when we're asking for significant behavioral changes. Research also suggests that we should try to avoid directly pointing out our audience's role in supporting the problems we're addressing. Doing so will motivate them to denigrate the victim in order to justify their own behavior.

For example, a college environmental group might pass out fliers on Earth Day that tell recipients how many trees are cut down each year to provide them with toilet paper, textbooks, paper bags, and other items. A campus animal advocacy group might pass out flyers that tell recipients how many animals suffer and are killed each year for their meals. A Students Against Sweatshops organization might pass out fliers that tell recipients about the suffering they've caused by purchasing clothing made in sweatshops. In each of these situations, the student activists have informed the recipient of their responsibility for the suffering and destruction. This may lead recipients to denigrate the victims in order to feel justified in their actions.

These student groups would likely be more effective if they focused their blame on the companies that are directly responsible, while at the same time urging recipients to make a change. Environmental pamphlets might describe how many trees major companies cut down each year to produce toilet paper, textbooks, and other items, and then encourage recipients to conserve paper. Animal advocacy fliers might talk about how much suffering animals endure every day on factory farms, then encourage recipients to cut meat out of their diet. Anti-sweatshop fliers might talk about how most major clothing companies exploit workers in foreign countries, then encourage people to buy brands not made with sweatshop labor. Recipients who haven't had their personal responsibility directly pointed out to them are less likely to denigrate the victim and should be more willing to make a change. While not directly blaming recipients for what's going on, the fliers must still have a clear call to action and point out recipients' ability to prevent the exploitation. Just getting them angry at corporations won't do much good.

Even with the most thoughtful efforts on our part, a large portion of our audience will still intentionally avoid feeling empathy for others and refuse to make changes in their lives. But by carrying out our activism with an awareness of these tendencies, we can accomplish more change and save more lives.

STATUS QUO BIAS

David Hume, an eighteenth-century Scottish philosopher, economist, and historian, was among the first to write about how people often take the mere existence of something as evidence that it's good and desirable. It wasn't until two hundred years later that researchers William Samuelson and Richard Zeckhauser coined the term *status quo bias* after demonstrating the existence of this phenomenon in a series of experiments.

The tendency to overvalue what is, and undervalue what could be, forms the basis of much of people's ethics. The judgments they make, and why they make them, come not from critical thought or personal experience, but from the mere existence and current popularity of those judgments in society.

Early research into status quo bias showed the tendency is partly due to peoples' preference for inaction when given a choice (Anderson 2003; Ritov and Baron 1992; Schweitzer 1994). This certainly isn't good for activists, who are in the business of changing behavior. Not only do we have to sway the other person to our point of view, we have to get them motivated enough to overcome their natural inertia. Buying fair-trade coffee doesn't just mean agreeing that fair prices should be paid to foreign farm-workers; it also means finding new places to buy coffee, which takes extra work. Status quo bias is also powerful because, as the number of alternatives to choose among increases, inertia grows as well (Kempf and Ruenzi 2006; Samuelson and Zeckhauser 1988). The more options that are presented to us—in company retirement accounts, in choices of entertainment, etc.—the more likely we are not to choose anything, or to stick with whatever we were doing before.

When trying to create change at a larger level—like a policy change at a business or school, or a value change in society—the collective inertia is even stronger. Almost all groups have a collective conservatism, a tendency to stick to established behaviors and values even when new needs arise (Thaler and Sunstein). Groups that pride themselves on being particularly liberal are usually no more tolerant of different opinions than any other group; they simply have a set of values that's further to the left on the political spectrum. A Green Party chapter is not likely to be more tolerant of a member's strong support for a ban on abortion than a Republican Party chapter is to be tolerant of a member's strong support for environmental protection.

Sometimes, inertia can actually work to our advantage as activists. As Richard Thaler and Cass Sunstein advise in their book *Nudge*: "First, never underestimate the power of inertia. Second, that power can be harnessed" (Thaler and Sunstein). When we're able to create a policy or values change, it's more likely that those changes will stay in place than be reversed. Furthermore, we can sometimes set up systems (in cafeterias, stores, public policies, and elsewhere) so that the default, inertia position is the one most beneficial to our cause.

For example, cafeterias seeking to promote healthy eating can put healthful options like fruits and vegetables in the most visible locations and on impulse-buy counters. One current political and ethical question is whether organ donation should be an "opt-in" or an "opt-out" system. Should people automatically be deemed organ donors unless they specify otherwise? Doing so would greatly increase the number of organ donors; but the question of which system is more ethical is up for debate. Sunstein and Thaler call the process of using inertia to the benefit of society *choice architecture*, and we'll discuss its usefulness later.

A second factor motivating status quo bias is loss-aversion, our fear of losing what we already have (Kahneman and Tversky 1984; Tversky and Kahneman 1991). In certain situations, the fear of losing something can be a much more powerful motivator than the hope of gaining something, in part because once we have something (an object, ethical value, etc.) we start to value it much more highly. In one experiment, students were asked whether they'd prefer to have a chocolate bar or a mug, items with equal monetary value. Pre-testing showed students had no preference for either item. The chocolate bars and mugs were then distributed randomly, so that half the students had one and half the other. Students were then asked if they'd trade in the item they'd been given for the item they hadn't been given. Despite having no initial preference, students were willing to trade for the other item only ten percent of the time (Thaler and Sunstein).

In a similar experiment, researcher Dan Ariely decided to find out whether Duke University students valued tickets to the school's basketball games more when they owned or didn't own the tickets. Duke basketball tickets are so highly prized that students who want them spend days camped in line outdoors, just to be able to sign up for the school's ticket-lottery system. Afterward, ticket winners are chosen at random, meaning that many students who waited patiently for days to sign up for the lottery won't even end up with tickets.

While fans wanted the tickets equally before the lottery had been drawn, after the tickets were given out the value students placed on them changed dramatically. Those who didn't win tickets were willing to pay $170 on average for scalped tickets. Those who'd won the tickets demanded an average of $2,400 for them when asked to sell. In other words those who received the tickets immediately valued them fourteen times more than those who didn't have them, even though both groups had valued the tickets equally before they were distributed (Ariely 132).

Considering how strongly loss-aversion influences our decisions when it comes to things like chocolate bars, basketball tickets, and money, just imagine the influence it has on people's values. As Ariely notes (137–138):

> Ownership is not limited to material things. It can also apply to points of view. Once we take ownership of an idea . . . we love it perhaps more than we should. We prize it more than its worth. And most frequently, we have trouble letting go of it because we can't stand the idea of its loss. What are we left with then? An ideology—rigid and unyielding.

The culturally and religiously conservative portion of the American public is a clear example of loss-aversion in action. That group's political priorities seem largely motivated by a fear of losing what they perceive as traditional aspects of society: traditional family values, traditional (heterosexual) marriage, traditional Christian religious beliefs, and (for some) traditional racial majorities and language monopolies.

Loss-aversion also has an impact on decisions we make about our lifestyle. Increasing our consumption, when we possess the money to do so, is psychologically very easy. Cutting back in any significant way (for example, moving to a smaller house or reducing the amount of appliances one owns) seems painful, even if in the past we'd been perfectly happy at that lower level of consumption.

It's important to note that loss-aversion only plays this powerful role once a person has experienced ownership of something. When it comes to advocacy messages, a meta-analysis published in the *Communication Yearbook* found that persuasive health messages framed in terms of loss were overall no more persuasive than those framed in terms of gain (O'Keefe and Jensen 2006). For example, a message such as "Smoking cuts an average of five years off your life" is likely to be no more effective than "Not smoking will add five years on to your life." Non-profits who frame their fundraising or advocacy messages in terms of loss aren't likely to see better results than had they framed those messages in terms of gain.

Inertia and loss-aversion aren't the only reasons the status quo bias exists. Research has shown that even when these factors are removed, people treat the existence of something as evidence of its goodness. In a set of five studies published in the *Journal of Personality and Social Psychology*, researchers Scott Eidelman, Christian Crandall, and Jennifer Pattershall demonstrated that people evaluate existing states more favorably than alternatives; that simply imagining something leads people to evaluate it more positively; and that even when it comes to purely subjective areas, such as food and art, the more prevalent the art form or food, the more attractive it is to people.

Eidelman, Crandall, and Pattershall's first few studies introduced participants to questions about school policies and corporate decisions that had no relevance to the participants (so their answers wouldn't be motivated by inertia or loss-aversion). When given two alternatives—one presented as the current state of affairs, one presented as a proposed change—participants expressed a clear preference for the status quo, regardless of which of the two alternatives was presented as the current state. We might assume that people have a preference for keeping things the way they are out of an assumption that the majority must be smart, and that policies are the way they are for good reason. While people do often make decisions on that basis, that thinking alone doesn't explain away what the researchers call the *existence bias*, the innate preference for whatever already exists.

As the researchers demonstrated in additional studies, our existence bias also operates in areas where choice is purely subjective and there's no right or wrong answer (so the majority opinion shouldn't matter at all). Participants were presented with different art patterns and foods, all of which were new to them and had been created by the researchers. Some of these patterns and foods were described to participants as long-established, and others were described as new forms and flavors. Overall, participants had a strong preference for the patterns and foods they believed to be more common (Eidelman, Crandall, and Pattershall 2009).

In one of his HBO specials, George Carlin, who research shows to be the funniest stand-up comedian of all time,[1] once riffed on the existence bias:

Don't be giving me all this shit about the sanctity of life. I mean, even if there were such a thing, I don't think it's something you can blame on God. No, you know where the sanctity of life came from? We made it up. You know why? 'Cuz we're alive. Self-interest. Living people have a strong interest in promoting the idea that somehow life is sacred. You don't see Abbott and Costello running around talking about this shit, do you? We're not hearing a whole lot from Mussolini on the subject. What's the latest from JFK? Not a goddamn thing. 'Cuz JFK, Mussolini, and Abbott and Costello are fucking dead. They're fucking dead. And dead people give less than a shit about the sanctity of life. Only living people care about it, so the whole thing grows out of a completely biased point of view (Back in Town 1996).

Another aspect of the status quo bias is that people will respond differently to a message depending on whether it represents a majority opinion or a minority one. When our stance on an issue represents a minority opinion, we face a number of additional challenges. Research shows that minorities are likely to be seen as illegitimate and biased (Kruglanski 1990; De Dreu and De Vries 2001). This reaction stems in part from group dynamics. The in-group (whatever group someone belongs to in terms of the question at hand) tends to denigrate what we might call the "out-group" and to form negative impressions of it. Majority groups in particular often overestimate how different minority opinions are from their own. This situation makes it difficult for someone with a minority opinion to be influential, because those holding the majority opinion will feel there's more difference between the two perspectives than there actually is.

Furthermore, in presenting its opinion, the minority has to be more concerned than the majority about presentation style and articulating valid concerns. A speaker presenting the opinion that natural resources (trees, land, rivers, etc.) should be used to benefit human society needn't worry about how logical their arguments are, or how eloquent their presentation is, since most of the audience will already agree. An environmentalist presenting a minority opinion that trees and rivers have value in and of themselves and that their inherent value is more important than economic growth, is going to face a very skeptical audience—one that will try to pick the speaker's argument apart any way it can. Those in the majority scrutinize minority opinions closely, whereas majority opinions are accepted as truth without much, if any, scrutiny (De Dreu and De Vries 2001).

When we as activists are trying to change current values or behaviors, the status quo bias will work strongly against us. On the other hand, when we're trying to maintain a current policy or encourage others to accept an already-popular value, the status quo bias can make our work a lot easier.

POWER

One quiet morning in Palo Alto, California, nine college students from Stanford University opened their doors to find armed officers of the Palo Alto Police Department waiting to arrest them for burglary and armed robbery. After being handcuffed and taken down to the police station for processing, they were deposited in a holding cell and left to await their fate. But these students hadn't actually broken the law—they had signed up as paid participants of a novel research experiment designed by Stanford University Professor Philip Zombardo. Their holding cell was actually the boarded-up basement of the Stanford Psychology building, and their prison guards were nine other students who'd also volunteered for the study.

The study's purpose was to examine what would happen to students when placed in the role of either prisoner or guard. The mock prison that Zombardo created mimicked real prison conditions as much as possible including confinement, inadequate nutrition, the forced wearing of uniforms, and the conducting of strip searches. The students serving as guards were allowed to come up with their own rules for running the prison and were (within reason) allowed to act as they wished to keep the prison orderly.

After a rebellion by the prisoners in which they barricaded themselves in one room, the guards attacked the prisoners with the contents of a fire extinguisher, stripped the prisoners naked, forced the ringleaders into separate cells, and began a campaign of harassment, punishment, and intimidation that lasted for days. Prisoners became increasingly stressed and upset, with several having emotional breakdowns, and one being released early because of his extreme level of distress. Although the experiment was intended to last two weeks, it was cut short after only six days.

The Stanford Prison Experiment showed the extent to which a person's situation and access to power can influence their behavior, regardless of their stated values and their typical behavior outside of that environment. While students who volunteered for the study were randomly assigned the role of guard or prisoner, once those roles had been established, students took to them with gusto. Those in positions of power (the guards) exercised that power in cruel and sadistic ways just days into the experiment (The Stanford Prison Experiment).

University of California-Berkeley psychologist Datcher Keltner has found that in many social situations, people with power act like patients who've suffered damage to their emotional brain. "The experience of power might be thought of as having someone open up your skull and take out that part of the brain so critical to empathy and socially appropriate behavior. You become very impulsive and insensitive, which is a bad combination" (Lehrer 187). To the extent people have power over others (and clearly they have near total power over animals and the environment), that feeling of power may help fuel destructive choices.

Widely publicized studies by researcher Stanley Milgram showed that people are often willing to commit serious acts of cruelty toward others simply because they have been directed to do so by a powerful authority figure. In a landmark study, participants were introduced to a second person who would also be taking part in the study. The second person was then taken to a separate room where they were strapped to a shock apparatus and given a series of questions to answer. Each time that person answered incorrectly, the participant was instructed by a white-coated lab researcher to flip a switch and send an electric shock through the man's body to provide negative reinforcement against incorrect answers. Although the shocks began at a very low voltage, these increased every time the second person answered a question incorrectly. A grand total of thirty shocks could be administered, concluding at an incredibly high 450 volts. What the participants didn't know was that the second person was actually an actor who was faking being shocked. The real purpose of the study was to see how far participants would go in inflicting pain upon someone just because a researcher had told them to do so.

Prior to conducting the study, Milgram polled thirty-nine psychiatrists and asked them to guess how many students would administer all thirty shocks. The psychiatrists estimated only about one in a thousand participants would go that far. But when the experiment was carried out, about two-thirds of the participants pulled every last switch, continuing to shock the second person even after he'd screamed that he wanted out of the study, and even after he'd passed out in pain (Milgram). While many participants did verbally protest the researcher's orders, and some refused to go beyond a certain point, the majority continued to flip the switches when the researcher told them the experiment had to be continued.

Milgram's experiment was designed to understand why so many Germans cooperated with the Holocaust. However, the study provided powerful evidence to suggest that such behavior reflected obedience to authority inherent in many people, and not a flaw unique to the German populace. In fact, this experiment was repeated in Germany and no significant difference was found between the actions of German and American participants. Further repetitions of the study revealed that there was also no difference between males and females, between young and old, or between citizens of different countries in their willingness to hurt others when an authority figure told them to do so (Meeus and Raaijmakers 1986).

The Milgrim study and the Stanford Prison Experiment looked at what happened when individuals were put in situations where they either had the power to act with disregard for the suffering of others, or were instructed by an authority figure to act with disregard. As people in industrialized countries have great power over most life (any animals, ecosystems, or societies that can be exploited), we can see similar results occurring on the societal level. The studies provide vivid research examples of being "drunk with power" and having "blind obedience," two phenomena that play a role in much of the world's injustice and cruelty.

THE MORE WHO SUFFER, THE LESS PEOPLE CARE

Psychologist Paul Slovic examined the relationship between the number of victims in a tragic situation and witness responses. He found that the greater the number of victims, the more depersonalized they were to the public and the less witnesses cared (Joy 121). As mass murderer and Soviet leader Joseph Stalin is reputed (probably incorrectly) to have stated: "The death of one man is a tragedy, the death of millions is a statistic." Because people are relatively insensitive to numbers and statistics, situations that involve large numbers of victims or huge quantities of environmental destruction can still have very little emotional impact on the public.

When social problems are large, they can also take away feelings of personal responsibility. People help more when they're directly asked to or when their actions have a clearly positive result. For most issues, because the problem is so widespread, people assume that it's not their responsibility and that others will or should intervene. Studies have shown that this sense of diffusion of responsibility occurs even when we're only imagining the presence of others (Garcia *et al.* 2002).

I'VE DONE MY PART

The *contribution ethic* refers to the feeling many people have that "I've done my part on issue A, so it's okay for me to ignore issues B, C, and D." During a Humane League campaign to get restaurants to stop purchasing products from a particularly cruel farm, owners would often tell us that they already do something to help animals ("We buy our eggs from a local farm," or "I donate to the ASPCA") so we shouldn't be bothering them. This phenomenon worked across issues too, as we often had owners or chefs tell us how they supported some other social cause so we should leave them alone about this one.

In addition to feeling like they've done their part and therefore don't need to do anything more, people often overestimate the amount of good they've done. Combined, these phenomena make it hard to move people beyond small actions for their one or two preferred causes (Thogersen and Crompton 2009).

THE ATTITUDE/BEHAVIOR GAP

Ask an American whether they think it's important to buy American-made products and they'll probably say "yes." But if you take a look around your house to see where your shoes, clothes, furniture, and other items were manufactured, and chances are most came from overseas. Ironically, many American flags being sold now even bear a "Made in China" sticker. A 2009 poll conducted by BIGresearch found that eighty-three percent of Americans say buying American-made products is important to them, but only fifty-seven percent make a conscious effort to buy them, and only thirty-seven percent said they were willing to pay even a little bit more to buy American (Dolliver 2009). If patriotic Americans aren't willing to put their beliefs into action and buy American-made products, that doesn't bode well for the likelihood of our getting people to adopt less popular behaviors, like biking to work or going vegetarian.

The gulf that exists between people's beliefs and their actions is referred to as the *attitude/behavior gap*. There's often little relationship between attitudes and behavior when it comes to environmental, animal protection, and human social justice issues.

This poses yet another problem for activists trying to get people to make more compassionate choices: increasing people's awareness or even their agreement on an issue won't necessarily translate into a change in behavior. This fact has been borne out in a variety of studies conducted both in the U.S. and abroad.

When five hundred people were interviewed about personal responsibility for picking up litter, ninety-four percent agreed that people should pick up litter. But in leaving the interview, only two percent picked up the litter that had been planted by researchers (Bickman 1972). Two large Swiss surveys found environmental knowledge and awareness were poorly associated with environmental behavior (Finger 1994). A Canadian study found that seventy-two percent of residents self-reported a gap between their intentions and their actions on conservation behaviors (Kennedy *et al.* 2009). Another study found that people strongly supportive of energy conservation were no more likely to conserve than those who hadn't expressed strong support (Archer *et al.* 1987). And a study of recyclers and non-recyclers found they didn't differ in their attitudes toward recycling (DeYoung 1989). For studies that have shown some relationship between pro-environmental attitudes and pro-environmental behavior, the relationships have been weak (Fransson 1999; Bamberg 2003; Bamberg 2007; Oskamp and Schultz).

Turning to the field of animal protection, a Gallup poll found that twenty-five percent of Americans say they believe animals should have the same rights as people (Gallup Poll 2003) even though most of those respondents still ate meat (less than four percent of the U.S. population is currently vegetarian) (McStay 2009). Unless eating one's neighbors is acceptable behavior, this demonstrates an obvious disconnect between stated attitudes and behavior. The Gallup poll and numerous others have also found that a large majority of the American public favors strict laws to protect farm animals from conditions of intensive confinement. Nevertheless, most people continue to buy products from farms that use such methods, even when alternative products can be purchased. Similar gaps between people's attitudes and their behaviors can be seen on issues such as child labor and buying what have become known as "blood diamonds."

This situation explains why information campaigns that focus only on changing attitudes often have little effect on behavior. Getting others to agree on an issue isn't the same as creating measurable change. Generating agreement may be a necessary first step in a campaign, but it should never be an end goal. People's behaviors don't match up with their attitudes enough for us to measure our success by attitudinal change alone. Our activism should be focused on creating specific behavioral or policy changes.

THE MEDIA

Although political conservatives blast what they perceive as a liberal bias in the media and political liberals mock the right-wing slant of Fox News, aside from the partisan divide, virtually all major media outlets are supportive of the basic economic, cultural, and political structures of the country. Studies of the media have concluded that, in general, the media frame issues in ways that do not threaten the existing social system. When problems do exist, they are portrayed as the result of ineptitude, accidents, malevolent acts, or individual wrong-doing (Nelkin 50; Andreasen *Social Marketing in the 21st Century* 50). Activists who believe that systemic problems exist that need to be addressed will find it hard to get positive coverage from any media outlet.

THINKING? NO THANK YOU!

In 1996, Princeton University political science professor Larry Bartels decided to ask a group of study participants who identified themselves as Republican what they thought happened to the budget deficit during President Clinton's first term in office. Although the budget deficit had actually declined by ninety percent, more than half of the Republican participants thought it had increased. The study found that high-information Republicans voters—those who read newspapers and watched the news regularly—were no better informed than low-information voters. As Bartels commented: "Voters think that they're thinking, but what they're really doing is inventing facts or ignoring facts so that they can rationalize decisions they've already made" (Lehrer 206).

Even when the stakes are high, people don't tend to spend enough time clearing aside the biases that prevent rational thinking (Camerer and Hogarth 1999). When they do try harder, they often simply embrace the incorrect belief with even more gusto (Shafir and LeBoeuf 2002). This is true even when people's beliefs prevent them from doing what would be in their own best interest (Christensen, Moran, and Wiebe 1999; Webley *et al.*).

In a pair of studies published in the *Journal of Personality and Social Psychology*, participants were divided up into groups of Christians or non-Christians and smokers or non-smokers. Each participant was asked to listen to a recorded message that was somewhat hard to hear due to static. In order to hear the message clearly, the participant had to press a button that would remove the static. The study found that Christians and smokers were more likely to tune out messages that criticized Christianity or that warned of the dangers of smoking (they tuned out the message by allowing the static to remain).

Similarly, non-smokers and non-Christians were more likely to tune out messages that disputed a link between cancer and cigarettes or that affirmed Christianity (Brock and Balloud 1967). People wanted to hear what they already believed and to ignore statements that contradicted their beliefs.

In 2004, Emory University Psychologist Drew Westen used a fMRI machine to get an inside look at what goes on in people's minds when they're exposed to information contradicting their beliefs. In the study, conducted around the time of the U.S. Presidential elections, Republican and Democratic participants were given two contradictory statements by Republican George Bush and two contradictory statements by Democrat John Kerry. Participants were then asked to rate how contradictory each of the statements was. As expected, participants almost uniformly rated their preferred candidate's statements as not contradictory and the opposing candidate's statements as very contradictory. While they made their judgments, their brains were scanned by the fMRI machine.

Westen found that when people were presented with the contradictory statements from their preferred candidate there was activation in their prefrontal cortex, the area responsible for logic, planning, and rationality. However, they didn't dispassionately analyze the facts. Instead, they searched for a justification for believing the statements not contradictory. When they found a justification, they were rewarded with a rush of pleasurable emotion. "Essentially, it appears as if partisans twirl the cognitive kaleidoscope until they get the conclusions they want, and then they get massively reinforced for it, with the elimination of negative emotional states and activation of positive ones," noted Westen (Lehrer 204).

People will often intentionally ignore messages that contradict what they believe— a phenomenon that makes it even harder to persuade others of our point of view if they already hold a different one. Furthermore, people often think they're logically considering an issue when they're not. That false thinking provides a pleasurable rush of emotion and leaves people even more strongly convinced they're right, since they believe they've been analyzing the facts and returning to their original conclusion. There are no easy ways for activists to get around this problem, but being aware of these processes can help us notice them when they're the reason we're unable to persuade someone.

ACTIVISTS WORKING to create social change quickly learn what an uphill battle it can be. Realizing how many psychological mechanisms stand in the way of persuading the public might makes the work seem even more daunting. But knowing what the obstacles look like will make it easier for us to avoid those that are avoidable. And as for those obstacles that aren't—well, at least we know what we're up against, and we won't be so mystified if people turn away from us without caring about our cause.

Having discussed why people are so resistant to changing their values and behaviors, the next question we have to ask is: Where do values and behaviors come from in the first place?

chapter three

WHERE BELIEFS ARE BORN

SOCIAL NORMS

Do you try to reduce the amount of energy being used in your household? If so, why?

It seems like a simple question with an obvious answer. Those who conserve energy are probably doing so either to save money or to reduce their impact on the environment. Ask a home-owner who conserves and they'll surely give you one of these answers. But, as with many issues surrounding human decision-making, the reality isn't that simple.

Researcher Robert Cialdini and colleagues wanted to test whether home-owners were aware of why they conserved energy. To do so, the researchers conducted a telephone survey in which they asked people to rank how important four different factors were in their decision to conserve. Those who answered the survey ranked the four factors in the order of most to least important: environmental concern, helping society, saving money, and because others do it. The main reasons they stated for conserving energy were altruistic (helping the environment and society) as opposed to self-serving (saving money) or conformist.

But Cialdini and company weren't going to take home-owners at their word, so they also polled them about how much value they placed on protecting the environment, how important saving money was, whether they thought most other people conserved energy, and related issues. These answers were correlated with the previous ones to provide insight into why home-owners actually conserved energy.

In stark contrast to the home-owners' stated reasons, the study showed that perceptions about how many other people conserve energy was the best predictor of how much a home-owner conserved. In other words, those who believed that most Americans conserve energy were themselves most likely to conserve. People who said they believed that saving money or protecting the environment were important behaviors were only slightly more likely to conserve. Those who expressed a strong belief in helping society were somewhat more likely to conserve energy, but not as much as those who believed conservation was the social norm. These results indicate that the study participants were largely unaware of what their actual motivation was for reducing household energy use. They pointed to altruistic reasons, yet it was a desire to conform to the social norm that made them most likely to conserve.

Since social norms are so influential in getting people to conserve energy, could they be useful for environmental activists who want the public to reduce their energy usage? Cialdini and colleagues wanted to find out. In the second half of their study, a separate group of home-owners were asked why they wanted to conserve energy. The respondents voted that social responsibility, helping the environment, and saving money were the most compelling reasons (in that order). Participants were next given one of four randomly selected brochures with a message that focused either on how conserving energy helped society, how it helped the environment, how it saved money, or that most other people were doing it. Researchers then tracked the actual energy usage of participants' houses over the following months. Want to take a guess as to which brochure led to the greatest reduction in energy use?

The brochure that established a social norm by stating that most people conserve produced a greater reduction in household energy-use than any of the other brochures. In fact, the people who received motivational brochures about environmental or societal reasons to conserve didn't save any more energy than a control group of households that was given no motivational message (Nolan *et al.* 913–924). Other studies conducted by Cialdini have also found invoking social norms to be more effective at creating sustainable behavior than giving a pro-environmental message (Goldstein, Cialdini, and Griskevicius 2008; Cialdini 2003).

As we can see, social norms play a powerful role in shaping beliefs. People view an attitude as correct to the degree they see others holding it, especially when those others are similar to them (Craig and Prkachin 1978; Altheide and Johnson 1977; O'Connor 1972; Bandura, Grusec, and Menlove 1967). As Cialdini's experiment demonstrated, most people are unaware of how powerful a role social norms play in influencing their behavior. Simply invoking them (when we can truthfully do so) can be more effective than focusing on what we consider the most compelling reasons to make a change.

This is counterintuitive, and it's hard to picture an environmental organization using brochures focused on the social norms of energy conservation and not the environmental benefits. Yet the research indicates that doing so can provide a bigger payoff, and there's no reason why social norms shouldn't be equally effective for other activist causes where most of society agrees with the issue. (Advocates of vegetarianism can't use social norms to promote their cause since most people aren't vegetarian, though animal activists can cite social norms about how most Americans want farm animals protected from cruelty.)

Another lesson to be learned from these studies is that asking people what they think would influence them (as is done in focus groups) may not provide good data on what messages activist groups should use in campaigning. People hold very inaccurate beliefs about what motivates them when it comes to conservation, and the same is likely true for other issues.

CONFORMITY

Immediate social norms—what those around a person are saying and doing at that moment—also have a significant impact on people's judgments. A number of conformity experiments have been conducted in which participants were asked to answer easy questions like "What color is this circle?" or "Which of these three lines is longest?" At times during the study, others in the room—research assistants who were posing as fellow participants—all gave the same wrong answer to the question. The actual participant was then called on for their opinion, and in many cases they too gave a wrong answer, conforming to the obviously incorrect majority. Additional experiments found that when people were asked their opinions on political or social topics, if other participants (again undercover researchers) all agreed one way then the actual participant was significantly more likely to agree (Thaler and Sunstein 55–56).

Subsequent experiments have provided a more nuanced view of how conformity

works. For example, it only takes about three or four others agreeing on a topic to create group consensus and sway another individual to conform. Adding additional people to the consensus does little to increase conformity any further; ten people judging
a circle to be blue won't create much more conformity in another individual than four
people judging a circle to be blue. Studies also found that getting a participant to conform was even more successful when two groups of three people both agreed on the
answer, as opposed to one group of six. On the other hand, the presence of even one
other person in a group who didn't voice the majority opinion led to an eighty percent
reduction in conformity among the study participants. This drop occurred regardless
of whether the majority opinion was either factually true or false (Brehm, Kassin, and
Fein 235–237).

Conformity in the experimental settings described here was clearly superficial: the participant didn't want to feel embarrassed about being the only one with a particular opinion,
so they simply repeated what the majority said, even if they didn't personally believe it at
the moment. But is it possible that over time conformity could actually alter perceptions so
that conforming participants eventually accept as true a belief that isn't?

Psychologist Mazafer Sherif arranged conformity experiments whereby groups
of participants had to decide how far a pinpoint of light had moved. Because the light
didn't actually move, responses were arbitrary guesses. When a researcher posing as a
participant spoke confidently and firmly in presenting his opinion on how far the light
had moved, his judgment had a strong influence on the group's overall decision.

What Sherif did that was unique among conformity experiments was that he continued to hold these experiments over many sessions and several years, with many participants returning for multiple sessions. What he found was that the group's judgment
from the first session became so internalized that people would adhere to it even when
responding alone in a later session. In fact, over a year later, when participants were put
into new groups where other group members offered new judgments, participants still
stuck close to their original assessment and, in turn, influenced the new groups to decide
similarly. The arbitrary decision of how far the light had moved—influenced in large
part by one undercover researcher in the first experiment—tended to stay the same
over generations of the experiment, even as new volunteers entered and old ones left.
Initial conformity had led people to internalize a false answer, and formed to the estab-
lishment of a group norm that was passed down from generation to generation of new
participants (Sherif 1937).

Could some of the beliefs that our society holds be the result of arbitrary (and possibly faulty) judgments made in the past that just got internalized and passed down as true? This phenomenon probably underlies many of the prejudices and superstitious beliefs that people embrace as true. Descartes' philosophical decision that animals lacked souls and the ability to feel pain became widely accepted as fact throughout Europe and led to invasive research on animals and a general disregard for their welfare. The concept that animals lack souls continues to be used to this day as a justification for their cruel treatment in Western societies.

Economists have even given a term to this phenomenon as it applies to consumer preference: *arbitrary coherence*. The choices that we make on what brands and styles of items to buy are largely a result of our memories of choices made in the past and a desire for consistency with those past decisions. Research has shown arbitrary coherence in a number of consumer decisions and taste preferences (Brouar and Sutan). Psychologists have found the process at work in romantic relationships, and sociologists examine ways that religious superstition is passed down from generation to generation as truth. Even looking at activism, we can see that there are many tactics passed down to newer activists that become internalized as the way to do things, yet which aren't and never have been effective at creating change.

TEACHING OURSELVES WHAT TO BELIEVE

Our tendency to embrace arbitrary coherence exists because of our mind's strong need for consistency. If we didn't have that need, every time we were making a choice our decision would be random. But that's not how our mind works. Once we've made a decision about a particular issue, most of us will continue to make the same decision in the future. There are several reasons for this: it makes decisions easier, it allows us to have a more definable self-identity, and it makes us look self-assured to others. The need for consistency plays a strong role in keeping values and behavior stable throughout a person's life.

Earlier, we discussed researcher Daniel Batson's experiment with a church group to see how they would respond when presented with evidence that contradicted their deeply held beliefs. Their reaction—a more tenacious grip on their belief-system—was the result of cognitive dissonance. When a person's beliefs and actions appear to them to be in conflict, that person has only a few options available to them in trying to reconcile the inconsistency: change their actions, change their beliefs, or change their perception of their actions so they don't seem to conflict with their beliefs. When people notice a conflict between their actions and their beliefs, the most common response is to come up with a rationalization that suggests there isn't really a conflict. When that isn't possible, people are more likely to change their beliefs than their actions (Brehm, Kassin, and Fein 213–223). What this means is that people often learn what their beliefs are by looking at their own actions.

We typically think things work the other way around. We consider people to be rational creatures, carefully deciding on a set of beliefs and then choosing behaviors accordingly. Similarly, in our advocacy work we usually operate under the assumption that we first have to change people's beliefs, which will in turn cause them to change their behavior. While this approach can certainly work, we can also be effective by (when circumstances permit) focusing on changing a person's behavior without worrying about their attitude. Not only does behavior alteration create change in the short term, but adopting the new behavior will cause some people to adopt a matching attitude as well—leading to long-term continuance of the behavior. Research shows that when people are gently coaxed into doing something and don't already have a particular opinion on the issue, they come to view themselves in ways that are consistent with the behavior (Chaiken and Baldwin 1981; Fazio 129–150; Schlenker and Trudeau 1990).

My first job after graduating from college was with the Urban Nutrition Initiative, a University of Pennsylvania project that held nutrition-education programs for inner-city high school students. One of the key programs was running lunchtime and after-school cooking clubs, where students would prepare and eat healthy recipes with a UNI worker. Instead of spending many classroom hours teaching students about the importance of cooking healthy food, hoping the message would sink in and that behavioral change would follow, the program simply had students engage in the desired behaviors, whether or not they initially cared about eating healthily. After students repeatedly prepared and ate healthy meals, cognitive dissonance would create the subconscious thought in many students' minds, "Why am I cooking and eating all this healthy food? It must be because eating healthily is important to me." So, while most students joined the program because they wanted to work in the food-service industry or make money from the paid after-school program, many of them did end up adopting healthier eating habits. Formal studies have documented that getting people to act out something or give a persuasive speech on a topic is more effective in persuading them to believe the idea than simply speaking to them about the issue (Janis 1968). Behavior creates attitude: in part because we learn more about the issue, but also because we decide how we feel about an issue by looking at the things we say and do.

Just as behavior can influence our attitudes, so can our expectations of whether or not we're going to like something. How something is presented affects both our experience and judgments of a situation. In one experiment, participants were given samples of two types of beer. One was a standard beer, the other had a small amount of balsamic vinegar added to it. After tasting both, participants could decide which one they liked better and receive a free beer of that flavor. When participants didn't know that vinegar was the secret ingredient in the second beer, they mostly chose that beer as their favorite. However, when they were told in advance that balsamic vinegar had been added, even after sampling both beers participants almost always chose the unadulterated one as their favorite (Ariely 158). Expectation affected their judgments. A lesson activists can take from this is never to tell someone they're about to experience something that could seem unpleasant ("You're not going to like this, but . . ."; "I know this is going to sound really hard to do . . .," etc.). When we do this, chances are that our audience is going to agree with us that our message is unpleasant—simply because they're expecting it.

It should be clear by now that beliefs are rarely based on reasoned decision-making. In fact, the emotional part of the brain often calls the shots, usually on an unconscious level. One interesting set of experiments showed that we often know something through our feelings (specifically, through chemical reactions) before we make a conscious decision on it. In these studies, participants' dopamine systems were analyzed as they tried to figure out which of the two pre-arranged piles of cards in front of them provided more wins in a game. This meant having to remember the previous cards selected, comparing the results from the competing piles, and trying to see a pattern. The studies showed that participants' dopamine systems acted up and seemed to "know" which deck was better before individuals consciously came to that knowledge (Lehrer 46).

We make most decisions in the emotional part of the brain, weighing the relative amounts of pleasure and pain we expect from each choice. When we're considering an ethical dilemma, the dopamine system automatically generates an emotional response. It's only then that the prefrontal cortex (where logic and reason reside) becomes activated, and people come up with reasons to justify the belief their emotional brain has told them is correct. Because of this, when we discuss values at length with other people we'll often reach a point where their justifications for belief have been stripped away and they offer arguments such as "Because it just *is*," or "It's just *wrong*, that's all." This state has been called *moral dumbfounding*, and it's clear evidence that the emotional brain generated the belief (Lehrer 172–174, 201).

THE AVAILABILITY BIAS

Ask the typical American what dangers they're afraid of and they'll probably mention events like crime and murder, terrorism, a house fire, or having their children be abducted. Fears such as these are common because, when we watch the news, these types of stories are reported on a daily basis. But are these dangers really the biggest threats to us? Smoking, overeating, and lack of physical exercise—all things that people do to themselves—are the leading causes of death in the U.S. And even though our murder rate dwarfs that of most countries, Americans are still nearly twice as likely to die from suicide as they are from homicide. Few of us have ever heard of septicemia—an infection of the bloodstream—but we're more likely to die of it than either suicide or homicide. And though our likelihood of dying from a terrorist attack is infinitesimal (we're about thirty times more likely to die from an accidental fall), the fear of such an attack has led billions of dollars to be spent on increased security measures in the U.S. (not to mention the hundreds of billions spent on wars to make our country theoretically more secure) (Deaths: Final Statistics for 2006).

People's fears are based on the threats that make the biggest impression on them, not on the threats that pose the most serious risk. Dramatic events like murders, terrorist attacks, and abductions stick in the mind, whereas health issues don't. Many families that would never live in an urban area for fear of being the victims of crime engage in daily behaviors like smoking and over-eating that are considerably more dangerous to their own existence than living in high-crime areas.

The *availability bias* is the phenomenon by which people perceive something to be correct based on how easily they can think of an example or supporting argument, and not on how many examples or arguments come to mind. Studies have shown that people report they use bikes more often after being asked to recall a few rather than many instances of bike-riding (Aarts and Dijksterhuis 1999). They hold an attitude with more confidence after generating a few rather than many supporting arguments (Haddock *et al.* 1999) and when the information is easy to bring to mind (Haddock *et al.* 1999; Tormata, Petty, and Briñol 2002). A set of studies published in *Advances in Experimental*

Social Psychology showed that encouraging people to consider an opinion opposite of their own was useful for persuasion only when picturing it was easy. When picturing the opposite opinion was difficult, the strategy backfired and people became even more resistant to it (Schwarz *et al.* 2007).

Because of the availability bias, getting others to consider an alternative way of doing things can be very difficult if examples of the alternative don't immediately come to mind. Asking someone to picture themselves as a vegetarian might have an effect opposite to what was intended; it might make the person think being a vegetarian was difficult because they couldn't easily picture the types of food they'd be eating. Congressional Representative Dennis Kucinich's idea for a Department of Peace sounds unappealing to many Americans in part because they can't envision what such a branch of government would do.

ADDRESSING IDENTITY AND VALUES

In addition to making decisions based on our brain's emotional responses to a situation, we also make decisions on the basis of self-identity: "What do people like me do in this situation?"

Are there aspects of people's identities that could cause them not to care about the messages activists are presenting? The World Wildlife Fund's U.K. office thinks so. They've done some great analysis on the ways that identity is connected to unsustainable behavior, and the consequences of ignoring identity when promoting sustainability. Although their focus is the environment, WWF U.K.'s findings can be applied to other progressive social causes as well.

Cross-cultural research by Shalom Schwartz and colleagues have identified about a dozen personal traits that consistently appear around the world (Schwarz 1992; Caprara *et al.* 2006). One of these traits is how much (or how little) a person is focused on wealth, status, achievement, and material goods. A study conducted across six nations found that people who highly value these things are more likely to have negative attitudes toward the environment and animals, to view humans as consumers of nature rather than part of it, and to have less concern about the impact environmental damage has on other people, children, future generations, and nonhuman life (Schultz *et al.* 2005). Studies in the U.S. (Good 2007) and Australia (Saunders and Munro 1995) showed the same correlation.

In the U.S. and England, studies have shown that adolescents and adults who strongly endorse materialistic goals are less likely to turn off lights, recycle, reuse paper, ride a bike, or buy second-hand items (Gatersleben *et al.* 2008; Brown and Kasser 2005; Richins and Dawson 1992). Materialism was also linked to greater ecological footprints from transportation, diet, and housing. A study published by the American Psychological Association that compared nations to one another found a correlation between how much a country values wealth and status and how high its carbon emissions are (even after controlling for Gross Domestic Product) (Kasser *et al.* 2004).

Another apparently universal trait is the way in which people cope with threats and fears. While fears can be confronted in a balanced and realistic manner, some people use defense mechanisms to suppress thoughts about anxiety-producing situations or protect their self-identity (Crompton and Kasser 2009). For example, people experience threats to their self-esteem when they're made aware of their complicity in societal problems like global warming. They also experience threats to their identity when they realize they'd have to change major aspects of their life if they wanted to help the situation. People who don't deal with the problem constructively will often cope in ways that lead to unsustainable behavior. These include the diversion strategies mentioned earlier: ignoring information, seeking pleasure, doing something small, claiming the threat is not that great, denying responsibility, pretending not to care, and acting as if there's nothing one can do to help.

Knowing that the trait of materialism and the use of coping behaviors to deal with threats are both linked to negative environmental behaviors (and probably other destructive behaviors as well), what implications does this have for our activism? For one thing, it means we should be careful about how we promote behavioral change. We don't want to accidentally support traits and coping mechanisms that lead to unsustainable behavior.

Instead of confronting destructive values, environmental organizations sometimes try to co-opt them for environmental purposes. Some promote green consumerism, appealing to people's desire for the newest and trendiest items. It's tempting to use appeals like these because they are sometimes more effective in the short term; but they end up promoting the same materialistic values that cause unsustainable behavior in the first place. Appeals like these also lead to the purchase of lots of unnecessary items that still have an environmental impact. Bamboo placemats, organic T-shirts with witty slogans, and solar-powered lawn lights may cause less environmental damage than their

cated issue, because the number of people in each category varies and some are easier to reach than others. Nevertheless, these surveys provide a clear example of how altruistic motivations are more likely to create significant behavioral change than self-centered ones. Activists should keep this in mind when considering which audiences to target and which messages to use in promoting behavioral change.

chapter four

TOOLS OF INFLUENCE, PART I: SIMPLE TOOLS

BY NOW YOU MIGHT BE FEELING A LITTLE DEPRESSED ABOUT your prospects for creating change; the psychological barriers are many and massive. People will often intentionally avoid feeling empathy, being predisposed to turn away from suffering when it's easy to do so. They tend to denigrate victims, and they have an innate bias to prefer the status quo. When people think they're thinking about an issue, they're usually just searching for justifications to support what they already feel. Powerful processes like social norms, conformity, and the role the emotional brain plays in decision-making can all serve as barriers that prevent people from adopting new beliefs. Even when you can get people to agree with you, chances are that agreement won't lead to a change in behavior.

But, obviously, change *does* happen. People *do* start buying fair-trade coffee, reducing their consumption, avoiding sweatshop clothing, and going vegetarian. Governments *do* adopt recycling programs and pass laws permitting same-sex marriage. Companies *do* switch to wind power, cease selling fur, stop experimenting on animals, and begin paying workers a living wage. Change happens much, much more slowly than we'd like it to; but it does happen. Sometimes it's the result of economics, new technology, or friends learning from friends. Often though, advocacy organizations play a pivotal role in creating change.

The previous few chapters have been somewhat one-sided, focusing on the mental biases that make it difficult to get people to adopt new behaviors. The good news is that there are plenty of psychological tendencies that can work in our favor. The next four chapters present various tools of influence that scientific research has shown effective and that can be used in a variety of ways for almost any activist cause. Some tools are useful for getting people to consent to things—saying "yes" when we want them to say "yes," voting the way we want them to vote, agreeing to volunteer their time, or donate money. Other tools are useful for creating behavioral change—for example, getting people to recycle or use public transportation. Activists should be familiar with all the psychological tools at their disposal, so they can choose the right ones in any given situation.

To start, let's take a look at some simple, easy-to-use tools of influence.

I WAS FRAMED!

Picture yourself sitting in the coffee shop of a local bookstore on your lunch break. You happen to have picked up a copy of *The Economist* magazine because you're taking an economics class and you want to see how what you're learning applies to the real world. As you flip through the pages you come across an advertisement for a one-year subscription to the magazine. You're given three choices: a web subscription for $59, a print subscription for $125, or a web-plus-print subscription for $125. Which one do you pick?

In an experiment based on this actual *Economist* ad, eighty-four percent of participants chose the last option, the web-plus-print subscription for $125. The remaining sixteen percent chose the first option, with no one choosing the second. You might be wondering why the magazine would be so stupid as to even include the second option—after all, who would order the print subscription alone when they could have that plus the web subscription for the same price? Let's just say the ad team at *The Economist* knows a little more about making money than we're giving them credit for.

When the middle option was removed in the experiment, the number of people who chose the more expensive option dropped from eighty-four to thirty-two percent. Somehow, including the seemingly worthless middle option sparked a huge increase in profits for *The Economist* by stimulating many more expensive subscriptions (Ariely 107). Why would this be the case?

The answer is *framing*. Put simply, framing means that we don't know what we want until we see it in context. Everything, including our judgments on how much something is worth, is relative and can be shaped by perceptual contrast (Cialdini 13). In the *Economist* advertisement, if you only have options one and three, then option one looks better in comparison, because it's less than half the price of option three. Once you add option two though, people are drawn to compare options two and three because they're so similar. Option three clearly seems better and it will be chosen by most people, who by now have forgotten about option one. This is an example of a type of framing called the *decoy effect*.

Framing and the decoy effect can be applied by activists in a lot of ways. One of the Humane League's current campaigns is trying to get universities to switch to cage-free eggs in their dining services. The only downside to this for students is the slight cost increase that accompanies a switch. One university's student government, when presented with this cost increase, was hesitant about the $5-per-term cost-increase for student meal-plans. In subsequent meetings with the student government, we re-framed the cost of going cage-free relative to the meal-plan cost-increase that already happens every year—on average, a $75 increase. The question for the student government was no longer: "Should we pay five dollars extra to go cage-free?" It was now: "Should we pay $75 and have no changes made at all, or should we pay $80 and have our school be cage-free?" Framing the issue this way helped generate support for the initiative, and the student government passed a near-unanimous vote encouraging their school to go cage-free.

Anytime activists are holding a vote on something or asking people to donate time or money, framing can come in handy as well. In our cage-free egg campaign we also worked with a campus group to develop a poll asking students how much extra they'd be willing to pay to have the school go cage-free. In offering different options of how much students would be willing to pay, we set out the following choices in this order: $5, $10, $20, $0. Instead of having $0 be first as it numerically should be, we included it last so that it would be framed by the $20 preceding it and seem inordinately low and out of line with the rest of the choices. Because this wasn't a scientific experiment, there was no control group to see just how much impact that ordering of choices had on how students voted. But the poll was successful in that only a small percentage of students chose $0. Framing may have helped that success.

In asking people to donate time or money, we might use the decoy effect by offering different personal incentives. For example, in requesting donations we might offer these options: donate $20; donate $50; donate $50 and get a free T-shirt. If this type of setup generated more high-level subscriptions for *The Economist* and for researchers studying the advertisement, it's likely to work for non-profits as well. And if you've ever gotten a donation-request form from a non-profit where the donation options varied back and forth between high and low amounts ($400, $45, $275, $100), that was framing at work as well.

ANCHORS: A WAY

Okay, imagination time again. Picture yourself sitting down at a small auction with a bid sheet in hand. Before things start, you're asked to write the last two digits of your social security number on the upper right corner of your bid sheet. The bidding begins. Based on the information I gave, do you think anything has occurred that will affect how high you bid on the auction items? In fact, there's one variable that could have made you bid up to three times higher than you otherwise would have: the last two digits of your social security number.

In an experimental auction testing this hypothesis, participants whose last two digits were high ("94," for example) bid three times more than participants whose last two digits were low. All the auction items were low-priced, well under $100, so writing down social security digits like "94" set a high "anchor" for the bids that were to follow. The same effect was found when participants spun a wheel before bidding: those who spun higher numbers went on to bid higher amounts of money. This phenomenon is called *anchoring*, and it's very similar to framing. If we have a number in mind for any reason, it can influence our numeric answers for other issues, even unrelated ones.

The applications of anchoring for activists are similar to those of framing. If seeking donations of time or money, or soliciting numeric answers in a poll, we might want to set an anchor that will generate answers closer to what we want. For the cage-free poll mentioned earlier, where we hoped for high responses on how much students would be willing to pay, we could have had students write their graduation year on the top of the sheet, or simply the number "99," to set a high anchor and draw answers upward. Similar anchors could be used on donation-request forms or when conducting auctions. If you've ever gotten a donation-request form from a non-profit and the donation option amounts started high and went lower ($100, $50, $35, $25), that was anchoring at work.

PRIME TIME

While anchoring deals with dollar amounts, the phenomenon of *priming* puts the same principles to work in a broader context. Priming involves giving cues meant to influence people's perceptions and behaviors. Priming can be done with words, images, and questions, among other things.

In one study, people who were asked to describe themselves in flattering terms later scored higher on self-esteem tests than those who were asked to describe themselves more modestly (Rhodewalt and Agustsdottir 1986). In another study, Asian-American women were divided into two groups. One group was asked race-related questions, while the other was asked gender-related questions. Both groups then took a math test. Those who had been asked race-related questions did better on the test (living out the stereotype that Asians are good at math) than those asked gender-related questions (who lived out the stereotype that women are not good at math) (Ariely 169). Researchers were able to influence participants' performance just by asking questions that primed them in a certain way.

A study published in the *Journal of Consumer Research* showed that college students were willing to spend twenty-nine percent more on mail-order catalog items, and donate two and a half times more to the United Way, when the room they were in contained some prominent MasterCard insignias—even when students were not paying by credit card (Feinberg 1986). Similarly, cash tips in restaurants were shown to be significantly higher when the trays for tips contained a credit-card insignia (McCall and Belmont 1996). Credit-card insignias prime people to be in a spending mood. A non-profit that puts prominent images of credit-card logos on their merchandise table should generate higher sales.

In other studies, the presence of briefcases and boardroom tables made participants more competitive and less generous, qualities associated with the business world. Study participants given iced coffee saw one another as more selfish, less sociable, and colder than those who were given hot coffee (Thaler and Sunstein 171).

Priming a person with certain words can also have an impact on judgment. In one experiment, participants who were first asked to memorize the words "reckless," "conceited," "aloof," and "stubborn" later formed negative impressions about the character of a fictitious story. Participants who were given the words "adventurous," "self-confident," "independent," and "persistent" formed positive impressions of the same character (Higgins 1977). In another study, students were given one of two descriptions of an upcoming guest lecturer: "Cold person, industrious, critical, practical, and determined," or "Warm person, industrious, critical, practical, and determined." Students had a much harsher view of the first person than the second, even though the descriptions were nearly identical. The first term—whether they were warm or cold—affected their perceptions of the other qualities listed (Larson *et al.* 1995).

Priming can be used by activists in a variety of ways. If a student environmental activist is meeting with an administrator at their university to encourage the school to switch to wind power, the activist can start off the meeting by prompting the administrator to talk about the university's current sustainability efforts. That should prime the administrator to be more supportive of other sustainability issues. In emails to students or administrators on the issue, the activist can pepper the first few sentences with phrases like "a good idea," "agree," and "on the same page" to help prime the other person for cooperation.

BREAK A PATTERN

To get someone's attention, it's very helpful to break a pattern. People are usually operating on autopilot, and if we can grab their full attention before making our pitch, we're more likely to get compliance. One research team has called this technique *disrupt and reframe.*

Door-to-door salesmen who announced the price of their product as three hundred pennies and then said "It's a bargain!" were twice as likely to sell Christmas cards as those who announced the price in dollars. Researchers who were selling cupcakes but instead called them "halfcakes" and then added, "They're delicious!" increased sales (Davis and Knowles 1999).

Vic Sjodin, a full-time leafleter who passes out booklets on vegetarianism at colleges across the country, will often say lines like "That's a lovely smile you have," "You look compassionate," or a variety of other things to students as they walk by. Since people aren't used to those types of personal comments from someone trying to give them a flyer, the comments increase the acceptance rate and probably also make recipients more receptive to the booklet's message. (Buttering them up doesn't hurt—as we'll discuss later, people will like you and listen to you more when they think you like them.) Strip club promoters in Las Vegas are well-known for making a popping sound with their fliers in order to get attention, making it easier to put a flier in someone's hand.

If the cause you're working on requires getting someone's attention and compliance, creatively breaking a pattern can make you more successful.

GIVE ME FEEDBACK

Earlier, we discussed loss-aversion, our fear of losing what we already have. The Duke basketball tickets study demonstrated just how powerful loss-aversion can be when it comes to financial and personal property issues. Providing feedback that shows the loss occurring can be a particularly powerful motivator for behavioral change.

Seeing a running meter of something—for example, the cost of a cab ride rising and rising, or calories burning off one by one on a digital counter while we exercise—has more of an impact than simply hearing the final price or number of calories burned. The Wattson, a popular item in the U.K., is a small device that displays in real time the amount of energy being used by a household and how much that energy is costing. Similar devices for sale in the U.S. show the electricity use and cost of individual appliances in real time. Watching the cost rise minute by minute can be a powerful motivator to lower energy consumption; the Wattson's creators claim the device cuts household energy usage by five to twenty-five percent simply by providing immediate feedback to home-owners.

Providing positive feedback on behavioral change that's already taken place can help increase that behavior. For example, signs posted on recycling containers that proudly mentioned how many cans had been collected the previous week increased subsequent recycling totals by sixty-five percent (Larson *et al.* 1995). In another study, households that were mailed letters about their reduced energy usage and financial savings subsequently decreased usage by another five percent, whereas a control group that didn't receive a letter actually increased their usage (Seligman and Darley 1977). Similarly, households in one town that got feedback on the number of pounds of materials they were recycling each week subsequently increased the amount of material they recycled by twenty-six percent (DeLeon and Fuqua 1995).

While these examples all deal with environmental issues, providing feedback can be useful for many types of behavioral change. Children's International, which has members "adopt" a child in a developing country for a monthly donation, has pictures and letters sent from the child to the adopter every few months. This ongoing positive feedback shows tangible results from the person's donation and is very effective for getting members to continue donating. Widgets to be placed on a person's social networking pages could be used by animal protection groups to show new vegetarians or semi-vegetarians how many animals have been spared a lifetime of misery that week, month, and year thanks to their change in diet. Similar widgets could also show the number of stray cats not killed in shelters because of the person's ongoing volunteer work with a trap–neuter–release program.

NARROW THEIR OPTIONS

When farmers are trying to herd animals from a larger area into a smaller one, they'll often create a chute that starts wide and gets narrower and narrower. Similarly, when we are trying to get someone to take an action, it's helpful to narrow their options. Offering people too many choices will make them more likely to choose nothing at all. A study of 800,000 workers found that the number of retirement funds offered by an employer was inversely related to the number of workers that signed up for any retirement fund (Iyengar, Huberman, and Jiang). The more retirement fund options they were given, the less likely workers were to choose any fund—which probably had negative consequences for workers and their families.

In another study, student participants were presented with two hypothetical choices for what they could do that evening: study in the library or attend a lecture by an author they admired who was in town for one night only. Only twenty-one percent opted to study, with seventy-nine percent choosing the more enjoyable activity. In the second round of this study, participants were presented with three options: the library, the author, and also watching a foreign film they'd wanted to see. In this second study, forty percent of participants decided to study, with sixty percent choosing one of the more enjoyable activities. Giving students two good alternatives to studying made them less likely to choose either (Redelmeier and Shafir 1995).

In trying to encourage people to do something positive, we're often tempted to give them an array of choices based on the idea that the more choices they have, the more likely they'll find one of them acceptable. Environmental campaigners might provide a list of twenty-five different things a person can do to help protect the planet. Gay-rights groups might create a similar list of actions people can take to promote equality. Health organizations might create a long list of foods rich in vitamins and minerals that should be part of a healthy diet. The research suggests that these groups would be more successful if they focused instead on promoting a few key actions.

Activists should also be aware that there's a big difference between education meant to stimulate thought and education meant to stimulate action. There are many shades of grey to every issue, and the more we think about an issue the more complexities we will see. If we are college professors and our goal is to hone our students' critical-thinking abilities, then ongoing discussion that examines every aspect of an issue is a good thing. But if we as activists are trying to educate people in order to motivate them to do something, then our communications need to simplify the issue and call for clear, specific action. We need to eliminate distractions and narrow options. One of the innate aspects of campaigning for policy change is that you're taking a grey issue and turning it into a black-and-white one. People can either support the change or they can oppose it. Campaigns convert unclear responsibility into clear responsibility, and convert non-urgent and broad issues into urgent and specific ones.

In 2008, two landmark ballot initiatives were put to voters in California: Proposition 8, which succeeded by a narrow margin in banning gay and lesbian marriages; and Proposition 2, which easily succeeded in banning the intensive confinement of farm animals. By and large, the media coverage and public dialogue on Proposition 2 were focused on a specific issue: whether farmers should be allowed to confine animals in cages so small the animals could barely move. Groups on either side debated the animal welfare, economic, and health impacts of the bill. The issue was clear and specific—cages or no cages—and the media coverage and public debate rarely strayed into more general philosophical arguments on animal rights. This may have been part of the reason for the bill's successful passage, a landmark event that will spare tens of millions of animals a great deal of suffering every year, once the law goes into effect in 2015.

On the other hand, media coverage and public debate over Proposition 8 centered on the conflict between religious beliefs and civil equality, a complex issue due to the diversity of beliefs people have on religion and its role in politics. Through no fault of gay-rights organizers, the question of what marriage means is so nuanced that gay marriage seemed to have too many possible implications for the majority of the public to support it. As a result Proposition 8 passed and same-sex marriages were made illegal in California, at least for the time being.

PROMPTS

Prompts are little reminders that can be helpful in getting people to do repetitive but easily forgettable behaviors that they already support, such as recycling, turning off lights when they leave a room, or buying environmentally friendly products. Prompts should be as close in time and space as possible to the targeted behavior. A prompt to recycle could be a sign on a recycling bin that's been placed next to a trash can—the container into which a person would otherwise throw their aluminum can. In contrast, prompts on street signs encouraging people to recycle will be much less effective. Prompts about which products are environmentally friendly could be put on store shelves next to specific products. This would be much more effective than passing out brochures to shoppers about which products are environmentally friendly.

TheHungerSite.com, which provides a food donation to needy people each time you click a button on the site, is more effective when it gets people to set the site as their home page or sign up for email reminders. While virtually everyone would be willing to take three seconds to click a button in order to help feed the poor, most people who hear about the site will use it several times then forget about it, because they're not repeatedly prompted to use it. Putting a note on the fridge to use TheHungerSite.com every day would not be a very effective prompt since it's separated in time and space from when a person would be online and able to visit the site. The refrigerator could, however, be a good place for a prompt on healthy eating, assuming you have healthy food in it and that the fridge is where you usually go when you're hungry.

Many colleges and buildings have prompts encouraging people to turn off lights when leaving a room, but they place these prompts on the light-switch covers. Although the prompts might be noticed when a person enters a room and turns on the light, when the person is leaving they may not look at the light switch and so may not see the prompt. Because of the poor choice of location, prompts like these are less effective than they would be if placed in a more visible spot, such as on the door.

When creating prompts, we should use ones that work in concert with people's current frames of reference. For example, when most people see a trash can, they think "This is where I throw my trash." When companies, schools, or cities use recycling bins that look just like trash cans but are labeled for recycling, people are going to throw trash in, because they won't always pay enough attention to realize the containers are recycling bins.

The way that prompts are designed can have a dramatic effect on how successful they are in creating behavioral change. Signs prompting Styrofoam recycling at one college had been having very little effect. Researchers made changes to the signs, including making the font size larger and more visible; placing them at eye level; making the language on the signs more specific, starting with the most important point first; showing physical examples of adequately cleaned Styrofoam plates and bowls; and having an extra prompt asking students to keep food contaminants out. Improving the prompt led to three times more recycling of Styrofoam products. It also led to the Styrofoam being scraped clean, whereas in the past, food contamination had been occurring regularly.

Prompting works by changing behaviors, not values (though as we discussed earlier, in some cases changing behavior can lead to a change in values). The researchers in the Styrofoam study surveyed students before and after improving the recycling prompts, and found that attitudes on recycling Styrofoam hadn't really changed. However, awareness of how to recycle and awareness of the presence of Styrofoam recycling bins had grown, and there was a huge increase in Styrofoam recycling (Werner, Rhodes, and Partain 1998).

When you're promoting a simple and repetitive behavior that people already support, using prompts can be a very effective way of countering forgetfulness and creating behavioral change. Because prompts don't require changing values, they're easy to use, and once put in place will continue to work on their own, as long as they're well-designed.

MIND THE GAP

Do you want to learn a great technique you can use to get someone's attention?

You've just seen it!

Behavioral economist George Loewenstein of Carnegie Mellon University has proposed what he calls the *gap theory of curiosity*. His theory is that curiosity happens when people feel a gap in their knowledge about something. In order to get someone to pay attention to us, we can stimulate their curiosity by creating a perceived gap in their knowledge. Laying out a question and inviting others to ponder it will help keep the individual's attention, because it gets them mentally involved and because there's an element of unexpectedness. This is why cliffhangers are often used at the end of television soap operas, to get viewers to tune in to the next episode, or at the end of chapters in a thriller to keep readers glued to the page.

Taking the gap theory a step further, Harvard physics professor Eric Mazur has developed a teaching tool he calls *concept testing*. Mazur has found that posing a question to stimulate curiosity and then asking students to vote publicly on the answer make them more engaged and curious about the outcome. Mazur has also found that fostering disagreement among students is particularly effective at stimulating interest. Not only has their curiosity been stimulated, but learning the answer now has personal relevance—it will show whether or not they're smarter than their classmates.

In trying to grab someone's attention, consider leading off with a question that piques their curiosity and that solicits a guess. In discussing the environmental impacts of factory farming, one might start off by stating:

> In the Gulf of Mexico there is an area 7,700 square miles in size—an area larger than the size of New Jersey—where virtually all the fish and other marine life have died off. This "dead zone" is the world's largest, and it came into existence just a few years ago. What could have created this terrible situation? A massive oil spill from a tanker? A nuclear disaster? If you knew this could be prevented from happening again, would you take action to prevent it?[2]

By putting the gap theory of curiosity to work for us, we can capture the attention and interest of our public as effectively as any good mystery writer.

MAKE A PLAN

Getting someone to make a plan for how they'll carry out the behavior you're promoting, or showing them very clearly how to do the behavior, can be helpful for getting them to follow through. It can help bridge the attitude/behavior gap in which people believe in something, yet don't act accordingly. Research published in the *Journal of Applied Psychology* shows that self-control, a very important element in adopting a new behavior, is most likely to occur when a person focuses on a specific and reachable goal (Loke, Bryan, and Kendall 1968; Kanfer and Goldstein 1975).

In the 1960s, Yale professor Howard Leventhal wanted to see whether high-fear or low-fear appeals would be more successful in convincing students to get tetanus shots from the campus health center. He prepared two different booklets on the subject, with the high-fear version containing graphic pictures of tetanus victims and extremely descriptive language evoking the horrors of tetanus. The low-fear booklet contained similar information but lacked pictures and descriptive language. The students who received the high-fear booklets were more convinced of the dangers of tetanus and the importance of getting shots. However, when Leventhal tracked actual behavior, he found that both booklets produced the same rate of compliance: a paltry three percent of students went to get a tetanus shot. In this situation, increased attitudinal change in the high-fear group didn't lead to increased behavioral change.

In a follow-up experiment, Leventhal added one seemingly minor change to the booklets. He added a campus map, with the health center circled, and listed the times that tetanus vaccines were available. He also asked students who received the booklets to make a plan for what time they'd go to get a shot and what route they'd take to get to the health center. Even though the students were seniors and probably knew where the health center was, simply adding the map and asking students to make a plan for when and how they'd go to get shots increased actual compliance from three to twenty-eight percent (with the low-fear booklets equally as effective as the high-fear booklets). In this situation, it wasn't greater attitudinal change that was needed, but clear instructions on how to make the change. In imagining the route they'd take and the time they'd arrive, students had made the process of getting a tetanus shot more mentally available to them and, therefore, made it seem more desirable and important (Leventhal, Singer, and Jones 1965).

Along the same lines, *implementation intentions* have been shown to be successful in maintaining behavioral change in areas where it's easy to stray. Implementation intentions are statements like "If a friend asks me to go out drinking, then I'll go to a coffee shop instead" (a useful implementation intention for a recovering alcoholic). Implementation intentions have been shown to be effective in increasing compliance with speed limits (Elliott and Armitage 2006), decreasing the amount people drive (Eriksson, Garvill, and Nordlund 2008), boosting the use of public transportation, and encouraging the patronage of stores that sell more eco-friendly products (Bamberg 2002).

Presenting clear instructions—even if the instructions should be obvious—and asking people to make a plan can be helpful in getting people to bridge the gap between attitudes and actions. If we're encouraging people to eat locally grown produce, providing a detailed map with the locations and times of nearby farmers markets is essential. Groups trying to prevent sexual assault might encourage people to develop implementation intentions such as "If I see a person too inebriated to take care of themselves, then I will help them get a cab home."

ANYTHING HELPS

Pointing out that even a small contribution makes a difference has been shown to be effective in getting more people to donate. In one study, researchers went door-to-door asking residents to donate to the American Cancer Society. For half the residents they appended: "Even a penny will help." Adding those five words increased the percentage of people donating from twenty-nine to fifty percent, and raised total donations from forty-four dollars to seventy-two dollars for every hundred people that were asked. This means that not only did many more people donate, but the average donation size stayed about the same, even though the researchers noted the value of small donations (Cialdini and Schroeder 1976).

Adding "Even a penny will help" or a similar phrase to solicitations for money should help us be more successful in our fundraising. Whether we're going door-to-door, canvassing on a street corner, tabling, or sending out a request by mail, this simple phrase should increase our fundraising totals. A similar phrase could also be effective in recruiting volunteers to lend additional time to your cause: for example, "In just ten minutes you could save a life!"

REVVING UP VOLUNTEERS

Most small activist organizations rely on volunteer labor to achieve their goals. Unfortunately, volunteers are notoriously fickle, expressing great interest one day and disappearing the next, never to be heard from again. While this general situation is unlikely to change, the scientific record does provide insight into strategies that might help activist groups strengthen the commitment of their core volunteers.

In one study, fifth graders who were praised for their hard work went on to do better and take on harder challenges than students who were praised for being smart. Those who were praised for their intelligence feared looking stupid later on, so they shied away from harder challenges and performed worse as the workload became heavier (Lehrer

53). It's not proven that the same process would operate with adult volunteers, but it's worth keeping in mind when deciding how to give your volunteers a pat on the back for their work.

Another tip that psychological research can provide is that, while we might be inclined to make things as easy as possible for volunteers, making them work hard and suffer for the cause or having them confront the opposition is likely to make them more committed. As a result of cognitive dissonance, the more that people work for something the more they will come to like it: "I just spent all day passing out flyers in the hot sun; I must really support what this non-profit is doing" (see Brehm, Kassin, and Fein 217).

This is why hazing continues to be so popular among fraternities, sororities, military groups and other small organizations. The more intense the initiation ordeal, the more committed a person will be to the group afterward. In a study published in the *Journal of Experimental Social Psychology*, women who endured pain or embarrassment to get into a sex-discussion group valued it much more highly than those who were admitted without having to endure those tribulations (Gerard and Mathewson 1996). A study of fifty-four native cultures found those with the harshest initiation ceremonies also had the greatest group solidarity (Young).

Furthermore, confrontation with an opposition force is a strong builder of group solidarity (Andreasen *Social Marketing in the 21st Century* 143). Protestors of disparate causes confronted by a line of club-wielding police at a protest at a World Trade Organization meeting suddenly find themselves feeling very unified with one another. (Though it also works the other way around; people watching the news who see windows being smashed by activists might become unified in condemning the protests.) Even group viewings of videos of animal cruelty, labor abuses, or other issues might make the viewers feel more unified with one another in their need to take action.

In the first chapter, we discussed why we and others become active for a particular cause. It's important to accept the fact that most volunteers aren't guided by pure altruism; they also have self-oriented motives, such as the desire to gain skills and find a social group. This isn't a problem in and of itself (though we have to be careful that our motives don't cause us to be less effective than we could be), and we should realize the importance that personal benefits play in volunteers' willingness to stay involved. A study of people who volunteered with AIDS organizations found that those who'd initially expressed self-oriented motives for volunteering—like gaining personal skills and an understanding of the issue—remained active longer than those who'd initially expressed altruistic motives, such as concern for the community (Omoto and Snyder 1995). Because of how our brains are hardwired, self-interest can sometimes keep volunteers (and ourselves) going when simple altruism would not. The feeling of competence that comes with success, the invigorating personal challenge to do more, and the sense of living a meaningful life can all provide strong motivation to keep going.

THE WALLS HAVE EYES

Imagine you're an office manager who cares about the environment. In one corner of the office sits a trash can, a paper-recycling bin, and a recycling bin for glass, plastic, and aluminum. Office policy states that all recyclable materials must be recycled by being deposited into the correct containers. While some employees are good about recycling, all too often you find paper and soda bottles in the garbage can. You've asked your employees several times to be more mindful, but things haven't gotten much better. What should you do?

For one thing, you could try putting either a mirror or a picture of a pair of eyes over the trash can and recycling bins. Research has found that if people see their own image or a pair of eyes, they act more ethically, as if there were another person in the room watching them.

In one experiment, trick-or-treating children were asked to take just one piece of candy from a bowl that had been left out on a porch. Sixty-six percent of the children complied by taking only one piece. However, when a mirror was put out on the porch so that children could see themselves as they put their hand in the candy bowl, ninety-one percent of children followed the rules and limited themselves to a single piece (Beaman *et al.* 1979). Another study found that showing participants a CCTV broadcast of their own image right before they left an experiment reduced their littering in the stairwell on the way out from forty-six to twenty-four percent (Kallgren, Reno, and Cialdini 2000). Placing a picture of eyes on the wall in a communal area where people were supposed to pay for coffee or tea they drank increased paying by an astonishing 250 percent (Bateson, Nettle, and Roberts 2006).

This technique has limited applicability for activists, but it could probably be used effectively in situations where prompts are already being used. As suggested, signs promoting recycling that have been placed by trash and recycling bins in a college cafeteria could have a mirror or a picture of eyes attached. Building entranceways where people are not supposed to smoke, but often do, could have mirrors installed to discourage such behavior.

GO MENTAL

Interested in improving your communication skills (or tennis skills, or any other skill)? For times and situations where you're not able to actually practice the skill, go mental!

A meta-analysis of thirty-five studies with over three thousand total participants found that carefully mentally rehearsing something produced about two-thirds of the benefits of actual physical practice. The benefits of mentally imagining the task were even higher for activities that weren't physically demanding (like public speaking or navigating a city) and a bit lower for activities that were mainly physical (like perfecting a golf swing) (Driskell, Copper, and Moran 1994).

A labor activist nervous about an upcoming negotiation meeting can imagine the back-and-forth dialogue in her head a number of times until she feels more confident in her ability to answer questions and make strong arguments. An amateur graphic designer who does volunteer work for a local SPCA can spend his train ride to work envisioning new design elements for the SPCA's print materials. An environmental activist nervous about an upcoming speech to an audience of three hundred people can mentally visualize herself in that setting while rehearsing the speech.

WHAT'S IN A NAME

Dale Carnegie famously wrote that nothing sounds sweeter to a person's ears than hearing their own name. This is why calling someone by their name is helpful for persuasion (for example, "Thanks, Judy, I appreciate it"). But the influence people's own names can have on them goes even further. Because people like things that are similar to them and things that are familiar, names can affect major life decisions people make and can even be used to gain compliance.

A study of dentists published in the *Journal of Personality and Social Psychology* found that they were forty-three percent more likely to be named Dennis than Jerry or Walter, even though the three names were equally popular during the years those dentists were born. Similarly, hardware store owners were found to be eighty percent more likely to have names starting with H than R, and roofers were seventy percent more likely to have names starting with R than H. People who moved to Florida or Louisiana are disproportionately named Florence and Louise. A similar connection to names has been found for the streets people live on, the towns they live in, and who they choose as romantic partners (Pelham, Mirenberg, and Jones 2002; Jones *et al.* 2004).

How can this strange phenomenon be used to our advantage? One creative researcher sent out surveys where the name of the sender was fabricated to look similar to the name of the recipient—for example, Cynthia Johnston and Cindy Johansen. The study found that making the sender's name similar to that of the recipient doubled the rate at which surveys were filled out and returned (Garner 2005). Activists willing to use this trick might do so on donation-request letters, on emails asking people to sign a petition, or on press releases to specific reporters. There are undoubtedly additional creative ways to use people's love of their own names to our advantage in gaining compliance.

Familiarity isn't the only influential aspect of words. Words that are simple, rhythmic, and easy to speak are more influential than those that aren't. You're probably familiar with rhyming maxims like "An apple a day keeps the doctor away," and if you're beyond a certain age you'll likely remember "If the glove doesn't fit, you must acquit." Research has found that statements that rhyme are perceived by people as more accurate than those that don't (McGlone and Tofighbakhsh 2000). People use *fluidity* as an indicator of accuracy—possibly because fluid statements stick in the mind and people prefer the familiar.

Investors, take note. A study published in the *Proceedings of the National Academy of Sciences* that followed stock names for a year after their launch found that those with the most easily pronounceable names performed much better than those with less fluent names, earning on average $330 more on a $1,000 investment. The same study also examined 750 companies on the New York Stock Exchange and American Stock Exchange and found that those with more fluid ticker symbols performed better than those without fluidity (for example, PIP vs. DTX) (Alter and Oppenheimer 2006).

The importance of fluidity should be taken into consideration when deciding on a name for your organization and a slogan for your campaign. One of the more active animal advocacy organizations in the U.S. in the 1980s and 1990s was called Trans-Species Unlimited, a confusing and hard-to-pronounce name that probably worked to their detriment. Easily pronounceable names, acronyms, and slogans may be helpful in garnering the public's support.

chapter five

TOOLS OF INFLUENCE, PART II: POWER TOOLS

DON'T BE AFRAID TO ASK

Do you plan to vote in the next election? If someone asked you that question a few days before the election, you'd become more likely to vote. Merely asking someone if they intend to do something can influence their likelihood of doing it.

In a study published in the *Journal of Applied Psychology*, it was found that approaching people the day before an election and asking them if they planned to vote increased voter turnout in that group by twenty-five percentage points (eighty-seven compared to sixty-two percent) (Greenwald *et al.* 1987). In another study, residents of Bloomington, Indiana were significantly more likely to volunteer time with the American Cancer Society (thirty-one vs. four percent) if a few days earlier they'd been asked whether they would hypothetically consider volunteering with the ACS (Sherman 1980).

Asking someone's intention to do something only increases their probability of doing it when they say they're likely to do it. When someone believes they're unlikely to do something, asking them their intention will make them even less likely to do it (Sherman 1980). The reason that asking intent often leads to an overall increase in the action being done is because people often over-predict how likely they are to do something. In the studies above, because of social norms nearly everyone answered "yes" when asked if they would volunteer with a cancer society or vote in an election. Once they'd said "yes," they were then more likely to do so. That's why asking their intent led to higher rates of volunteering and voting.

In a study polling tens of thousands of households across the country on car and computer purchases, researchers believed that people would over-predict their likelihood of purchasing those products in the next six months. After being polled, each household's purchases were tracked for the next six months and the researchers' predictions were confirmed. For buying a car, a huge financial decision, simply asking intent increased purchasing by thirty-one percent. For household computers, purchasing increased by eighteen percent when people were asked their intention.

This same study also examined the effects of repeated polling on behavior. It found that repeated polling made those with high intent to buy only slightly more likely to do so. On the other hand, repeated polling made those who had little intent to buy drastically less likely to do so. Those who had a low initial intent to buy a car were sixty-nine percent less likely to do so when polled multiple times than when they were polled only once. The figure was forty-seven percent less for computers (Morwitz, Johnson, and Schmittlein 1993). If a non-profit wanted to deter its audience from engaging in an unlikely behavior ("Do you intend to use heroin in the next six months?"), it would be most successful by polling its audience several times. On the other hand, a non-profit that wants people to engage in a particular behavior ("Do you intend to eat more vegetables next month?") should only ask the question once; repeat polling would cause only a few more people to do so, and many more people to avoid doing so.

Why does asking intent influence behavior so significantly? Think back to the availability bias discussed earlier: the easier we can bring something to mind, the more we tend to value it. Answering a question about intention makes a person's attitude on the behavior more mentally accessible. Saying they intend to do something also causes a person to feel like they've made a commitment. Both of these lead the person to think more highly of the behavior, therefore becoming more likely to buy a car, vote in an election, etc.

Being able to picture one's self engaging in the behavior is key, even when that picturing is done unconsciously or automatically. If people can't picture themselves doing it, asking their intention won't increase the likelihood that they're going to do it. Research participants who were asked how much they expected others to floss their teeth didn't themselves increase that behavior, since the question didn't lead people to picture themselves flossing. Similarly, participants who were asked "How likely are you to avoid fatty foods in the next week?" were twice as likely to do so as participants who were asked "How likely are you to not eat fatty foods in the next week?" The latter question had little impact on behavior because it's hard to picture oneself not doing something (Levav and Fitzsimons 2006).

These studies suggest some serious opportunities for activists trying to create behavioral change. Asking people if they plan to donate to your non-profit in the future should increase their likelihood of donating. Volunteers asked if they'd be willing to take part in a charity walk if the organization holds one would be more likely to do so when the organization does decide to go ahead with the walk.

Any situation where we expect people to over-report their likelihood of doing the desired behavior is a good opportunity for using this tool. Because people over-report their likelihood of doing most socially smiled-upon behaviors (like volunteering, voting, or caring for the environment), we should be able to get people to do these things more often by asking them if they plan to do them. For example, asking people if they plan to recycle this year should increase their likelihood of recycling. The same should hold true for working at a soup kitchen or volunteering at an animal shelter. And because asking someone's intention is so easy, so subtle, and appears to have such a big payoff in the right circumstances, it could be a powerful tool in any activist's toolkit.

A word of warning though: we should steer clear of asking people's intent when they will probably under-report their likelihood of doing something, or when most will say they don't plan on doing it. For example, asking the public if they plan to go vegetarian would probably backfire, because most people would say "no" and there's no social norm that would encourage people to over-report their likelihood of going vegetarian. On the other hand, if animal activists could identify a group of people who'd expressed interest in going vegetarian, asking them their intent should increase their likelihood of carrying out the switch.

A more nuanced situation would be polling home-owners on whether they intend to install solar panels. The vast majority of people have little intent to do this, and asking them would make them even less likely to do so. On the other hand, adding solar panels is seen as a socially popular action right now, so people might over-report their likelihood of doing so, making some people more likely to install panels. Deciding whether it's useful to ask intent in situations like this would take careful consideration, and would benefit from preliminary testing.

COMMITTED

Getting a person to commit to doing something is a good way to ensure they'll follow through. We often put this into effect in our personal lives: "You sure you'll be able to help me move next Saturday?" Because no one wants to look like a flake, once they've verbally committed to something they're more likely to follow through. Research has shown simple verbal commitments to be effective. A restaurant that started telling customers who called to make phone reservations, "Will you please call us if you change your plans?" and waited for a response, saw their no-show rate drop from thirty to ten percent (Cialdini 1998). Another study found that people making reminder calls about a blood drive who ended by adding, "We'll count on seeing you then, okay?" and waiting for a response, increased the show-up rate by almost thirty percent (Lipsitz *et al.* 1989). The power of commitment can be put to very good use by activists in getting people to follow through on behaviors that they support but might not prioritize: for example, recycling, making a donation to a charity, or conserving energy.

A study by social marketers Doug McKenzie-Mohr and colleagues examined different ways to promote bus ridership, dividing study participants into four groups. The first group was given route and schedule information about the bus system. Participants in the second group were asked to make a verbal pledge to ride the bus. The third group was given ten free bus tickets and told they could receive more later. The final group was both asked for the verbal pledge and given the free bus tickets. Which of these four methods do you think had the greatest success in increasing ridership on the city's buses?

While all four of the initiatives increased bus usage, the largest gains were found in the second and fourth groups: those who'd been asked for a verbal commitment, and those who'd both been asked for the verbal commitment and had been given free tickets. The second and fourth group showed equal increases in bus usage—demonstrating that it was the verbal commitment, and not the free tickets, that played the key role. When researchers checked in on participants three weeks and three months later, the effects of the intervention remained the same (McKenzie-Mohr, Smith, and Smith 1999).

Other studies have demonstrated the power of written commitments. Signed commitments increased recycling in Salt Lake City more than a flyer, phone call, or personal contact alone (Werner *et al.* 1995). A separate recycling study that requested either verbal or written commitments from participants found that only those who had committed in writing were still recycling when a follow-up visit was conducted (Pardini and Katzev 1983–4).

Having a commitment be public can make it even more effective. In one study, those who agreed to a public commitment to household energy conservation (their names would be published in a local newspaper) saved significantly more energy than those who made a private one. Even after learning that their names would not actually be published, these individuals continued to save more household energy than those who had made a private commitment (Pallak, Cook, and Sullivan 1980).

Group commitments can also be very effective in situations where there's good group cohesion and individuals care how they're viewed by others. When members of a retirement home were asked to make a group commitment to recycling, there was a forty-seven percent increase in paper recycling (Wang and Katzev 1990).

Asking people to commit to being spokespeople for a behavioral change has also been shown to be effective in spreading the behavior. In one study, a group asked to commit to grass cycling (spreading cut grass over one's lawn instead of bagging it and disposing of it as garbage) didn't increase this behavior. A second group was asked to commit to grass cycling but also instructed to ask their neighbors to do the same. In this condition, both participants and their neighbors increased grass cycling. This increase was still observable when researchers checked back twelve months later. Two lessons can be learned here. The first is that getting people to be spokespersons makes them more likely to adopt the behavior they're encouraging in others. Secondly, people are more likely to follow through on a verbal commitment they make to their neighbor than a verbal commitment they make to a stranger (in this case a researcher).

When we're trying to create change as activists, we're more likely to succeed if we can get others to make a commitment. Rory Freedman, co-author of the bestseller *Skinny Bitch* and a strong promoter of veganism, sometimes finishes public talks by asking people in the audience to make a "pinkie pledge" to try going vegetarian or vegan for thirty days. Other vegetarian advocates sometimes hold a "Veg Week," where they encourage people to sign a written pledge to eat vegetarian food for one week. Many colleges hold a competition each year, where residence halls are pitted against one another to see who can save the most electricity over the course of a week or a month. Residents of each hall are asked to make a group commitment to reduce energy usage in order to help the environment and/or to help the hall win the prize that sometimes accompanies these competitions. College alumni magazines that list the names of donors aren't just doing so to thank them or to demonstrate a social norm that alumni are supposed to donate. They're also making public each donor's commitment to supporting the college, which makes those individuals more likely to continue donating in the future.

Commitments can also be helpful for creating policy changes at the institutional level. When we at the Humane League are able to convince a business, school, hospital, restaurant, or other institution to make a change that benefits animals, unless there are other overriding factors we like to make that commitment public by putting out a press release and trying to get media coverage. Having the institution's decision made public lessens the likelihood that it will later go back on its word; doing so would make it look like it was indecisive or that it had made a mistake.

FOOT IN THE DOOR

Imagine you hear a knock on your door one day and upon answering it you find a couple of men who'd like to put an ugly sign in your front yard. The sign says "Drive carefully" and the men claim to be working for a non-profit that promotes safe driving. Would you allow them to put the sign in your yard? Chances are you wouldn't; when researchers carried out this experiment only seventeen percent of home-owners agreed to the request.

However, the researchers thought they knew a way to get more people to say "yes." They visited a second group of home-owners and instead of bringing the yard signs they carried three-inch-by-three-inch window stickers encouraging safe driving. When the researchers asked home-owners to place the small signs in their windows, virtually all agreed. A few weeks later, the researchers returned with the ugly yard signs in tow. They asked the home-owners if they'd be willing to put the signs in their yards, and this time a whopping seventy-six percent said "yes." What had happened to increase compliance from seventeen to seventy-six percent? The researchers had gotten their foot in the door (Freedman and Fraser 1966).

The *foot-in-the-door technique* is one of the most common business tricks used to increase sales and acquire new customers. It's a technique that activists can use to create behavioral change, improve policies, recruit volunteers, and acquire donors. The basic mechanism of the foot-in-the-door technique is to make a small initial request to which a person is likely to say "yes." After they've said "yes" and some time has passed, you make a second, larger request that's similar in nature to the first. The person is now more likely to say "yes" to the larger request than they would have been if you hadn't already gotten your foot in the door with the small initial request.

Individuals previously asked to wear a Canadian Cancer Society pin were about twice as likely to donate to the CCS than those who hadn't been asked to wear the pin (Pliner *et al.* 1974). When asked if they'd financially support a recreation center for the handicapped, fifty-three percent of people who'd never previously been approached about the issue agreed to make a donation. In contrast, ninety-two percent of people who'd previously been asked to sign a petition supporting the facility agreed to make a donation (Schwarzwald, Raz, and Zyibel 1979).

The foot-in-the-door technique works by altering self-perception. As was mentioned in our discussion of cognitive dissonance, people often look at their own behavior to decide what their beliefs are (Bem 1972; Vallacher and Wegner). In getting somebody to agree to your small initial request, you've helped shape their self-perception to include the belief that "I'm the sort of person who _____." They're now much more likely to comply with other requests that are consistent with that self-concept. For example, asking a person to wear a small pin about breast cancer awareness may do little in and of itself, but the person who agreed to wear it is now more likely to believe "I'm the sort of person who cares about breast cancer." That belief makes it easier for breast-cancer groups to later solicit that person to volunteer time or donate money to combat breast cancer.

A thorough meta-analysis of foot-in-the-door studies, conducted for the journal *Personality and Social Psychology Review* by researcher Jerry Burger, found that on average this technique increases compliance rates by about thirteen percent, though sometimes the number is much higher. The foot-in-the-door technique works even when a sub-stantial amount of time passes between the first and second request, and even when the two requests are made by different people. In fact, this technique has been shown to work better when a different person presents the second request, and to work better when there's more of a delay between the two requests.

Burger's meta-analysis uncovered a few other general rules about the foot-in-the-door technique. For example, it works particularly well for behaviors where the first and second requests are very similar in nature. It also works particularly well when the first request requires more active involvement from the participant. For the technique to work, the initial commitment has to be freely and actively chosen. Forcing someone to do something doesn't change their self-image, and so it won't lead them to comply with a later request.

Social norms also influence how effective the technique is. If people think most others are doing something (for example, signing a petition or donating) they're more likely to do the same and more likely to comply with the second request. However, the reverse is also true: saying "Thanks for stopping, nobody else seems to care about saving the rainforest" will make you less effective when following up with a second request because you've informed the signer that the issue is an unimportant one, at least according to social norms (Burger 1999).

A person's perception as to why they complied with the first request also influences how successful the second request will be. One study found that donors to a charity who were told they were a very generous person later gave seventy-five percent more when asked for a donation by an unrelated charity (Kraut 1973). Once a person began to perceive themselves as generous, they were inclined to give more regardless of who was asking. In another study, people who were paid as a "thank you" for their compliance with an initial request were less likely to comply with a second request. They attributed their initial compliance to the financial benefit, so there was no motivation to comply with the second request since no additional money was offered (Burger 1999).

Using the foot-in-the-door technique is likely to make our efforts to create behavioral change more successful. We can get volunteers and donors involved by first requesting something small like a petition signature, a dollar donation, putting a bumper sticker on a car, or sending a protest email to a CEO. We can then follow up with progressively larger requests of their time, effort, and money. Not everyone will continue up the ladder of greater and greater involvement, but we'll achieve more substantial commitments this way than if we'd asked for the large commitment from the start. To be as successful as possible, we should try to have the first request be personally involving, but not so large as to be a major commitment (for example, have them mail a letter instead of signing a petition); invoke social norms by noting that many people are complying ("Over one thousand have already signed!"); tell the person why they're complying ("You must really care about the environment!"); and have the second request be similar in nature.

No studies have been done on the effect of the foot-in-the-door technique when it comes to changes on the institutional level. For example, if you can convince a university to switch the office paper they're buying to thirty-percent recycled stock, will that make it easier or harder to convince them to switch to one hundred percent recycled paper if you make that request a few years later? On the one hand, since they made the initial change, the decision-makers on this issue are more likely to have the self-perception that "We are a school that is concerned with sustainability," which should then make it easier to convince them to switch to one hundred percent recycled paper. But because institutions don't operate exactly the same as individuals, and because institutional policy changes carry more consequences than donating a few hours of time or putting a sign in your front yard, we can't draw any hard and fast conclusions about how foot-in-the-door applies to creating institutional change.

Institutions are not as susceptible to influence as individuals because of the number of decision-makers involved and the bureaucracy that must be dealt with to achieve any significant change. Another complicating factor is that institutions will rarely answer "yes" or "no" right away, like an individual does. They'll deliberate on the issue for a long time, and getting compliance with even a small request is likely to take a significant amount of time and effort on the part of the activist organization pushing for the change. Foot-in-the-door would suggest that concluding the first change makes the second change easier, but research has not been conducted to demonstrate this.

ALWAYS BE NORMAL

We like to think we're independent and make choices based on what *we* want to do, not what others are doing. However, research on social norms—information about what most other people are doing—suggests we're influenced by the majority opinion much more than we think. Invoking social norms can help activists succeed in changing attitudes and behaviors.

Earlier, we discussed how invoking social norms was more successful at getting home-owners to conserve energy than appeals to financial savings, community benefit, or environmental protection. In another study, famed persuasion researcher Robert Cialdini and his colleagues worked with a hotel to make changes to room signs encouraging the reuse of towels. Previously, the signs had asked guests to reuse towels to help protect the environment, but Cialdini and his team replaced these with signs that simply noted that the majority of guests reused towels. After switching from an environmental message to a social-norms message, towel reuse increased by twenty-six percent. When the signs noted that most guests of that particular room reused towels, reuse increased by thirty-three percent (Goldstein, Cialdini, and Griskevicius 2008).

This same effect has been shown in numerous other studies. White college students who were told they had more stereotyped perceptions of African-Americans than their peers later endorsed fewer stereotypes (Stangor, Sechrist, and Jost 2001). An Oklahoma anti-littering ad campaign that showed littering to be a violation of social norms got the percentage of residents who said they'd feel guilty if they littered to rise from thirty-seven to sixty-seven percent in just a few years (Grosmick et al. 1991).

Statements of social norms can be used for any activist efforts where the behavior being promoted is already in the majority. Distributing door hangers that point out the majority of residents in a community spay and neuter their companion animals should increase the amount of spaying and neutering going on in that community. Noting that millions of people donated to fight cancer last year should help increase the number of people donating to a cancer-prevention organization. Advertisements stating that most Americans know their HIV status should cause many who don't know their status to get tested. Combining a statement of what the social norm is with a specific request ("Get HIV tested"; "Spay or neuter your animal") is particularly effective (Cialdini 2003).

Another method of using social norms is modeling. When individuals—either community leaders or regular people—engage in a particular behavior, other people take hints from them as to how they're supposed to act in that situation. In a study published in the *Journal of Environmental Systems*, researchers at the University of Santa Cruz wanted to see how they could encourage students to take more environmentally friendly showers. The school's hope was that students would turn on the water to get wet, turn the water off while they soaped up, then turn the water back on to wash off. Placing a sign about the issue on the locker-room door led only six percent of students to comply. However, having the sign plus one person in the shower modeling this behavior (without speaking to or even looking at other students) increased compliance to forty-nine percent, and having two people modeling the behavior increased compliance to sixty-seven percent (Aronson and O'Leary 1983).

In another study, showing photos of students participating in a previous blood drive led student participation in a current blood drive to increase by seventeen percent (Sarason *et al.* 1991). Another study found that children who saw a film depicting a child's positive visit to a dentist's office lowered their own anxiety about their dental visit when they were about the same age as the child in the film (Melamed *et al.* 1978).

When we activists distribute leaflets to large crowds of people, one of our biggest problems is "throw-down"—the leaflets that get tossed onto the ground by people uninterested in them. One of the Humane League's current outreach activities is distributing booklets on factory farming and vegetarianism at the Warped Tour, a traveling concert series that draws nearly half a million attendees each summer. At an average Warped Tour date we'll distribute about seven thousand booklets, a portion of which will get thrown down.

The portion being discarded in this way varies greatly depending on how many other leaflets are on the ground. If we clean up regularly so there are few or no booklets on the ground, very few people will throw their own down, because it doesn't seem like anyone else is doing so. On the other hand, if we're lax in cleaning and the ground is covered with booklets, concertgoers are drastically more likely to throw their booklets down because doing so seems acceptable or even expected. Identical results have been found in controlled scientific studies on littering (Cialdini, Reno, and Kallgren 1990).

When passing out leaflets, we should also be aware that people will tend to model what the person in front of them did: if that person took a leaflet, they're more likely to do so. If the person in front of them didn't take a leaflet, and especially if several people in a row did the same, they're less likely to do so. When you're passing out leaflets and several people in a row turn you down, it's helpful to pause and let a few people pass before resuming offering leaflets.

Additionally, if you're sitting behind an outreach table at a festival or on the street, it's helpful to have one or two friends standing on the other side of the table posing as interested passersby. Their presence models the idea that your table is interesting and that other people should come check it out. If you have a sign-up sheet on the table, it's best to fill in the first line or two with fake names and addresses; doing so provides a social norm for people who visit your table to feel that they, too, should sign up. If you've got a donation jar on the table, it's best to fill it at least halfway with cash, including some larger bills. This provides a social norm as to what visitors to your table should do. While none of these practices has been formally tested, they fit in with the principle of social norms and in the Humane League's experience they've been very effective.

Social norms can be modeled by public figures. This is why endorsements of political candidates can have an effect on the outcome of elections, and why having well-known people endorsing your cause can be helpful in garnering support. TV shows that modeled ways to conserve energy have led to documented reductions in energy use (Winett *et al.* 1985), and social marketers have successfully promoted family-planning and child-health initiatives by incorporating these issues into the storylines of popular soap operas (Andreasen *Marketing Social Change*).

Social norms can also be modeled by community leaders. One study found that households visited by a block leader about recycling were thirty-three percent more likely to recycle than those who received prompts, and three hundred percent more likely to recycle than those who only received an informational brochure (Hopper and Nielsen 1991). Another recycling study found that having a block leader visit homes to encourage recycling increased the activity by twenty-eight percent, in comparison to a twelve percent increase in homes that only received a written appeal (Burns 1991).

While social norms can be a very powerful tool for persuasion, be careful not to use them in a counterproductive way. For example, promotional materials should not say "Many people are doing [the undesirable thing]" (driving to work every day, eating meat, buying items made in sweatshops). Doing so encourages the undesirable behavior because it affirms that most people are doing it. In situations where the desired behavior is not in the majority, either focus on attitude norms ("Ninety-two percent of Americans think sweatshop labor is bad"; "Eighty-six percent of Americans think farm animals should be protected from cruelty") or simply skip using social norms in favor of another tool of influence.

We must also be sure to praise the minority who are engaging in the positive behavior. In a study of household electric use, home-owners who found out they used less electricity than their neighbors subsequently increased their usage by nine percent. However, when the information they received about their less-than-average electric use included a smiley face (a simple recognition of doing something good), home-owners didn't increase consumption (Schultz *et al.* 2007). Patting the backs of those who've made a change is usually quite easy to do and can be very helpful in getting them to maintain the change.

THE RULE OF RECIPROCITY

Game theorists are researchers who study the complex interactions of two or more people, each of whom is acting in their own self-interest. (We'll discuss game theory in more detail in a later chapter.) One strategy of interaction that game theorists have found to be particularly effective is called *tit for tat*. The way that tit for tat works is you start by cooperating with the other person, and after that you simply copy what they've just done to you. If they've just cooperated with you, you cooperate back. If they've just been uncooperative, you be uncooperative back. Game theorists have found that players who use tit for tat or similar strategies often get very positive results for themselves.

Evolutionary psychologists believe this principle can help explain why there's cooperation among humans and other animals. Operating in a tit-for-tat manner often leads to good results for each person involved. As a result, people have an ingrained tendency toward what is called the *rule of reciprocity*: when someone does something nice for us, we feel compelled to return the favor.

An undercover researcher who brought study participants a can of soda without them asking for it later got those people to buy more raffle tickets than a control group of participants who weren't given sodas. The rule of reciprocity was so strong that people bought more tickets even when they didn't like the undercover researcher (Regan 1971). A study published in the *Journal of Consumer Research* examined what happened when a hotel posted signs in each room saying a donation had been made to an environmental group on behalf of its guests to thank them for reusing towels. The signs asked guests to reciprocate by reusing their towels, and the hotel succeeded in increasing towel re-use by forty-five percent. When, instead, the signs offered to donate to an environmental group if guests re-used their towels, there was no increase in reuse (Goldstein, Cialdini, and Griskevicius 2008). By donating first, the hotel invoked the rule of reciprocity and got many guests to return the favor by reusing towels.

Unexpected or personalized gifts are particularly effective for invoking the rule of reciprocity. In a study carried out at a restaurant, servers who left a piece of candy for each diner increased their tips by three percent. When two candies were left for each diner, tips increased by fourteen percent. When servers put one candy out for each diner, turned to leave, then doubled back and put out one more candy per person, tips increased by twenty-three percent (Strohetz *et al.* 2002). In another study, handwritten sticky notes increased the response rate to a survey from thirty-six to seventy-five percent in one test and thirty-four to sixty-nine percent in another. The sticky notes were much more effective than simply handwriting a message directly on the survey (Garner 2005).

As activists, we'll be more successful if we go out of our way to do small favors to those we're seeking to influence. Josh Balk, a campaign director at the Humane Society of the U.S., once bought presents for the dog of an important executive he was meeting with, even remembering the dog's name from prior conversations—scoring major points and displaying a kindness that was later reciprocated. Similarly, a student environmental organization might drop a batch of cookies off with school administrators they're hoping to persuade on a sustainability initiative. Sending handwritten "thank you" notes or letters to donors and volunteers shows you really appreciate their support, and leads to increased involvement. And it seems that a thick pad of sticky notes would be a good investment for any activist organization.

The rule of reciprocity operates in a few other interesting ways. For example, when we find out that someone likes us we tend to find that person more likable (after all, they clearly have good taste). So letting others know with our words and our facial expressions that we like them is helpful in getting them to like us, and therefore be more easily influenced by us. Additionally, research has revealed that the impact of a favor on the recipient declines over time, and ultimately is forgotten; so we should pay the favor shortly before our request (Flynn 2003).

Furthermore, research has found that if someone has previously persuaded you to change your mind about something then they're likely to reciprocate by letting you persuade them about something else (Cialdini, Green, and Rusch 1992). When talking one-on-one with a person we're trying to influence, we should concede some of their side arguments as true. That will make them more likely to be persuaded by us when it comes to our main point. Furthermore, if we do reach a resolution with them (a policy alteration, behavioral change, etc.), the back-and-forth reciprocity will lead the other person to feel more responsible for the outcome, and therefore happier with it and more likely to keep their end of the deal (Benton, Kelley and Liebling 1972; Schindler 1998).

DOOR IN THE FACE

We've discussed the effectiveness of the foot-in-the-door technique, where we make a small request that people are likely to say "yes" to and then later make a similar but larger request. Another effective technique for getting people to comply that works in the opposite direction is called the *door-in-the-face method*. We start by making a very big request that's likely to be turned down. We then follow up asking for something similar but much smaller. Because the person feels bad for rejecting our initial request (slamming the door in our face), and because we were willing to reduce our request, the person feels compelled to reciprocate by agreeing to our second request. Door-in-the-face also works because of framing: compared to a very large request, a subsequent small request seems much more agreeable.

In one study, college students were asked to commit to spending two hours a week for the next two years volunteering with juvenile delinquents; none agreed. They were then asked to help take juvenile delinquents on a two-hour field trip, and fifty percent agreed. A second group of students was asked only the second question, and only seventeen percent agreed. Using the door-in-the-face technique had nearly tripled the number of college students willing to volunteer for the field trip. The study found a smaller but still noticeable increase in volunteering among a third group of students who didn't have to say "no" to the first request before hearing the second one: twenty-five percent of these students agreed to volunteer for the field trip (Cialdini 1975).

In a nearly identical study, students were much more willing to volunteer for two hours with a mental-health agency when they were first given the larger request of volunteering two hours a week for two years. Compliance increased from twenty-nine percent to seventy-six percent when students were first asked the larger request. Furthermore, those who heard the larger request and later agreed to the smaller one were more likely to follow through: eighty-five percent showed up to volunteer, compared to only fifty percent of those who were not asked the initial request (Miller *et al.* 1976). In a study of a student blood drive, adding an initial request to donate a pint of blood every six weeks for three years nearly doubled the likelihood that students complied with a subsequent request for a one-time blood donation (Cialdini and Ascani 1976).

It should be noted that door-in-the-face doesn't work if a different person makes the second request, since there's no longer the need for reciprocity. It also doesn't work if the first request is so large it seems insincere (Regan 1971). Asking for a $10,000 donation to your organization and then following up by asking for $10 isn't likely to benefit from the principles at work in the door-in-the-face technique. Asking for $100 and then asking for $10 if the first request is turned down should succeed in increasing donations.

Activist organizations can use the door-in-the-face technique for trying to recruit new volunteers and for soliciting donations from members of the public. It's possible that door-in-the-face could work for behavioral changes as well, though research to demonstrate this has yet to be done. For example, an environmental organization might approach members of the public with an initial request that they stop using their car to get to work and instead bike or take public transportation. After this first request is turned down, they could then follow up by asking people to commit to using alternative means of transportation to get to work one day a week. Door-in-the-face research suggests this method would make activists more successful in getting people to leave their car at home one day a week than if they'd asked for a one-day-a-week commitment from the start.

SWEET EMOTIONS

We like to think that we're rational creatures, making decisions and holding beliefs based on careful reasoning. In reality, we usually base our decisions on emotions and then use logic to justify them—not the other way around. Because of this, it's useful to draw out people's emotions with anecdotal stories when trying to persuade. Stories are particularly effective when they focus on one individual.

A study by researchers Deborah Small, George Loewenstein, and Paul Slovic examined the impact different types of appeals had on charitable giving to a hunger-relief organization. The first appeal asked donors to help Rokia, a young girl from Mali who was very poor and faced starvation. The second appeal presented facts and statistics about the millions of hungry children facing starvation in African countries. The third appeal included both the personal story and the facts about widespread starvation. Which of these three ads would you guess generated the largest amount of donations from study participants?

People shown the personal story donated twice as much money overall as those given the facts and figures. The third appeal—the combination of the personal story and statistics—worked only slightly better than the facts-only appeal. In a variation on the study, researchers introduced participants to both Rokia and a starving African boy named Moussa. If participants were asked to donate to help one of the children, they remained generous. But if the participants were asked to donate to help both of them, the amount of donations declined.

If our minds worked logically, then learning the statistics on how millions of children are starving (or even learning that two children are starving) should make us give more than learning about the plight of one individual child; yet the opposite results were found. The study's researchers theorized that when people are thinking analytically (in terms of logic, statistics, and problem-solving), they tend to care less and therefore give less.

To test this idea, Small, Loewenstein, and Slovic conducted a second study where half of the participants were given analytic questions to answer and the other half were asked to write about their feelings. Afterward, both groups were given the personal story of Rokia and her battle with starvation. Participants who were first asked to write about their emotions gave nearly two times as much as those who'd answered analytic questions. Answering analytic questions had almost the same effect in reducing donations as including only facts and statistics in the appeal. These results suggest that the researchers were right: thinking analytically reduces most people's generosity (Small, Loewenstein, and Slovic 2005).

The implications of this research for activists is clear when it comes to fundraising efforts. While internally we should measure our success based on data (think back to the bottom line discussed in the first chapter), in promoting our organization to the public and in requesting donations we'll be more successful if we focus on individual stories instead of statistics. Non-profits like Children International and Farm Sanctuary do a great job at focusing on individual children or individual rescued animals, even running popular "adopt a child" or "adopt an animal" programs that pair individual donors with individual children or animals.

Research has shown that images that generate extreme, negative emotions produced the largest donations of money and volunteer time—more so than images that generated weaker negative or positive emotions. Because images can usually evoke emotional responses more easily than words, appeals that included images also had a stronger impact than those that just contained a narrative description (Burt and Strongman 2004; Eayrs 1990; Brock and Keller 1995; Maheswaran and Meyers-Levy 1990; Rothman et al. 1993). As an aside, it's worth mentioning that fundraising appeals that include information about the likelihood of achieving a fundraising goal have been shown to increase recipients' intentions to donate as well (Das Kerkhof and Kuiper 2008).

Outside of the fundraising arena, research is mixed on whether statistical or narrative information is more effective at persuading people. The most thorough meta-analysis of studies on this topic found that, overall, narrative appeals were about ten percent more effective than statistical appeals in creating attitudinal change—however, this increase didn't carry over into behavioral intention (Reinhart and Feeley 2007). In other words, people given narrative appeals felt more in agreement with the message, but didn't state they were more likely to do what the appeal asked of them. With the exception of fundraising appeals, there are no clear data on what circumstances cause narrative appeals to create behavioral and not just attitudinal change.

While behavioral change should, of course, be our focus as activists, we can at least conclude from the research that focusing on individuals is likely to be more effective than focusing on statistics when trying to change people's attitudes. An anti-sweatshop activist who tells the story of one child laboring in a factory in Bangladesh is likely to be more persuasive in changing attitudes than an activist who focuses on the number of sweatshop workers around the world, how many are under the age of ten, and other statistics. Animal activists are likely to be more effective in changing attitudes about testing on animals by describing a week in the life of a specific beagle in a laboratory (and giving the beagle a name) than they are by focusing on how many animals are experimented on each year, how the majority are used in non-medical research, and other facts. It's not as easy for environmental activists to focus on an individual, but they could still point to specific old-growth trees or rivers that are imperiled. The image of a polar bear adrift in the waters of the once-frozen Arctic makes a compelling emotional argument regarding the dangers of global warming, even though the impact of global warming is exponentially larger than the harm being done to that one polar bear.

SAY IT LOUD, SAY IT OFTEN

We've spoken several times about the power of social norms. For some issues, the social norm is clear cut: most people think it's acceptable to kill and eat animals and most people think recycling is a good thing. In other situations, how the larger group (a classroom, city, or country) feels on the issue is harder to tell. Research suggests that even if we are in the minority on a position, if we constantly repeat our belief and do so vocally our opinion may seem to the public to be the majority opinion or close to it. Because of the power of social norms, having our opinion appear to be prevalent can be very help- ful for creating change.

A study by Kimberlee Weaver published in the *Journal of Personality and Social Psy- chology* found that hearing the same thing over and over from one person can be just as persuasive as hearing it from many different people. Because we assess the likelihood that something is true by how easily it comes to mind, and because we'll often forget where we heard it, our brains can be tricked into thinking we heard a statement from a variety of people when in fact we heard about it repeatedly from the same source.

Weaver's study found that three people expressing the same opinion were only slightly more influential on the perceptions of other group members than one person expressing their opinion three times. The participant reiterating their belief was ninety percent as effective in convincing other group members what the majority opinion of the group was. The impact of repetition was strongest when group members didn't yet know what others thought about the issue. If they did already know a group's position, repetition had little impact in the short term; however, it did lead to greater influence in the long term as group members forgot who said what.

Weaver's study found that even reading an email message where the same statement was printed three times (seemingly by accident as a function of the email program) led recipients to estimate greater support for the idea among the group to which the sender belonged. In other words, simple repetition of a statement from one individual—by accident—was enough to affect the recipient's judgments on how an entire group felt about the issue (Weaver *et al.* 2007).

A separate study found another persuasive benefit to repetition. In this study, partic- ipants were presented with either two or five statements that the wax used to line Cup- O-Noodles soup cups had been shown to cause cancer in rats. Participants were then asked to guess whether this story had been reported in the *National Enquirer* (a tabloid filled with phony stories) or the highly esteemed *Consumer Reports* magazine. The study found that the more often the statement was heard, the more likely participants were to guess it came from a credible source—in this case *Consumer Reports* (Fragale and Heath 2004). (By the way, the Cup-O-Noodles story was made up by researchers—it never appeared in any publication.) In addition to making people think a particular idea represents the majority opinion, mere repetition of a statement can also make people believe it came from a credible source.

Advocacy organizations often strive to repeat their message in any available outlet. Many large environmental and animal protection organizations hire full-time staffers whose sole job is to submit letters over and over again on the same subjects to editors of newspapers and magazines across the country. In trying to convince legislators to vote a certain way on an issue, advocacy groups will attempt to activate their members to make as many phone calls and send as many letters as possible. A simple poll should provide the most accurate information on whether the public supports a bill, yet non-profits rarely rely on polls alone to convince legislators. Even when a majority of the public supports a non-profit's position on the issue, the organization will still encourage letters and phone calls because repetition of the message is important in convincing the legislator what the majority opinion is.

When we as activists are not in the majority on a particular issue, or when the majority doesn't feel strongly in either direction, we can still sometimes create the appearance that the majority supports our cause. A student environmental group at a large university near me was recently campaigning to create a five-dollar "Green Fee" for all students, with the money going to fund sustainability improvements on campus. Given the relatively small cost, it was thought that a small portion of the student body would strongly support it, a small portion would oppose it, and the rest would care little either way. However, by spending time approaching students on campus and asking them to sign a petition of support, the group was able to get thousands of signatures and demonstrate what looked like strong student support for the issue. Had another group been sufficiently motivated to stop the Green Fee from being put into place, they probably could have gotten thousands of signatures of opposition. This would have suggested there was probably not a majority opinion on this issue.

Several lessons can be learned here. The first is that if the majority has no strong feelings on an issue, it's fairly easy for us as activists to make it appear that an overwhelming majority agrees with our position. Activists shouldn't feel discouraged from taking up a cause just because they think most others in their school or community aren't concerned about it. Organizational grunt work on your part can create the appearance of (and in some cases actually create) strong majority support and can lead to the implementation of the change you're seeking.

The second lesson is that we should continue to repeat ourselves and our position as often as possible. Repetition will sway perception of the group norm and therefore individual behavior, both in the short and long term. Instead of calling a consumer hotline to voice your opinion once, call three times. When discussing things in a group, give your opinion several times instead of just once (though don't become so much of an annoyance that people start to dislike your position because they dislike you). And if you're trying to convince a legislator, administrator, or someone else that your opinion is the majority opinion, you just might want to have the message "accidentally" repeated a few times in the body of your email to them.

chapter six

TOOLS OF INFLUENCE, PART III: TOOLS OF PERSUASION

MAKE IT STICKY

When writing an appeal for donations, how should you craft your letter? In trying to garner sympathy for your cause, what approach is most likely to get the public's attention? Several pop psychology books that have topped the charts in recent years, including Malcolm Gladwell's *The Tipping Point* and Chip and Dan Heath's *Made to Stick*, emphasize the importance of making your messages as *sticky* as possible. What they mean is that content and presentation matter a lot in getting attention, and sometimes what works is counterintuitive. Key sticky traits these authors emphasize include: simplicity, unexpectedness, concrete imagery, having people be able to test the idea for themselves ("Doesn't it seem like this is true?"), emotional charge, and the use of stories. Things that are dangerously un-sticky include: losing the main point in the midst of lots of information, and focusing only on presentation style while neglecting content. The authors point out that we don't have to invent new ways of being sticky—we need simply observe which ideas, consumer products, and cultural trends are sticky and why, and adopt similar techniques.

These books rely heavily on anecdotes to demonstrate their main points, so their accuracy is really up to their readers to judge. However, one informal study that Chip and Dan Heath discuss is worth mentioning here. Chip is a professor at Stanford University, and in one of his classes he had students prepare one-minute persuasive speeches. Analyzing the speeches, he found that on average each one used two-and-a-half statistics, while only one in ten speeches told a story. He also found that the speakers deemed most persuasive by their classmates were those who were the most poised, smooth, and confident in their delivery—traits we typically associate with being persuasive. However, when quizzed about what they remembered from the speeches a short while later, only five percent of the students remembered any individual statistic from any of the speeches, whereas sixty-three percent of students remembered the stories. When it came to getting the message to stick, the use of stories was much more important than anything else, including how poised and confident the speaker was.

People relate to many things in life through stories, which are much more memorable than statistics or ideas. Stories allow for the use of emotionally powerful imagery, providing a shortcut to understanding. They allow people to insert themselves mentally into the situation, making it more vivid. When you are preparing a speech or pamphlet, or talking with someone about an issue, stories are likely to stick with the listener much longer than statistics or ideas. Describing the situation of a child in Iraq whose limbs were torn off in a U.S. bomb blast, and explaining what his daily life is now like as a result, will stick with the listener and probably have more of an impact than saying that tens of thousands of civilians have been killed since the war began. Detailing a story of your own visit to an animal-testing laboratory, and what you saw and smelled and felt there, will be more persuasive to your cause than simply listing the conditions common in such places.

YOU TAKE THE HIGH ROUTE, I'LL TAKE THE LOW ROUTE

Is it more important for your campaign materials to look slick and professional or for them to have convincing rational arguments? If Tide detergent can increase its sales just by using colorful, creative advertising, can't we as activists do the same thing in persuading people to adopt new behaviors?

Not usually. The way that people make low-involvement decisions like what brand of detergent to buy is different from the way they make high-involvement decisions like what beliefs to hold and whether to adopt significant behavioral changes. Persuasive techniques that work for one type of decision will often not work for the other.

Low-involvement decisions are often made through what is called the *peripheral route*: instead of evaluating the message based on its content, people rely on emotional cues and mental rules of thumb. Such evaluations are often the most efficient way to come to a decision for relatively unimportant issues (Gigerenzer and Goldstein 1996). If you're stopping by the grocery store to pick up a jar of peanut butter and they're out of your favorite brand, you don't need to consult *Consumer Reports* before deciding which other brand to purchase. Cues like popularity and package design are enough to go on for this unimportant decision.

Messages, especially about low-involvement decisions, are more persuasive when the message's speaker has a good reputation, when the message is spoken or written fluently, when there is a long list of arguments or statistics, when experts are involved, when the message is familiar, and when the message's speaker seems to be arguing against their own interest. All of these factors provide subtle mental clues that the message is correct and should be accepted (Wells and Petty 1980).

High-involvement decisions are made through what psychologists call the central route: people gather information, they think about the decision for some time, and they're often emotionally involved, since their decision will affect their self-perception (Andreasen *Marketing Social Change* 143; Chaiken 1987; Cacioppo and Petty 1987). Because people are processing the information more systematically, the message conveyed to them needs to use sound logic and supporting evidence. This doesn't mean that presentation style is irrelevant when you're trying to persuade people about high-involvement decisions. It still matters a lot, and without an attractive presentation style people are unlikely to pay enough attention to hear the substance of your argument. In fact, a brochure or lecture about a high-involvement decision should incorporate as much as possible the characteristics that make low-involvement appeals persuasive. But these characteristics alone aren't sufficient to be persuasive for high-involvement decisions.

If a representative from a Sierra Club chapter is speaking at a city-council meeting on an important environmental issue, the speaker will need both style and substance to be as persuasive as possible. A brochure encouraging a significant behavioral change like eating locally raised foods or volunteering with the overseas non-profit Doctors Without Borders will also need both style and substance, as these are high-involvement decisions. On the other hand, a student activist running for president of the student government should probably just focus on the peripheral routes to persuasion. Most students voting in student government elections see it as a low-involvement decision that will have little if any impact on them. Similarly, an Amnesty International chapter tabling at a college to get students to sign postcards to political prisoners should focus on the peripheral style issues, since signing a postcard is such a low-involvement decision.

COME WITHOUT WARNING

As part of my work with the Humane League, I make presentations to high school and college classes on factory farming and its impact on animals, the environment, and human health. I don't directly advocate vegetarianism during the presentations, but I do very clearly detail the reasons why many people become vegetarian, and I teach students that what they eat has a major impact on animals (and the environment and their health).

Part of my reason for not directly encouraging students to go vegetarian is because I'm concerned that doing so would reduce the number of schools that invite me back to speak. But the bigger reason is that I know I'll be more persuasive when I act like an expert whose mission is to present facts on the issue (higher credibility) than when I make clear I'm an advocate whose mission is to persuade people (lower credibility—who really trusts salespeople?) (Eagly, Wood, and Chaiken 1978). Of course, I'm very much trying to change students' minds and eating habits. But telling them that's my purpose would be counterproductive.

Usually the class teacher will introduce me by saying that I'm there to talk about factory farming, animal agriculture, the impact farms have on the environment, animal ethics, or vegetarian nutrition. However, in a couple of classrooms, teachers have introduced me by saying, "He's here to tell you why you should become a vegetarian." This has sometimes led to a large collective groan from portions of the class who don't want to be told what to do—especially on an issue that's such an established part of their life.

Research has confirmed my own personal experience, that when people are told someone is about to try to influence them on a topic that matters to them, they are less likely to be influenced. Researchers Jonathan Freedman and David Sears carried out an experiment where they had a speaker present to three hundred high school students on the subject of teenage driving. While pre-polling showed that every student believed teenagers should have the right to drive, the presenter spoke about why teenage driving should be banned. Some of the students were told ten minutes ahead of time that this was the opinion the presenter would be advocating; other students were told two minutes ahead of time; and still other students didn't know the speaker's position at all until he was introduced and began speaking. Afterward, the researchers again polled students to find out if their beliefs on the issue had shifted.

The data showed that those who received no advance warning that the speaker would be advocating a ban on teenage driving were significantly more likely to be influenced by his presentation. Sixty-seven percent of the students who received no warning shifted their opinions to be more sympathetic toward restrictions on teenage driving, whereas only fifty-eight percent of those who received a two-minute warning and fifty-two percent of students with the ten-minute warning showed such a shift. The researchers theorized that the advance warning gave students time to think about counter-arguments to the upcoming presentation, making it less persuasive. The study also found that those warned in advance believed the speaker to be more biased (Freedman and Sears 1965). Other studies have similarly found that people who are informed they're about to hear a persuasive communication are less likely to be persuaded if the issue is important to them (Allyn and Festinger 1961). Conversely, people who are told in advance that they're going to receive a persuasive message about a topic that's unimportant to them are actually more likely to be persuaded by the message (Wood and Quinn 2003).

Why are people less influenced when they know a persuasive speech is coming on a topic important to them? What compels people to develop counter-arguments and to decide the speaker is biased? And why are people more likely to agree when warned in advance if the subject is one that doesn't matter to them?

Earlier, we discussed cognitive dissonance and how people have a strong desire to see themselves as consistent. If we hold one idea, and we know that we'll soon be presented with someone advocating an opposite idea, we have a dilemma. The possibility that someone else may have better judgment than we do is a threat to our ego. Accepting the other person's opinion feels like admitting we're inconsistent, uninformed, or submissive. The more palatable alternative is to cling to one's current belief. Thinking up counter-arguments and deciding the speaker is biased make this alternative easier, by providing justifications for ignoring the other person's arguments.

On the other hand, when the issue is one that isn't important to us and therefore one we don't hold a strong opinion for or against, as soon as we learn that the persuasive message is coming we start mentally agreeing with it. That way, when the message does arrive, we don't feel like we're being influenced by it—we already believed the same thing. This keeps us feeling consistent and knowledgeable, and not like the sort of person who quickly changes beliefs when someone else tells them to.

The cause that we as activists are advocating for might be one that has personal importance to the audience or it might be one that doesn't matter much to them. That variable dictates whether it would be helpful to notify your audience that you're going to try to persuade them or whether you should avoid doing so. A gay rights activist speaking to a general audience in support of gay marriage laws should not preface his presentation with, "I hope that by the end of this talk you will agree that marriage is a fundamental right that all citizens are entitled to, regardless of sexual orientation." Because marriage is an important issue to most people (whatever their position), an introductory statement like that would make audience members who don't agree with the speaker more resistant to the speaker's message. On the other hand, an environmental campaigner trying to win public support for a little-known ballot initiative that would affect the policies of a few polluting companies might benefit by stating her intention to persuade. The issue wouldn't affect most people, so if the campaigner states from the start, "I'm going to explain to you why you should vote 'yes' on this ballot question," it should make the audience more likely to agree.

An interesting sidebar to this issue comes from a study by researchers Sergio Moscovici and Patricia Neve, published in the *European Journal of Social Psychology*. In the study, participants were more likely to accept another person's judgments after that person had left the room, and more likely to reject those judgments when the person remained in the room (Moscovici and Neve 1971). In other words, a person can be more persuasive when they're absent than when they're present. Once the persuader gives his opinion and then leaves, it becomes psychologically easier for the receiver to consider and agree with that opinion. Since the persuader is not present, the receiver feels that if they change their opinion, they're doing so because it's what they believe, not because someone else is telling them to. After all, no one present is trying to influence them. This situation makes adopting the new idea less threatening to a person's self-esteem. Other studies have found that negotiations are often stalled by both parties being afraid to lose face, and that negotiations benefit by having the parties spend time apart from one another to consider the opposing side's arguments in private (Pruitt and Johnson 1970).

In light of these findings, when I'm giving my humane education presentations, it would be a mistake to conclude by asking the students how many of them will now consider going vegetarian. Because the source of persuasion (me) is still in the room, students will be compelled not to agree since it might make them look inconsistent and easily swayed. On the other hand, if I simply leave without asking that question, they'll be able to consider the issues on their own. If they do think about switching, they'll feel like they're doing so because they want to, not because I told them to.

This principle may explain why books and brochures can be very effective at changing people's minds. Because there's no other person present trying to influence them, people may find written materials less threatening and the messages more easily acceptable. A woman I know tried for years to get her friend to go vegetarian, explaining all the cruelties done to farm animals, but was unable to get him to change. Then one day he picked up a copy of a vegetarian magazine from a news-stand box on the street, and after reading it he immediately went vegetarian. He didn't have to save face with a magazine as he felt he had to with his friend when she was trying to change him. Reading a magazine on the issue enabled him to feel that he was deciding on his own—not because someone told him to.

AGAINST MYSELF

In discussing the peripheral route to persuasion, we mentioned a few tricks that are helpful in changing attitudes and behavior. One of these is making statements that seem to go against our own interests.

People are swayed more by experts who seem to be impartial than they are by those who have something to gain (Eagly, Wood, and Chaiken 1978). While this effect is strongest in regards to salespeople, it still applies to non-profits that are trying to change attitudes and behaviors. To make it look like we're impartial, it's helpful to argue against our own interest on one or two small points. By establishing that we're truthful on minor issues, we'll be seen as more believable when we present our key arguments (Hunt, Domzal, and Kernan; Settle and Godon 1974; Smith and Hunt 1978).

An anti-war protestor could become more persuasive by first agreeing that the war in Afghanistan has granted women in that country more freedom, and then going on to detail all the overwhelmingly negative effects the war has had. An environmental activist promoting a much higher gas tax to reduce driving could note that they drive to work each day and it's going to cost them a lot more too, but that the tax hike is necessary to cut carbon emissions.

LOOKING GOOD

Like it or not, attractiveness matters. According to economists, attractive individuals in the U.S. and Canada get paid twelve to fourteen percent more on average than their unattractive coworkers (Hamermesh and Biddle 1994). A study published in the *Journal of Applied Social Psychology* found that good-looking defendants were twice as likely to avoid jail time as unattractive defendants charged with the same crime (Stewart 1980), and other studies have confirmed attractive people receive highly favorable treatment in the legal system (Castellow, Wuencsh, and Moore 1990; Downs and Lyons 1990). A study of elections found that attractive candidates received two and a half times as many votes as unattractive candidates, even though most voters who were surveyed vehemently denied the possibility that looks influenced their decision (Efran and Patterson 1976).

The power of attractiveness carries over to activism as well. In one research study, college-student participants approached other students with a petition encouraging the university cafeteria to stop serving meat for breakfast and lunch. Attractive student participants were successful in getting a signature twenty-eight percent more often than unattractive participants (Chaiken 1979). Another study found that attractive people are more likely to receive help than unattractive people (Benson, Karabenick, and Lerner 1976). One of the reasons attractiveness has such influence is that people tend to automatically assign traits like talent, kindness, honesty, and intelligence to attractive people, without even being aware that looks played a part in their judgment (Eagly *et al.* 1991).

On occasions where we're interacting with the public, we should make ourselves look as attractive as possible. That requires having at least one good outfit suitable for professional meetings, and clothes of whatever style that's currently popular for situations where we're interacting with the public—even if it violates our personal fashion sense. Staying in good physical shape is also important, not to mention good for our health. Lastly, if we're working with other activists on a campaign, then personal attractiveness should be one factor taken into consideration when deciding which role each individual should play.

Statements like this might set off alarm bells in those who are understandably worried about "lookism," devaluing individuals because of how they look. Without a doubt, the public's focus on physical attractiveness causes a lot of suffering. Those who feel unattractive or are deemed unattractive can have low self-esteem, become depressed, and have their entire life experience altered by society's standards of beauty. Those who are deemed very attractive can get their way so often that they never (or only later in life) develop emotionally from having to deal with rejection. There is, and should be, a whole field of activism focused on changing public perceptions of what beauty is, and encouraging people to value others for who they are and not just what they look like. In light of all this, it might seem that considering attractiveness when deciding how to go about our activism is just perpetuating the problem of lookism. Trying to look as attractive as possible or trying to recruit more attractive volunteers to do public outreach work might seem to be perpetuating a stereotype.

However, the fact is that whether you use more or less attractive people to publicly promote your cause through methods like getting petitions signed or passing out leaflets, and whether you yourself look more or less attractive, the public has no idea of your motives. Their attitudes on beauty and personal value won't be changed regardless of your choice. So incorporating attractiveness as one consideration among many when deciding who will work on what activity doesn't promote lookism among the general public. The only potential harm it could do would be bruising the ego of some activists, including at times ourselves. Hopefully though, our and others' desire to be as successful as possible in our activist work will prevent us from taking this personally.

In contrast to the very small personal cost it has for activists, utilizing attractive volunteers and trying to be as personally attractive as possible can do a great deal of good for our cause: feeding starving people, saving animals, protecting trees, etc. The small cost to our egos of admitting that attractiveness varies from person to person and that we're not the most beautiful person in the world can save lives and reduce a great deal of suffering. Attractiveness certainly shouldn't be the only consideration, but because of its power it should be considered when making strategy and lifestyle decisions.

RESPECT MY AUTHORITY

Things that signify authority are very useful in helping to gain compliance with a request. Similar to the issue of attractiveness, people consistently underestimate the extent to which they're influenced by the trappings of authority.

Clothes and uniforms are one way of signaling authority. In an experiment, a person on the street instructed passersby to "Pick up this bag for me!" or stated "That fellow is over-parked at the meter but doesn't have any change—give him a dime!" When the person giving the commands was dressed in casual clothing, people complied only a third of the time. When the person giving the commands was dressed in a security-guard uniform, compliance rose to nearly ninety percent (Bickman 1974). In another study, police officers dressed in traditional uniforms were rated by observers as more fair, helpful, intelligent, honest, and good than officers not in uniform (Mauro 1984).

Clothing and other items that convey wealth can also lead to greater influence. One study found that pedestrians were three-and-a-half times more likely to follow a man jaywalking into an intersection when that man was wearing a suit than when he was wearing a work shirt and pants (Lefkowitz, Mouton, and Srygley 1955). In another study, a researcher in an old economy car repeatedly drove up to a red light and then remained at a standstill for some time, even after the light had turned green. Nearly all of the cars stuck behind him honked at least once, and two of them rammed the researcher's bumper. Later, the experiment was repeated, but this time with the researcher driving a new luxury automobile. Half of the cars that were stuck behind the luxury vehicle never honked once; instead, they patiently waited for the vehicle to move (Doob and Gross 1968).

Titles and credentials can also imply authority and lead to greater compliance (Peters and Ceci 1982; Ross 39–43). If you received a pamphlet on healthy eating that stated a vegetarian diet adds three years to a person's life span, would you take that claim more seriously if it was coming from John Smith, M.D., Cleveland Health Research Institute, or if it was coming from the Rutgers University Students for Animal Rights[3] (Adventist Health Studies 2010)?

The connection between height and authority has led to some surprising research findings. Because height and titles are both symbols of authority, a study found that people perceive those with impressive titles to be taller than they actually are. In one study, a man was introduced to some college classes as a Cambridge student. To other classes he was introduced as a Cambridge professor. The classes that thought he was a professor guessed him to be two-and-a-half inches taller than the classes that thought he was a student (Wilson 1968). Another study found that politicians are perceived to be taller immediately after winning an election (Higham and Carment 1992). Yet another study, conducted in 1984, found that the U.S. Presidency was won by the taller of the ent of the time between 1900 and 1984 (Lynn and

to the trappings of authority is not a very good trait
;ed. But as long as this is one of the principles guiding
ignoring it will have a negative impact on the people,
ying to protect.

; with decision-makers should always dress as nicely as
ıg. Even for activists with little money, it's easy to "fake it
for good business clothes at a thrift store or inexpensive
e non-profits that hold protests ask all protestors to dress
ııı ᵥᵤ..   ıile policies like this can draw the ire of some participants,
they are usually a good idea and will make the public and the protest's target consider
the message more seriously. Using authoritative titles can also be helpful for activists,
as can invoking statements in support of your cause from people who hold such titles.
And if you have a few tall volunteers, keep height in mind as one consideration when
deciding who to send to a meeting, lecture, or any other situation where you're seeking
to persuade.

YOUR FRIENDLY NEIGHBORHOOD ACTIVIST

One of the most important keys to influence is being friendly. Friendliness isn't automatically going to change minds or policies, but it's always going to get us a few steps
further toward that goal. Being likable and having the other person know (or think) we
like them is a vital part of persuasion.

Research shows that as a general rule people tend to believe praise and to like those
who give it, even when it's probably untrue, and even when they know the other person stands to gain something by being liked—so long as the other person isn't being
clearly manipulative (Drachman, deCarufel, and Insko 1978; Bryne, Rasche, and Kelley
1974). Research has also shown that prefacing a request with "How are you feeling?"
increases compliance (Howard 1990).

Beyond these types of studies, the research record is thin as to the exact aspects of
friendliness that lead to persuasion. Nevertheless, bookstores and the Internet are filled
with pop psychology advice on how to get others to like you, with most content overlap-
ping around a few central ideas. Here are some of the key points emphasized repeatedly,

from classics such as Dale Carnegie's *How to Win Friends and Influence People* to the more recent *How to Make People Like You in 90 Seconds or Less*. While there hasn't been a great deal of research done to demonstrate how well these methods work, you'll likely see their effectiveness if you incorporate them into your own efforts at persuasion.

First, always be kind and courteous, even if the other person is not. Those for whom we're advocating gain nothing if we become defensive or argumentative, and it's possible that even people who act with hostility toward us will later change their mind if we keep our cool. (One of the best grassroots animal advocates I know used to chase vegetarians around throwing meatballs at them when he was in high school.) Also, never tell someone they're wrong. If you have to correct a misperception, do so gently and by presenting new information. This allows the other person to save face and makes it easier for them to accept a change in perspective.

Second, we need to enroll and not cajole. By asking questions and letting the other person answer we can learn what it is about our position that they agree and/or disagree with—important knowledge for moving forward in persuading them. Doing these things also shows that we care what the other person thinks and that we take their opinions seriously, which should lead them to consider ours more seriously as well. We should respond to questions honestly, but without letting the conversation stray too far from our central message.

Third, we must be optimistic and outgoing. In his bestseller *The Tipping Point*, Malcolm Gladwell notes that the people who are highly influential are almost always friendly, optimistic, and interested in others. Think positively, make sure you're smiling, be upbeat, and interact with others as if you know they like you and that they'll be interested in what you have to say. If we indicate with our body language and tone of voice that we don't think the other person will agree to our request, or that we don't think the other person likes us, that makes the other person more likely to disagree with or dislike us. If you don't feel confident going into an interaction, breathe deeply and make confident physical movements—both can help you become authentically confident.

Fourth, we should point out how our idea or request is consistent with who the other person is and what they already believe. Everyone has ways in which they care for animals, the environment, and other people. Drawing these ways out and showing how your request is in line with what they already believe will make other people feel like their motivation for making a change is internal, and not that they're easily swayed.

In one study, researchers had participants take a survey about civic involvement.

They then told one randomly selected group of participants that the survey showed they were "above-average citizens likely to vote and participate in political events," and another randomly selected group that they could be categorized as average in this regard. A week later, members of the first group were fifteen percent more likely to vote in that day's election (Tybout and Yalch 1980). Labeling others as already concerned with politics, world hunger, the environment, or any other issue can influence their self-perception and consequently their behavior in that direction.

Fifth, express agreement or acceptance as much as possible, including on minor points that individuals make that you don't actually agree with. Debating minor points can quickly derail an otherwise effective conversation. Realize that no one is going to agree with all or even many of your beliefs. Focus on the key change you're advocating, and simply nod and smile to acknowledge the other person's opinions when they make statements you disagree with on issues that won't impact their acceptance of the key change you're advocating.

As an example of putting these principles into action, let me describe a meeting I had recently with the dining director and purchasing director of a small liberal arts college that we were encouraging to switch to cage-free eggs.

I attended the meeting dressed is my nicest business attire: button-up shirt and tie, dress pants and belt, business shoes, and gelled hair. I also brought to the meeting the optimistic assumption that the directors would agree with me that this was an important and valuable issue, and the confidence that I'd be able to lead them to make a change (the only question being *how quickly*).

I started off the meeting by thanking the directors for their interest in this issue, praising them for already caring about sustainability (as evidenced by some policy statements on their website), and telling them that I thought the cage-free issue would really be something they'd be interested in. After a brief explanation of some of the benefits of cage-free, and invoking social norms by mentioning all the other local schools that had gone cage-free, I asked if they had questions or concerns on the issue. By asking this question several times throughout the meeting, I was able to learn what their main concerns were and the hot-button phrases that would have the most impact on them.

When they had misperceptions about a particular aspect of the issue, I would (after I was sure they were finished talking) begin my response with phrases like "It would seem like . . ." or "Conventional egg farms certainly like to give the impression that . . ." in order to validate their intelligence and not act as if I was calling them uninformed. Only then would I present the actual facts of the situation, invoking statements by experts and other authoritative sources as much as possible.

At one point, the dining director stated that she really didn't care about chickens, but that the food safety and environmental benefits of going cage-free were important to her. While I could have argued with her on this point, and could have attempted to persuade her that animals feel pain and deserve ethical consideration, doing so didn't seem necessary for getting a policy change to cage-free. If I was really concerned about the long-term effects of her opinions on this issue, I could just wait until after the policy change was made and then try to alter her attitude about farm animals. Doing so at this point would have interrupted the positive flow of the discussion. So, after her statement about chickens, I focused for the rest of the meeting on the issues that mattered to her: food safety and sustainability.

Toward the end of the meeting I praised the directors for their reputation of having higher-quality food than other local colleges, which they clearly appreciated and which led them to talk about why they thought food quality was so important. I was then able to point out that, by going cage-free, they would re-assert their commitment to food quality and take a step ahead of (or at least be equal to) other colleges in this regard.

I also tried to lay out in their minds the agenda for what would need to happen for them to go cage-free. Based on the directors' statements during the conversation, aside from price concerns (which I discussed honestly but tried to minimize in importance) the main thing that they agreed needed to happen for them to make the change was being assured that students supported the switch. From my experience at other schools, I know this would be something easy for us to demonstrate through getting students to sign letters and petitions. Since I was able to focus the director and manager on student support as the key issue in deciding whether to go cage-free, when I was able to demonstrate this support to them later I knew they'd be more likely to follow through with the change than if we'd focused on other issues which I couldn't control (like price).

A few hours after the meeting I sent a follow-up email to the directors thanking them for meeting and for their interest in the issue. I re-iterated how great I thought it was that they were concerned with food safety and sustainability and added that I looked forward to working with them to show student support and make this change happen at their college. I also asked for (because I expected they would give it, and they later did) a verbal commitment that they were indeed interested in making the switch.

While this particular situation was a meeting about cage-free eggs, these same principles of friendliness and persuasion should be used in any personal interaction where you're advocating for your cause.

I'M JUST LIKE YOU

It's sometimes said that opposites attract, but this is rarely true for romantic relationships and even rarer when it comes to friendships. The more similar people are to us in age, gender, dress, income, personality, and other traits, the more we tend to like them. Because likeability is very helpful for persuasion, we can use this principle to our advantage in trying to create change. By making ourselves look or act as similar as possible to those we're trying to influence, it becomes more probable that our audience will accept the behavioral change we're promoting.

Researchers who asked passersby for a dime were more likely to receive it when they were dressed similarly to the person they asked (Emswiller, Deaux, and Willits 1971). A survey of sales records from an insurance company found that customers were more likely to buy insurance when the salesperson was similar to them in age, religion, politics, and cigarette-smoking habits (Evans 1963). Another study showed that repeating a customer's order back to them in a restaurant increased tips by seventy percent (Van Baaren *et al.* 2003).

As activists, we should try to look as similar as possible to those we're attempting to influence. If an Amnesty International volunteer is passing out leaflets outside of a punk-rock concert, being dressed in khakis and a polo shirt is not a good idea. If a neighborhood recycling organization is asked to speak to residents of a retirement home about the importance of recycling, they'll most probably be more successful in persuading the residents if they have an elderly volunteer give the presentation than if they have a young person do so.

In speaking one-on-one with someone you're trying to persuade, it's best never to reveal that your political or religious views are different from theirs (unless, of course, you're trying to persuade them about a political or religious idea). Doing so puts another barrier in the way of changing that person's mind: "Why would I listen to a Democrat? They're wrong about everything!"

We can also cultivate similarity by matching the other person's posture, gestures, and speech patterns. If they speak quickly and to the point, we should do the same. If they speak more slowly and like to tell anecdotes, we can too. Several studies have

shown that mirroring a customer's body posture, mood, and verbal style leads to positive results in sales and negotiations (Chartrand and Bargh 1999; Locke and Horowitz
1990; Woodside and Davenport 1974; Maddux, Mullen, and Galinsky 2008). However, we have to be careful not to overdo it; if it's obvious that we're acting like the other
person on purpose, the technique will backfire.

Other similarities, including shared experiences and mutual acquaintances, are also
helpful for developing rapport. Similarities are especially useful when they're relevant
to what we're discussing, though they're still helpful when irrelevant. When I meet with
decision-makers I'm trying to persuade, I always try to find commonalities to mention.
For example, I recently met with a company whose website noted they worked with a
local foundation with whom I also work. I made sure to bring the foundation up in conversation, and it went over well. Similarly, when meeting with administrators at schools,
I always mention that someone I know is a student or an alumnus. For important meetings, I'll often Google-search the individual's name in advance of the meeting to learn
what I can about them, what their interests and hobbies are, etc. Company and institutional websites often contain biographies with some of this information, and sites like
Facebook have made intelligence-gathering even easier.

Because rapport is developed best through personal interaction with someone,
meeting to discuss an issue in person is much better than doing so over the phone or by
email. Even if it means spending a lot of extra time driving or flying to be able to meet
face-to-face, making a personal connection is essential for first meetings. A study of simulated negotiations found that those who were negotiating by email had a harder time
establishing rapport and reaching a consensus than those who interacted face-to-face,
because less personal information was shared (Morris *et al.* 2002). However, exchang-
ing personal information first (such as a photo or a list of interests) increased the success
of the email-only negotiations (Moore *et al.* 1999). So, while meeting in person is crucial, it's okay to follow up with mostly emails and phone calls.

HI, IT'S ME AGAIN

Another way to increase your likeability and therefore be more influential on key decision-makers is through repeat exposure. Because people like things that are familiar to
them (remember the existence bias), the more we interact with someone the more they
will probably like us (Zajonc 1968).

In a study published in the *Journal of Personality and Social Psychology*, when faces were flashed on a screen so quickly that they couldn't be recognized, participants still liked, and were more persuaded by, the opinions of those whose faces had appeared more often (Bornstein, Leone, and Galley 1987). Other studies have found that repeated exposure to people, places, and things increased likeability (Bornstein 1989; Harrison 1977).

As an important caveat, this principle only works if the interactions are positive. Continued exposure to a person in unpleasant situations such as conflict or competition leads to decreased likeability (Burgess and Sales 1971; Swap 1977). That's why presenting yourself as being in cooperation with the other person is important for getting them to like you. In trying to create a policy change, we should stress mutual benefits so that it seems like we're working with the other person and not against them. In meeting with decision-makers, we should always state that we're happy to be working with them on the change—even if they seem to be reluctant to work with us or to make the change.

A student activist trying to get their university to use renewable energy sources shouldn't hesitate to email key administrators with updates or news articles pertinent to the subject (within reason, of course: too many emails could get annoying). The activist might also try to show up at school functions like symposiums and athletic events that the administrator is likely to attend for an opportunity to "accidentally" run into them, say hello, and ask what progress is being made.

THE LAW OF ASSOCIATION

By pairing ourselves with pleasurable stimuli we can become more persuasive. This is known as the *law of association* or the *good mood effect*. People's enjoyment of something else gets paired with us and our message, and they come to associate us with that positive feeling.

Studies have shown that people are more willing to help when they're experiencing pleasurable stimuli like sunshine, delicious aromas, eating a cookie, or listening to a comedian (Wilson 1981; Isen 1970; Isen and Levin 1972; Wilson 1981; Rosenhan, Salovey, and Hargis 1981). In one study, people were more likely to agree with a series of controversial statements when they were given peanuts and soda to snack on (Janis, Kaye, and Kirschner 1965). Other studies have confirmed that participants become fonder of people and things they experienced while eating, which may be part of the reason why lunch meetings are so popular (Razran 1940; Razran 1938). Positive feelings activate the peripheral route to persuasion, causing people to let down their guard and be more generous and sociable.

When possible, activists should pair themselves with enjoyable stimuli. An environmental activist speaking to a high school class about the importance of using public transportation—not a particularly appealing idea for most teenagers—might be more successful in getting the message accepted if they first pass out snacks to the audience to eat during the presentation. A college social justice organization trying to recruit new members by tabling near a major walkway might play some popular music to put passersby in a good mood and make them more receptive to signing up. Distributing leaflets where people are bound to be in a good mood, like sunny summer festivals or music concerts, should be a bit more effective (excluding other factors) than leafleting in situations where people aren't as happy, like on cold winter days.

The law of association can also work in the reverse. If we unwittingly get paired with a negative stimulus, the other person can end up liking us less (Lott and Lott 1965). This is why people do actually tend to dislike a person who brings bad news, even if that person is just the messenger (Manis, Cornell, and Moore 1974). Therefore, we should try to talk to people when they're likely to be in a good, or at least a neutral, mood. Meeting with someone at nine a.m. on Monday is probably not the best idea, since many people aren't happy to be back at work after the weekend. It would be worse still if the person you're meeting with just trudged into work soaked from the rain. I was once asked to reschedule a meeting I'd set up with a hospital administrator from the morning to the afternoon because the administrator had to attend a funeral in the morning. Not wanting to meet with her a few hours after the funeral for fear of being paired with negative emotions, I rescheduled for another day entirely and had a positive meeting.

chapter seven

TOOLS OF INFLUENCE, PART IV: HANDLE WITH CARE

DON'T DENY IT

When trying to correct a misunderstanding the public holds on an issue, it's a bad idea to deny something, to say "XYZ is not true." Denials and clarifications that are meant to clear up rumors can actually bolster them because they require repeating the false information. This makes the false information more accessible in peoples' minds, and as we discussed earlier, the more accessible a thought is the more likely people are to believe it to be true. Instead of denying false statements, we should simply assert the truth.

Research has found that non-profits who use denials to try to educate the public can end up doing more harm than good. The most vivid demonstration of this comes from a study conducted by social psychologist Norbert Schwarz. Schwarz wanted to examine the impact of an actual Centers for Disease Control flyer that was created to clear up misconceptions about the benefits and dangers of flu vaccines. The flyer contained a number of true statements labeled "True" and a number of false statements labeled "False." This type of presentation (sometimes presented as *Facts and Myths*) is often used by non-profits and government agencies to disseminate information.

In the study, Schwarz gave the flyer to participants to read and then tested how much they accurately remembered. By and large, the participants understood the information on the flyer; immediately after reading it, only four percent of the false statements were thought to be true, and only three percent of the true statements were thought to be false. However, that understanding soon declined. Only thirty minutes after reading the flyer, about twenty-eight percent of older participants incorrectly remembered the false statement as true. After three days, that number had risen to forty percent. Younger participants did a better job of remembering at first, but after three days even they mistakenly believed thirty percent of the false statements to be true.

While the number of false facts believed to be true rose dramatically over three days, the number of true facts believed to be false didn't. This suggests that once the memories of which statements were labeled true and which false began to fade, statements that were familiar (because they'd been read) were more likely to be accepted as true. Furthermore, all of the participants believed that the source of their knowledge, including their incorrect beliefs about many key points, was the trustworthy Centers for Disease Control. This led them to be even surer that their beliefs were correct when, in fact, many of them were incorrect (Schwarz *et al.* 2007). It's possible that, overall, the flyer increased more than it decreased understanding, if people were extremely uninformed about the issue to begin with. However, the CDC would have been much more effective at increasing understanding if they'd simply presented the facts of the issue instead of presenting both true and false statements.

The Internet is filled with Facts and Myths pages for every social issue imaginable, from marijuana use (Myths and Facts about Marijuana) to the Israeli–Arab conflict (Hertz), from health care reform (AARP) to global warming (Global Warming Myths and Facts). Prominent non-profits as varied as the Environmental Defense Fund (Global Warming Myths and Facts), the AARP (AARP—Health Action Now!), and the NRA (NRA–ILA: Fables, Myths and Other Tall Tales) all use the facts-and-myths format to state their case, and news sources like National Geographic (Koerth-Barker) and ABC (The Vaccine–Autism Link: Facts and Myths) use it to present information on misunderstood issues.

A whole host of government agencies also use this format (Facts and Myths about Generic Drugs; Security and Prosperity Myths vs. Facts; Diesel Idling Facts and Myths; Residential Sprinkler Myths and Facts). Despite the findings of the Schwarz study, the U.S. Department of Health and Human Services continues to publicize a list of myths and facts about flu vaccines at www.flu.gov/myths. This site, like many other Facts and Myths pages and pamphlets, may be doing more to confuse the public than to bring clarity.

The Facts and Myths presentation is especially dangerous for older audiences. In addition to the Schwarz study, a second study found that older adults were much more likely to confuse true and false facts given to them, especially after time had passed. Because older adults' memories were not as good when it came to remembering which statements were labeled true and which false, they were more likely to accept false statements as true because the statements sounded familiar to them (Skrunik *et al.* 2005).

Experiments by cognitive social psychologist Ruth Mayo also found that in trying to correct a falsehood, it's more effective simply to state what is true and make no reference to the original myth. This carries over to how we word things as well. Mayo found that the statement "I am innocent" was more convincing than "I am not guilty," because with the latter the speaker gets paired with the idea of guilt in the audience's mind (Mayo, Schul and Burnstein 2004). Richard Nixon's infamous statement, "I am not a crook," is nowadays invoked by those who want to emphasize how crooked someone actually is.

The clear lesson that activists can learn from this research is that we shouldn't use a Facts and Myths format in presenting information to the public. Instead, we should simply state what's true. But there are additional implications for those willing to be somewhat insidious and use misunderstanding to advance their agenda. If thirty to forty percent of facts labeled as false are going to be remembered as true, then if we present five false but personally advantageous statements to the public, and say they are falsehoods, the chances are that one or two of them will later be remembered as true by the audience. Yet we'll be left looking perfectly innocent—because, after all, we did say that the statements were false.

Conservative news network Fox News has often been criticized for using a variation on this technique in its broadcasts. Critics contend the station poses outrageous questions for which the actual answer is clearly "no"; yet simply asking the question instills in some viewers the belief that the question has validity and may be true. For example, in an April 2, 2009 broadcast pundit Glenn Beck aired photos of Adolf Hitler, Joseph Stalin, and Vladimir Lenin and asked "Is this where we're heading?" in the midst of criticizing the Obama administration (Fox News). Other questions posed repeatedly in recent years have included "Did the 9/11 hijackers have links to Iraq?" and "Is President Obama's birth certificate a fake?" Even though the answer to all of those questions is pretty clearly "no," repeatedly asking the question surely helped spread incorrect beliefs on these issues.

EDUCATION ISN'T EVERYTHING

"If only people knew about _____, then they would _____." So goes a common activist lament. We earnestly believe that if only people knew what was going on in sweatshops, mountain-top coal-mining sites, factory farms, and other places, they'd stop supporting these industries. A popular slogan in the animal protection movement is: "If slaughterhouses had glass walls, everyone would be a vegetarian."

We also think that if people were taught how to make changes—where to go to buy sweatshop-free clothing, how to sign up for wind energy, how to eat vegetarian— they would. Non-profits often create and distribute how-to pamphlets on making these types of changes.

Educating the public about an issue and providing resources for action are both extremely important. After all, few of us would have made more compassionate life-style choices if we hadn't first had our eyes opened by someone. And social marketing research makes clear that showing people how to do something is critical in creating behavioral change (Andreasen *Social Marketing in the 21st Century*). But just because education plays an important role in the situations where we achieve success doesn't mean that education alone will always lead to that success.

Numerous studies document cases where education had little or no effect on eliciting sustainable behaviors. In one study, home-owners were provided three-hour workshops about energy conservation and ways to reduce energy use. While the workshops did result in participants having greater awareness and willingness to implement changes, very little actual behavioral change occurred (Geller 1981). A Dutch study found that providing households with information about energy conservation didn't reduce energy use (Milden *et al.* 1983). High school students who attended a six-day workshop on environmental issues were no more likely to be engaging in sustainable behaviors two months later than those who hadn't been at the workshop (Jordon, Hungerford, and Tomera 1986). In another study, households given a detailed handbook on water efficiency didn't decrease their water usage (Geller, Erickson, and Buttram 1983).

In contrast to these studies, educational efforts can be, and in some cases are, successful in creating change. An analysis by researchers Andreas Diekmann and Peter

Preisendorfer found that people who became more environmentally conscious were slightly more likely to engage in pro-environmental behaviors, especially easy ones (Diekmann and Preisendorfer 1998). Animal protection groups distribute educational booklets on the whys and hows of vegetarian eating and receive a lot of feedback showing the booklets have caused people to change their diets. Many people have altered their driving habits after watching Al Gore's *An Inconvenient Truth* and learning some of the scientific data on the impacts of climate change. There are countless other examples of educational efforts having a degree of success.

Because many factors are involved, it's impossible to pinpoint the reasons why some education-only efforts succeed and others fail, without delving into the specifics of each effort. The important lesson to be learned, however, is that we cannot assume that because we're educating people about an issue we're achieving change. Educational efforts are extremely important, a bedrock of most activists' efforts. Nonetheless, it's essential that we monitor the results of our educational efforts to see whether or not they're having an impact on people's behavior. If they're not, we have to figure out what to do differently in order to succeed.

A college Amnesty International chapter might find that passing out flyers to classmates educating them about political repression and asking them to write a letter to a political prisoner don't result in many letters being written. They might then decide to re-design their flyer to be more persuasive, or they might try to target the types of students likely to be persuaded to write a letter. Alternatively, they might decide to abandon typical educational outreach in favor of another method of getting people to write letters. For example, they might try having a movie night with free popcorn and asking attendees to write a quick letter to a prisoner before the movie starts. Whatever the Amnesty International chapter does, what is most important is that they pay attention to what effect their outreach is having and its impact on their ultimate goal: supporting and freeing political prisoners. Assuming that education alone will bring about a desired behavioral change is a dangerous mistake made far too often by advocacy organizations.

FEAR FACTOR

Imagine you're the principal at a suburban high school and prom night is approaching. You want to hold an assembly to educate seniors about the dangers of drinking and driving, but you're not sure of the best way to persuade them. Should you simply talk to them about drunk driving, giving statistics about how many teenagers are killed in car crashes each year? Or should you show the bloody car crash videos that many administrators of the past used to encourage safe driving? Will such footage persuade them, or will it cause them to turn away and ignore your message? Perhaps there's a workable middle ground, like showing videos of crash test dummies?

Now imagine you're a doctor trying to convince one of your patients to stop smoking. Is showing a gory video of a lung-cancer operation likely to help convince your patient to quit their habit, or is it likely to turn them off and cause them to ignore your advice? Would it be better to show a more upbeat video, or give statistics about the consequences of smoking?

For both of these situations the underlying question is whether scare tactics are effective at creating behavioral change. The answer is . . . "yes!" Studies have found that gory lung-cancer operation ads and bloody-accident ads are more effective than statistics and crash-test-dummy videos in turning people against smoking and drunk driving (Leventhal *et al.* 1967; Rogers and Mewborn 1976).

Research shows that appeals using high levels of fear do motivate change, in part by increasing people's incentive to think carefully about the persuasive arguments. For *fear appeals* to be effective they must include strong arguments that the threats are real and—most importantly—they must provide clear instructions on how the listener can avoid the threatened danger. If the listener feels little control over the situation, the fear appeal will be ineffective, because it will scare them out of paying attention and taking action (Keller 1999; Leventhal 1970; Rogers and Mewborn 1976). A meta-analysis of decades of research on fear appeals, published in the *Journal of Applied Social Psychology*, found that how strongly people believed they could avoid the threat by changing their behavior was the most important element of a fear appeal's success. Providing clear, effective ways to avoid a threat had more of an impact on people than presenting particularly scary messages (Milne, Sheeran and Orbell 1998). Furthermore, once people are familiar with the problem it's wise to mostly move on to dealing with the solution; otherwise, people become so habituated to the message that the fear appeal loses its impact.

Fear appeals can be very useful to activist groups promoting behavioral changes that affect personal health and well-being. In addition to the smoking and drunk-driving examples mentioned earlier, fear appeals could promote safe sex to prevent the spread of HIV and sexually transmitted diseases, encourage prostate exams or breast-cancer screenings, and discourage the use of hard drugs. Any group using fear appeals should include clear guidance on how people can avoid the threat.

THAT'S DISGUSTING

Most studies examining fear appeals have focused on behaviors that directly affect the listener. The listener can choose to smoke or not, drive drunk or avoid doing so, and they will bear the consequences of their decisions. But what about appeals where the threats mentioned impact others and not the person hearing the appeal? For example, activist flyers might show graphic depictions of landmine victims, child soldiers, or animals in product-testing labs. Messages such as these have been called *disgust appeals* by some researchers because of the feeling they elicit at what's going on in the world.

The question of whether to be graphic or not is one that many non-profits deliberate over in choosing which images to use in their materials. Are anti-abortion groups more effective in persuading the public when they use images of mutilated fetuses, or are they more effective when they use images of healthy children in utero? Are anti-war groups likely to persuade their audience with pictures of children seriously injured and maimed by U.S. bombs? Should animal protection groups use graphic images of animals in slaughterhouses (as PETA did for many years with its classic image of a bloody, dripping cow's head) or should they use cute pictures of baby farm animals? One animal protection group, Vegan Outreach, distributes two booklets that are virtually identical on the inside, but which have very different covers. One shows a picture of happy chickens in a field, the other contains stark images of farm animals confined in metal cages.

The concern that non-profits have is that if images are too graphic the recipient will simply throw their flyer in the trash, exit their website, or otherwise turn away without having received the other key elements: strong arguments and clear advice on how to prevent the threatened outcome. Graphic imagery might also be deemed as inappropriate by some viewers, generating hostility toward the non-profit that used it.

Unfortunately, not enough studies have been conducted to provide clear answers on the impact of disgust appeals. In a study published in *Communication Quarterly*, participants were shown a video that gave arguments for and against animal experimentation. The study found that the more graphic the images of animal experimentation presented, the more the video caused people to disagree with animal experimentation (Nabi 1998). One factor that limits the applicability of this study to most activist work is that participants had to watch the entire video. In many real-world situations the public can turn away from images they find upsetting, which could prevent the messages that go with them from having an impact on people's behaviors.

Little other research has been done on the effect of graphic imagery in activist appeals. However, based on the above study and the success of fear appeals, it seems likely that graphic imagery can help activists persuade the public, as long as the images aren't so graphic that they cause people to turn away and ignore the corresponding message. Hopefully, in the future non-profits and researchers will conduct case studies to better understand the impact of such images on changing behavior.

TO GUILT OR NOT TO GUILT?

One related area where the research is crystal clear is that using guilt in advertisements and materials is not persuasive. Guilt can be a powerful influencer for interpersonal relationships (Baumeister, Stillwell, and Heatherton 1994; Vangelisti, Daly, and Rudnick 1991) and the popularity of terms like "Catholic guilt" and "Jewish guilt" suggests the role guilt plays in enforcing religious morality. Nonetheless, studies have consistently found that as non-profits or commercial advertisers increase the amount of guilt in messages, their persuasiveness drops (Dillard, Kinney, and Cruz 1996; Coulter and Pinto 1995).

Using straight *guilt appeals* will backfire on us in trying to change people's attitudes and behaviors. Among activist causes, the animal advocacy movement has been notorious for occasionally using guilt-laden messages. In the 1980s and 1990s, many posters proclaimed "Meat is Murder." One animal rights T-shirt has a picture of a cow with the slogan, "I died for your sins." Messages like these might be popular among animal activists and might help a non-profit raise funds, but research suggests they're not ideal for persuading others.

The only relevant exception to this is a situation where people notice their own hypocrisy on a particular issue without it being pointed out to them. In a study published in the *Personality and Social Psychology Bulletin*, some participants were asked to record a message for high school students promoting safe sex and were then asked to privately recall to the researcher times they failed to have safe sex. Other participants were only asked to record a message, and a third group was only asked about their personal history. Participants were then paid for participating in the study and offered condoms for sale. The participants who'd recorded the message and later recalled unsafe personal behaviors were more likely to buy condoms and to buy more of them than participants who only recorded the message or who were only asked about their personal behaviors (Stone *et al.* 1994). Realizing their own inconsistency led the first group of students to feel guilty about having unsafe sex and to purchase more condoms in order to prevent future unsafe behavior. The situation was effective in creating behavioral change because no one was trying to make the participants feel guilty; the conflict was internal.

Activists conducting humane education programs will sometimes start their presentations by asking students about their companion animals, why they care about them, and whether they think cruelty to animals is wrong. Humane educators will then talk about issues like animal agriculture or testing on animals, allowing students to notice on their own the disjunction between their concern for some animals and their prior non-consideration of others. The research discussed earlier suggests that this sort of tactic should help increase behavioral change, since it makes people aware of a personal hypocrisy without explicitly stating it or attempting to make the audience feel guilty.

Environmental advocacy and social justice groups can use the same tactics in speeches, presentations, and materials. A person encouraging the boycott of products made by child labor might start off a talk by asking the audience about their own children and how much they love them, and by discussing how everyone agrees that children deserve protection. The speaker can then begin revealing the conditions for child laborers making soccer balls, sneakers, and other items sold in the U.S. The audience will see the disjunction between their attitudes and actions when it comes to protecting all children from exploitation, and that may stimulate a behavioral change, such as boycotting goods made in sweatshops. The speaker shouldn't directly point out to the audience: "You care about children here in the U.S., but you don't seem to care about children in sweatshops in Bangladesh." A straight guilt appeal such as that is sure to backfire.

SPILLOVER: A SECOND FOOT IN THE DOOR?

To the extent they seek to alter individual behavior, should environmental organizations continue down the path most are on now of encouraging small and relatively painless behavioral changes, like switching to compact fluorescent light bulbs, turning off the light switches when you leave the room, and recycling? Clearly, more people will comply with easy changes like these than seemingly difficult changes that do much more environmental good (like getting rid of one's car or going vegan).

Similarly, should animal advocates promote vegetarianism and veganism (a major change that fewer people will agree to) or should they promote a reduction in the amount of meat consumed (a smaller change that probably more people would agree to)? Depending on the issue, getting a majority of the population to make a small change may or may not do more good in the short term than getting a minority of the population to make a large change.

Earlier, we discussed the foot-in-the-door technique and how people are more likely to agree to a larger request if they've first agreed to a similar but smaller request. But does that mean that, as a general rule, those who undertake a small change subsequently become more likely to make larger changes? This is a hotly debated question in the world of advocacy, with some activists arguing that encouraging small changes is bad because it makes the public complacent and dissuades them from more meaningful changes. Others argue that not only do small changes produce immediate good, but they make it more likely that people will later engage in larger changes. So, which side is correct?

Foot-in-the-door research shows that people will be more likely to agree to a larger change if they first agree to a small one. Individuals who've already switched to compact fluorescent bulbs or taken part in the Humane Society's "Meatless Monday" program should be more likely than a control group to take larger steps in energy conservation and meat reduction if later encouraged to do so. However, we need to be aware of several caveats.

The first is that foot-in-the-door only works if a second request is made. If we encourage someone to switch to compact fluorescents or eat less meat and they comply, we shouldn't assume that they're then going to take further steps on their own. We have to allow time to pass and then make the second, larger request. For example, those who've switched to CFLs might be challenged later to try to reduce their home energy usage by twenty percent. Those who've given up meat one day a week might be encouraged to become vegetarian or semi-vegetarian. If the second, larger request isn't made then the foot-in-the-door technique isn't being used—we're simply encouraging a small change.

We cannot assume that when people make small changes it will spill over into additional positive changes. The results of research on *spillover* in the adoption of sustainable behaviors have been very mixed. Some studies have found that pro-environmental behaviors do tend to spill over, so that once you engage in one or two you are likely to engage in more (Thogersen 1999). For example, home-owners given a shower-flow restrictor and pamphlet were more likely to install the restrictor and engage in other conservation actions mentioned in the pamphlet than home-owners who were only given a pamphlet (Hutton 1982). Evidence for spillover seems particularly strong among behaviors that are equally easy; spillover into more arduous environmental behaviors seems to occur only in those who have strong pro-environmental attitudes (Diekmann and Preisendorfer 1998).

However, a survey of one thousand Danish citizens found that recycling didn't lead them to be more concerned with related pro-environmental behaviors like buying products with minimal packaging. In fact, recycling led them to care less about this issue. Curiously, while there was negative spillover in terms of attitude, in terms of behavior there was a positive outcome. People who were recycling said they cared less about buying products with minimal packaging, yet they engaged in this behavior more (Thogersen 1999). A separate survey that followed people's behaviors over the course of two years found some spillover between environmentally friendly behaviors like eating organic foods, recycling, and decreased driving. But spillover was small and only in some areas, and some possible negative spillover was found (Thogersen and Olander 2003). Still other research has found little evidence of either positive or negative spillover of environmentally beneficial behavior (McKenzie-Mohr and Oskamp 1995; Pickett, Kangun, and Grove 1993).

Several reasons may be suggested as to why little or sometimes negative spillover has been found for sustainable behaviors. Spillover can be thwarted by the *contribution ethic* that many people have, which leads them to adopt the idea that "I'm doing my part by undertaking A, so I don't have to worry about B, C, or D" (Diekmann and Preisendorfer 1998). Promoting actions that are already part of the social norm, such as recycling or eating less red meat, will likely fail to create spillover. People who engage in the new behavior will believe they're only doing it because everyone else is, and their self-perception won't be changed (Thogersen and Crompton 2009).

Negative spillover can occur when people adopt pro-environmental behaviors for non-environmental reasons. As was discussed earlier, someone might cut back their energy usage by ten percent in order to save money. Since their motive was financial and not environmental, they might use the money they saved to take a flight across the country for vacation, an activity with a heavy carbon footprint. Similarly, someone who stops eating beef or pork for health reasons may increase their consumption of chicken and fish, causing even more animals to suffer (since these animals are smaller and you get much less meat per animal than you would with beef or pork).

The effectiveness of the foot-in-the-door technique is well documented when it comes to influencing relatively easy behavioral changes. However, we shouldn't be under the illusion that getting people to make a small change will automatically get them to make other or larger changes down the line. If that's what we're seeking, we have to be very clear in making a second, larger request later on. Leaving it up to individuals to realize they should do more will only occasionally result in spillover into other positive behaviors, and may result in spillover into negative ones. Furthermore, in promoting behavioral changes we should emphasize the altruistic reasons for making the change: protecting the environment is very important, all workers should be protected from exploitation, animal suffering is bad, etc.

OUT WITH THE OUT-GROUP

Humans have a natural tendency to greatly value their own social group and ignore and denigrate those not in it. That's why people root for the home team, why they consider their city or country the best in the world, and why ethnic and racial tensions are so common across societies. It's one reason why Americans acted with such shock and horror when several thousand people died in the September 11, 2001 attacks, but barely notice when similar acts claim hundreds or thousands of lives in other countries. While people don't consciously consider who's in their ingroup and who's not, judgments in this area have a profound effect on people's behaviors.

Activists are often speaking up for members of an out-group. Starving people in Africa, Palestinians, the rivers and trees that make up our ecosystem, and animals on farms and in labs are all (perhaps unconsciously) considered by most Americans to be part of the out-group. Because people have little concern for out-group members, it can be hard for activists to get people to care about these individuals.

How can we help people see these others as part of their ingroup? One way is through encouraging people to put themselves in others' shoes. Research has shown that perspective-taking makes people more likely to help members of an out-group (Batson, Ahmad, and Lishner 417–24; Esses and Dovidio 2002; Galinsky and Ku 2004). Many homeless-advocacy groups hold events where supporters sleep outside (sometimes in the cold) to acquire a taste of what homelessness feels like. The groups hope that after experiencing this perspective participants will become more likely to donate and volunteer to help the homeless.

Another way to generate sympathy for members of an out-group is to put people in close contact with them, creating an experience of connection (Whitley and Kite). Farm Sanctuary, a farm animal–rescue organization with shelters in New York and California, hosts thousands of visitors each year who come to hang out with rescued pigs, sheep, turkeys, and other animals. For many visitors, being in close proximity to the animals break downs negative stereotypes and helps create attitudinal change so that the animals are seen as friends and not food.

Bias against members of an out-group can also be reduced if people come to perceive themselves and others as part of a common group (Gaertner and Dovidio). Sports and music helped break down racial barriers in the U.S. by uniting people of different races in a common passion. The desegregation of the armed forces had the same effect. Some churches, schools, and cities have "sister" churches, schools, and cities in other areas or other parts of the world as a way to break down barriers between the rich and poor. The popular documentary *Earthlings* points out both in its title and its narration that all animals (humans and others) share space on this planet, and as such we should treat nonhuman animals with respect. Emphasizing animals' similarity to humans— their experiences of certain emotions, intelligence, and their unique personalities—is a popular and effective method of breaking down barriers and getting people to give more ethical regard to animals.

HOW MUCH IS TOO MUCH?

When we're trying to persuade someone to make a change, how much should we ask for? Often, when trying to change behaviors and attitudes we're unsure about just how extreme we should make our message. If a person really wants to reduce their impact on the environment they shouldn't reproduce, and should go vegan, eat mostly local foods, and stop driving. But if you're passing out fliers about Earth Day or giving a talk to an assembly about environmentalism, are you really going to ask your audience to do all these things? Or should you ask for smaller and easier behavioral changes like reducing household energy use and biking to work one day a week? Which message is likely to be more persuasive and do more good?

Should an animal advocate speaking to a high school or college class assert that animals need to be given rights and afforded the same protection from exploitation, killing, and cruelty as humans? Or should they present a softer appeal, saying that institutional cruelty to animals is something society should pay attention to? Which appeal will have more of an impact in changing attitudes and behaviors? Is it better to ask for more so that you get more, or ask for less so that you don't get rejected?

Message discrepancy refers to the distance between the message of the speaker and the belief of the listener. Picture a continuum of differing beliefs on a social issue like environmental protection. At the far left end are those who believe that humans should have as little impact on the environment as possible, and we should abandon industrialism and return to a local, small-scale livelihood within our biosphere. Further to the right are environmentalists who favor strong laws to protect the environment, like mandating renewable energy and making cities car-free.

Further still, are those with weaker environmental beliefs; until you reach those who believe that we should have no concern for our impact on the environment and that we should mine, drill, and otherwise exploit the planet for every resource that can benefit humans in the short term. The distance between a speaker's stated position on the continuum and the audience's position is the message discrepancy. When the speaker and listener have fairly similar views there is low message discrepancy; when the speaker advocates an idea very different from the listener's beliefs there is high message discrepancy.

Of course, people have some flexibility in their beliefs. Wherever they may be positioned on the continuum, people have a range of beliefs to their left and right that they might consider moving toward. For example, someone in the center of the continuum might be swayed into thinking environmental protection is only important when it impacts the quality of human life (going further to the right). On the other hand, they might also be persuaded that renewable energy is necessary to stop the impacts of global warming (going further to the left). The beliefs to the left and right of our current position that we'd be willing to consider represent our *area of acceptance.*

Studies have found that for issues related to values, beliefs, and self-identity, the impact of message discrepancy on persuasiveness follows a *discrepancy curve* that looks like an inverted "U" (Aronson, Turner, and Carlsmith 1963; Bochner and Insko 1996; Sherif, Sherif, and Nebergall, 1965; Whittaker 1967). Initially, the greater the message discrepancy the more attitude and behavioral change the message will create. Once message discrepancy goes beyond a certain point, however—once it goes past the edge of the audience's area of acceptance—the amount of attitude and behavioral change quickly declines. Once the message is outside the area of acceptance, listeners will start to discount it, argue against it in their heads, and perceive it to be far too different from their current belief to be reasonable. If message discrepancy is too high, the message's persuasiveness will drop to almost zero. An environmentalist encouraging college students to drop out of school and move to the wilderness to live in huts as hunter-gatherers is unlikely to win many converts, no matter how polished their speaking skills.

The more strongly held people's beliefs are on a particular issue, the smaller their area of acceptance will be. In these cases, attitudinal change will increase with message discrepancy for only a short while. Soon, the message will be out of the listener's area of acceptance and its impact on attitude and behavior will start to decline.

On the other hand, if the subject being discussed is one that doesn't have to do with someone's values, attitudes, or self-concept, research has found that the greater the message discrepancy the more the message will change attitudes (Anderson 1971; Anderson *Methods of Information Integration Theory*; Hunter, Danes, and Cohen). Because self-identity and personal values are not at stake, people find it psychologically much easier to change their attitude, so their area of acceptance widens. If a message is so discrepant that it seems completely unbelievable, then persuasiveness can decline. But as a general principle, for subjects that don't have personal importance, the greater the message discrepancy the greater the attitudinal change (Dillard and Pfau).

Most of our work as activists does involve changing values. Thus, if we want the message we present to be as persuasive as possible then we should tailor the message to broaden the audience's area of acceptance, but not by too much. We can go outside of that area, and changing attitudes and behaviors does sometimes require moving people to a belief they'd never have agreed with before. But since attitude and behavioral change will start to decline at that point, we need to keep in mind that the further we stray, the less we will create that attitude and behavioral change.

In order to target your message, you'll need to know the general beliefs of your audience. While a few people in every audience will hold unique beliefs, it's obvious that in general a room full of Democrats will hold different areas of acceptance on abortion than a room full of Republicans. An audience comprised of student environmental activists will have a different average area of acceptance on conservation issues than a college English classroom.

Earlier, we discussed whether it's better to encourage small behavioral changes that most people would be willing to make or large behavioral changes that fewer people would be willing to make. Those questions remain, and the discrepancy curve doesn't provide easy answers. Is an AIDS-prevention organization better assisted by getting one college student to become a committed volunteer or twenty college students agreeing to be tested for HIV? Does an animal advocacy organization help more animals by getting one person to go vegan or by encouraging ten people to reduce their meat consumption slightly? Presenting highly discrepant messages ("AIDS prevention is so important that you should devote your nights and weekends to helping out"; "You should go vegan to prevent animal suffering") will significantly reduce your persuasiveness for most members of your audience, but will have a maximal impact on the one or two audience members whose area of acceptance encompasses those beliefs. Deciding which outcome is better, and operating within the most effective amount of message discrepancy, will depend on the issue and the audience. It's safe to say, however, that arguing for very small changes or very large changes isn't ideal when trying to create behavioral change.

Finally, it should be noted that how discrepant a message feels to the audience can vary based on circumstances (Fink, Kaplowitz, and Bauer 1983). At a conference on gender equality, most members of the audience would perceive a speaker who agrees with most feminist ideas but argues that women shouldn't serve on the front lines as having a discrepant message, since the speaker deviated from the homogenous beliefs of most attendees. If that speaker gave the same talk as a guest on a morning radio show that typically objectified women, feminist listeners would likely perceive the speaker as having beliefs very similar to theirs.

You can use circumstances such as these to make your audience feel like your position is really not far from theirs, which should increase persuasiveness. A pro-environmental booklet might begin by discussing a few conservative politicians who want current laws repealed and who support the most damaging mining, drilling, and deforesting projects. By emphasizing the most extreme opposing position, environmentalists will make the audience perceive there to be less discrepancy between their own beliefs and those advocated in the booklet. Activists against the death penalty help sway the public toward their position by often focusing on states like Texas, which put prisoners to death with a frequency most Americans find upsetting. Politicians on both sides of the political spectrum use this same tactic to make their opponent's message seem extreme and theirs seem more closely aligned to their audience's beliefs.

REACT NOW

Activists spend most of their time attempting to persuade people to choose new attitudes and behaviors. But when campaigning for policy changes, sometimes we seek to remove people's ability to do certain things. For example, environmental campaigners might work to prevent four-wheeler enthusiasts from being permitted to go off-roading in state forests. Animal activists have been able to outlaw fur farming and foie gras production (a food item produced by force-feeding ducks and geese) in several countries in Europe. Bans such as these represent momentous victories, codifying new ethical values into laws. When campaigning for such bans, activists need to be aware that they will face an extra challenge: a reaction from those affected by the regulation.

People hate to lose the freedoms they currently possess. *Psychological reactance* is the phenomenon by which, when a particular freedom is threatened, the desire to retain that freedom makes people value it more than before (Brehm 1966; Brehm and Brehm 1981). After Dade County, Florida (the county where Miami is located) disallowed the use of cleaning products containing phosphates in order to protect the environment, the majority of Miami consumers came to see phosphate cleaners as better products than before. Compared to residents of Tampa, who were unaffected by the prohibition, Miami residents rated phosphate detergents gentler, more effective in cold water, better whiteners and fresheners, more powerful on stains, and even claimed they poured more easily (Masiz 1975; Masiz, Settle and Leslie 1973). As a result of this attitude shift, many people chose to smuggle in phosphate detergents from neighboring counties.

The principle of reactance holds true for information as well. Our response to learning a particular perspective has been suppressed is to want that information more and become more supportive of that perspective—even when we only know the general topic and not its specific content (Ashmore, Ramchandra, and Jones 1971; Wicklund and Brehm 1974; Worchel and Arnold 1973). For example, when University of North Carolina students learned a speech opposing co-ed dorms would not be permitted, they became more opposed to the idea of co-ed dorms (Worchel, Arnold, and Baker 1975). In a study, thirty experimental juries were presented with a case where a careless driver had injured a victim. When the prosecuting attorney noted that the careless driver had liability insurance (meaning the insurance company would be paying damages), the jury awarded the victim an average of $4,000 more. However, when the judge told some juries to disregard the attorney's statement about insurance because it was inadmissible as evidence, those juries awarded the victim an average of $13,000 more. Being told they weren't supposed to know something made that jury consider the information even more important in deciding on damages (Broeder 1959).

In pursuing restrictions on particular practices we should expect a degree of reactance from those who'd be affected, and we should try to reduce that reactance as much as possible. We might do so by framing the ban in empowering terms. For example, instead of promoting "House Bill 112, Banning Soda in Public Schools," we might promote "House Bill 112, Ensuring Healthy Beverages for All Public School Students." Our talking points to the press and our flyers on the issue could be similarly phrased.

Along the same lines, if a campus Green Party group is holding a forum on military spending and a Republican audience member wants to voice an opposing opinion, the group shouldn't prevent that person from doing so. Aside from the general benefits of open debate, refusing to allow that opinion to be expressed will make audience members on the fence about the issue more likely to agree with the dissenter.

HOW HARD TO CAMPAIGN?

If gentler attempts at persuasion haven't been successful, you may find yourself starting a campaign against a particular target. The Rainforest Action Network targets major banks to convince them to stop funding environmentally destructive practices. Animal advocates campaign against certain clothing lines and department stores to convince them to no longer sell fur or fur-trimmed garments. Students Against Sweatshops chapters work to stop their school stores selling clothing made in sweatshops.

Just how hard-hitting should these types of campaigns be? As a general rule of thumb, they should be only as hard-hitting as necessary to create the desired change. Martin Luther King, Jr. advocated the use of escalating tactics to achieve civil rights for African-Americans. Early campaign tactics would be soft and non-confrontational, but if these didn't produce results then harder-hitting tactics would gradually be employed, to eventually create "a situation so crisis-packed that it will inevitably open the door to negotiation" (Garrow 246). While launching a campaign with a fury can have some benefits (if the target thinks that anger will be sustained for a long period of time, they might agree to your campaign demands more quickly), the escalating strategy used by King is typically the better choice—for a number of reasons.

First, as a general human characteristic, people accept inner responsibility for a choice only in the absence of a strong external pressure to make that choice. Boys given a mild warning not to play with a toy were much less likely to play with it six weeks later than boys who'd been threatened from the outset with serious punishment if they played with it (Freedman 1965). To achieve long-term compliance, pressure should only be as strong as necessary to achieve the change. If we can get decision-makers to change policies with just a small amount of pressure, they're more likely to attribute the change to their own desire to do so and are therefore more likely to maintain the new policy into the future. If the pressure exerted is extremely high, then even if they do change, they'll see their decision as nothing more than a response to pressure—meaning they're more likely to backslide when pressure is no longer being placed on them.

Another psychological phenomenon that campaigners should be aware of is "good cop/bad cop." This technique is used by police officers because it often works. One reason is framing: compared to the mean, threatening officer, the good cop looks like someone you'd want to align yourself with. The other reason that good cop/bad cop works is the *rule of reciprocity*. The good cop seems likable, acts as if he's trying to get the best possible result for you. The good cop will often perform small favors for you, such as providing you with food or a cigarette. In return, you may feel compelled to confess to a crime or give the officer whatever other information he wants.

The good cop/bad cop strategy can be put to use in deciding how hard to campaign. If multiple non-profits are working on an issue, one or several can play the good cop and engage in nothing but friendly dialogue and gentle nudging with the target while another non-profit engages in more confrontational tactics that place intense pressure on the target. When your organization is the only one running a campaign, you can still set up a good cop/bad cop dynamic. In every personal interaction with key decision-makers, be unfailingly polite and professional. At the same time (as it becomes necessary), use tactics that put serious pressure on the target—launching websites that publicly shame them, holding protests or gathering petitions asking for a change, using boycotts, etc. The Humane League has experienced many occasions where our street protests led to an angry response from the target company; but when I afterwards met with company representatives and was very polite, a policy change was made. With companies that receive nothing but the friendly meeting, policy change occurs far less frequently.

As per King's escalation of tactics, the best approach is always to start with a friendly meeting or set of meetings. Sometimes they'll succeed. When they don't lead anywhere, follow up with pressure tactics that gradually increase in intensity—while at the same time continuing to engage in warm and friendly dialogue with the key decision-makers.

MINORITY INFLUENCE

All new ideas start off being advocated by a minority group (a statistical minority, not a racial one). If the idea spreads through society, eventually it becomes the majority opinion. In the United States, the beliefs that recycling is important and child labor is bad have already embraced by the majority of Americans. On the other hand, beliefs that animals shouldn't be eaten or that gays and lesbians should have the right to marry are still minority opinions. Many of the goals that activists are pursuing represent minority opinions, which is why our work is both valuable and also somewhat difficult.

People tend to have biases in favor of the majority opinion and against the minority opinion on any given topic, because they evaluate messages from each group differently (Festinger 1950; Levine 1989; Watts and Holt 1979). As we've noted, studies have found that regardless of how relevant or irrelevant an issue was, and regardless of initial differences in opinion, hearing that a message stemmed from a majority led people to have more favorable attitudes toward it (Erb *et al.* 1998). One of the reasons for this is that when we hear most people agree on an issue, our brain assumes the majority is probably right and we process the majority opinion with less scrutiny (De Dreu and De Vries 2001). Minority opinions on the other hand are scoured for any perceived faults.

While these biases can make it harder to persuade, there are ways to help overcome them. One useful strategy that activists should be aware of is *first conform, then dissent*. People will only doubt their current beliefs when they find themselves in disagreement with someone who they'd expect to agree with, someone who's similar to them. If people perceive an activist to be very different from them (based on their looks, lifestyle, or other factors), then the activist will be seen as a member of the out-group. Since out-groups are expected to hold the wrong opinion on things, the activist's message won't cause people to reconsider their beliefs (Dreu and De Vries 2001).

This is why dressing and acting similar to our audience is so important, and why studies have repeatedly found that people are more willing to help those who appear similar to themselves. It's also part of the reason why former cattle rancher Howard Lyman is a particularly compelling spokesperson for veganism, and why corporate CEOs can be particularly compelling spokespeople for strict pollution regulations. Such individuals conformed first, establishing themselves as industry insiders before raising a dissenting viewpoint. (Another reason they're particularly persuasive is because they appear to be arguing against their own self-interest, which makes them appear more trustworthy.) As activists, we should do and say whatever we can to appear similar to those we're trying to influence, cementing ourselves as part of the ingroup.

Consistent dissent is also important. Activists who hold a minority opinion on their issue should be persistent in repeatedly advocating their message, while at the same time taking care not to appear rigid or close-minded. Studies have shown that even when a minority advocated a factually incorrect position (stating a green image was blue, for example), if they were consistent in stating their faulty position at every opportunity they were able to sway others to agree nearly ten percent of the time (Moscovici and Zavalloni 1969; Clark 2001; Crano 2000). The reason consistent dissent is effective is that by appearing confident, you make others begin to doubt their own position—causing them to re-examine their belief, and to actively consider yours.

Finding a balance between consistency and rigidity can be a delicate process. Those you're interacting with need to know that you wholeheartedly believe your position is correct, but at the same time know that you don't have a "my way or the highway" approach (Jones and Davis 1965; Moscovici, Mugny, and Van Avermaet; Moskowitz 1996; Brehm, Kassin, and Fein 240; Stangor and Ruble 1989). In the animal protection movement, a few activists believe that advocating anything less than veganism (for example, promoting a reduction in meat-eating or working to ban practices in the intensive confinement of farm animals) is ultimately counterproductive because it sends a mixed message to the public. These activists believe that advocating only one thing (veganism) in every situation will ultimately win the most gains for animals.

The scientific record, however, points quite clearly in the opposite direction, and suggests that this sort of rigidity—especially when coming from a minority opinion—reduces influence. A consistent but non-rigid alternative message, and the one espoused by most animal activists, is that the suffering of an animal is bad and anything (any law, personal behavioral change, policy change, etc.) that reduces that distress is a step in the right direction.

Those advocating a minority position were also shown to be more effective when they had a consistent behavioral style (De Dreu and De Vries); when their message couldn't be attributed to self-interest (Moskowitz 1996); and when they agreed with the majority on a side point (Baker and Petty 1994). Research has found a number of additional ways that you can persuade your audience to consider the minority message you're presenting: you can make your message extremely relevant to them; cause them to feel less confident in their own knowledge or belief about the issue (De Drew and De Vries); point out similarities between yourself and them (Hinsz, Tindale and Vollrath 1997); or surprise them by agreeing on issues they don't expect you to agree on (Jones and Davies 1965; Stangor and Ruble 1989). In one study, researchers got participants to alter their initially stated beliefs by pointing out that the Ku Klux Klan shared that belief. Not wanting to be associated with the much-despised organization, participants shifted their stated opinions (Wood *et al.* 1994).

Other studies have found that although presenting a minority message can (if done well) get people to re-examine their beliefs, it also causes them to consider other alternatives—not just the one you're promoting (Nemeth and Kwan 1987). College activists passing out flyers about school apparel being made in sweatshops might get passersby to make changes on related issues (such as buying fair-trade coffee) even if those passersby aren't motivated enough to boycott the campus clothing store. Environmentalists encouraging people to stop driving may inadvertently persuade some members of the public to reduce their home energy use, yet continue driving as much as before. Animal activists promoting veganism will always spark in some members of the public the decision to switch to organic or pastured animal products, no matter how explicitly materials are worded (De Dreu and De Vries).

Part of the reason some people will make these alternate changes is their desire to do something easier than what's being promoted. Adopting a similar but distinct change is also easier because people haven't raised their defenses on those other issues. As we discussed earlier, people don't want to feel like they've been persuaded into doing something. Making a similar but different behavioral change than the one being advocated allows people to feel independent while at the same time partially addressing the problem being discussed—such as unfair labor practices or environmental destruction (Crano and Alvaro 1997). In one study, liberal subjects who were exposed to a conservative minority message opposing gays in the military weren't swayed in their beliefs on that issue; but subsequently they expressed greater support for another conservative minority position (opposing gun control) than they'd initially indicated. The process worked in reverse as well: when other participants were presented with a minority message opposing gun control, they weren't swayed; but they subsequently expressed greater support for a minority position opposing gays in the military (De Dreu and De Vries).

When you feel that you've failed to persuade someone to accept a minority opinion, know that it's possible you've influenced them in other, related areas. This shouldn't make us content with failing to persuade others; but it can provide a silver lining to our sometimes frustrated public outreach efforts.

chapter eight

SPREADING
SOCIAL CHANGE

SOCIAL NETWORKS

A few years ago, obesity passed smoking to become the number one killer of Americans, with over 400,000 people in the U.S. dying each year from obesity-related diseases like heart attacks, heart disease, and diabetes. The vast majority of these deaths could have been prevented by healthy eating habits and exercise.

The spread of obesity is sometimes referred to as the "obesity epidemic"; but is "epidemic" really an accurate term? After all, for most people obesity is the result of personal lifestyle choices, and for a small percentage of people the result of their genetic make-up. Obesity isn't spread from person to person like AIDS and other epidemics—is it?

In 2007, the *New England Journal of Medicine* published a groundbreaking study by researchers Nicholas Christakis and James Fowler (Christakis and Fowler 2007). The pair had spent several years combing through data collected by the Framingham Heart Study, which had followed the medical histories over the course of thirty-two years of 15,000 people, most of whom lived in Framingham, Massachusetts. In addition to monitoring the health of each participant, the Framingham study kept records of who the participants' friends, co-workers, and family members were at any given time. Christakis and Fowler had one burning question they hoped the data would answer: Was obesity socially contagious? If a person became overweight, would that make it more likely that their friends and co-workers would follow down the same path?

The answer was a resounding "yes." The data showed that when one person became obese, their friends were fifty-seven percent more likely than the average person to become obese. However, the influence didn't end there. Friends of friends were twenty percent more likely to become obese, and their friends—people removed by three degrees of separation from the first individual—were ten percent more likely to become obese. When one person began to gain weight, they didn't just put their own health in jeopardy, they also threatened the health of their friends, their friends' friends, and even their friends' friends' friends.

This ripple of influence wasn't confined to obesity. Christakis and Fowler found that when an individual began smoking, it increased their friends' chances of smoking by thirty-six percent, and their friends' friends' friends chances of smoking by eleven percent. Alcohol consumption and happiness were found to spread in the same way, having an impact on others that faded away after three degrees of separation. This phenomenon is known as the *Three Degrees of Influence rule*. The researchers note that it applies to a broad range of attitudes and behaviors including political views, creativity, and job recommendations (Christakis and Fowler *Connected* 28). Other phenomena shown to spread in clusters of varying size include back pain, suicide, eating disorders (Christakis and Fowler *Connected* 120), and pregnancy (Thompson 2009).

The spread of traits through a social network is not caused by *homophily*, the tendency for people to befriend those who are similar to them. While it's true that smokers tend to gravitate toward other smokers, and optimists tend to gravitate toward other happy people, these tendencies don't explain the spread of traits. Christakis and Fowler took homophily into account by analyzing who each study participant was friends with. Even when this variable was controlled for, the tendency for obesity and other traits to spread through a social network remained (Christakis and Fowler *Connected* 109).

The spread of obesity was also not caused by *confounding*, the process by which friends or family members share common experiences that influence them in a similar way. An example of confounding would be that, if several fast-food restaurants opened up in one neighborhood, making fatty foods more accessible, we could expect that people in that neighborhood to be more likely to become obese. Even after Christakis and Fowler controlled for confounding, the tendency for obesity to spread through social networks remained (Christakis and Fowler *Connected* 109).

So what causes the epidemic-like quality of obesity, smoking, happiness, political views, and other traits? Christakis and Fowler suggest that they spread in part through subconscious social signals about what is normal. If the person sitting next to you is eating more, chances are you will, too. If several of your friends are overweight, you'll begin to see that as a socially acceptable condition (Thompson 2009). Behaviors don't spread as quickly and directly as a physical disease; they spread through a more complex process, often involving reinforcement from multiple sources (Christakis and Fowler *Connected* 23). Because of this, behaviors can pass from a person to his or her friend's friend without changing the intermediary friend's behavior (Thompson 2009).

Because we look to those closest to us for guidance on social norms, traits are spread along links of close relationships: spouses, siblings, very close friends, and those who work together at small companies. Christakis and Fowler found that for two close friends who each named the other as a best friend, when one became obese it tripled the likelihood that the other would also (compare that to the fifty-seven percent increase in risk for general friends). For unequal friendships—where Person A named Person B as a best friend, but Person B didn't name Person A as a friend—if Person B became obese, Person A was twice as likely to do the same. On the other hand, if Person A became obese, Person B (who didn't claim to be friends with Person A) wasn't influenced. So we're only influenced by those we consider ourselves close to. The closer we are, the more we're influenced (Christakis and Fowler *Connected* 109–110).

While Christakis and Fowler's research has focused primarily on obesity, smoking, and happiness, those aren't the only traits spread through social networks. As mentioned, political views, eating habits, and other traits spread in a similar fashion. This has major implications for our work as activists. After all, one of the primary goals of activism is to change the behaviors of as much of society as possible. Though they haven't been formally studied, many of the behaviors we're encouraging probably spread through society in the same way. When one person begins carrying a reusable water bottle instead of purchasing bottled water each day, that person's friends, their friends' friends, and their friends' friends' friends should become more likely to do so. When one person begins to publicly support same-sex marriage, the same ripple effect should be found.

One implication of the spread of traits through social networks is that every time we get one person to make a change, that will likely lead others to make a change as well—meaning we're more successful than we think. This is cause for celebration, especially considering how hard it can be to change people's behavior. Fowler points out that most people are within three degrees of separation of one thousand people, all of whom become more likely to recycle, donate to starving children, or spay their dog when the first individual makes such a change.

How much of a ripple effect is created depends on the particular issue, and data would have to be carefully gathered to find out the specifics. This isn't practical for most non-profits to do, but it would make for a very interesting research project. For example, let's say data gathering found that the average American has a three percent chance of going vegetarian, and also found that if a person goes vegetarian it increases their friends' likelihood of doing so to four percent. Friends' friends' likelihood of going vegetarian was found to increase to 3.5 percent, and friends' friends' friends' likelihood to increase to 3.2 percent. Using this hypothetical data, and assuming that the average American has about ten friends, one person going vegetarian would lead a couple of others to do the same.[4]

Of course, people who are engaging in a behavior we don't like will also influence others to do the same. If most people in a social network drive gas-guzzling SUVs, that makes it likely that most of the people in that network will continue doing so. This is the power of social norms, which we discussed at length earlier. And it explains why it can be so difficult to get a person to break from the mainstream and adopt a less common attitude. One inherent property of networks like the human social network is that they tend to magnify whatever properties are already common, a "rich get richer" dynamic (Christakis and Fowler Connected 31). If most people in a small town are Christian, that puts social pressure on all town members to become or remain Christian, and when they do so, that in turn creates even more social pressure.

However, environmental factors and the "fitness" of an idea matter as well. Lower food prices, growing wealth, and the influx of fast foods and fattening packaged foods have shifted the social dynamics over the past sixty years to cause obesity to spread from a small segment of the population (about thirteen percent) to a much larger one (about thirty-five percent) (NCHS Health E-Stat 2006). Similarly, new beliefs that are more "fit" than older ones can radiate as more and more people gradually adopt those beliefs. New religious beliefs take hold (as do the reverse—witness the sharp rise in atheism and agnosticism in the U.S. over the past twenty years); new social ideas like women's rights or civil rights embed themselves. If conditions are right, these "fitter" ideas gradually replace older beliefs for a substantial portion of society. Activists play an important role in seeding society with new (or neglected older) ideas and initiating their spread through social networks.

USING SOCIAL NETWORKS TO SPREAD CHANGE

In taking a hypothetical look at the spread of vegetarianism, we made an assumption that the average person has about ten friends, each of those people has about ten friends, and so on. In the real world, however, the number of friends a person has varies significantly from individual to individual. Someone who's particularly social might have many dozens of friends; someone who's shy and reserved may have only one or two. Malcolm Gladwell uses the term *connectors* to describe people who have large numbers of friends and acquaintances. Other authors call these individual *hubs*. Either way, these highly connected individuals sit at the center of vast social circles.

It's because of connectors that "Six Degrees of Kevin Bacon" actually works. For those not familiar with the game, "Six Degrees" involves trying to connect the actor Kevin Bacon to any other actor or actress based on the movies they've been in. For example, if Kevin Bacon was in a movie with Danny DeVito, and Danny DeVito was in a movie with Jim Carrey, then Bacon would be two degrees away from Jim Carrey. In fact, Bacon can be connected to almost any other American actor or actress in only three or four links. The reason for this is connectors—the small number of actors who've been in a large number of movies (Barabasi).

Researcher Stanley Milgram wanted to find out how many links it would take to go from one randomly selected person in the U.S. to another. In other words, he wanted to find out how connected we are. To do so, he mailed out letters to randomly selected individuals in Nebraska and Kansas. In the letters, he described the experiment and instructed the recipients that their goal was to get those same letters to a target person in Boston. The target's name and information were given, but recipients were instructed to forward the letter to that person only if they knew him personally. Otherwise, they were instructed to forward the letter to whichever friend of theirs they thought most likely to know the target person in Boston. So the letter was passed on from one friend to another, getting closer and closer to the target person. Want to take a guess as to how many times each letter was forwarded on before reaching its intended recipient?

On average, the letter reached the target person after being forwarded only six times. So there are about six degrees of separation between any two randomly selected people in the U.S. It's a small world after all—thanks in large part to connectors. Of the letters that reached the target person at his home, two-thirds were sent to him by one man, a prominent clothing merchant. Of the letters that reached the target person at his office, half were sent by two other men. Connectors such as these individuals make the world a much smaller place (Travers and Milgram 1969).

One of the fundamental properties of the human social network is that most people have a small number of links (that is, friendships), but some have a large number of links. In fact, about twenty percent of people hold about eighty percent of the links (Barabasi and Laslo), and research has found that genetics play a significant role in how connected a person is (Christakis and Fowler *Connected* 233). This 80/20 principle of uneven distribution holds roughly true for other issues as well, including the distribution of population among cities in the U.S., the size of businesses, the length of rivers (Rank-size distribution 2010), and the distribution of wealth (as of 2007, twenty percent of the U.S. population controlled ninety-three percent of the country's financial resources) (Domhoff 2010). Networks such as the human social network, in which links are distributed unevenly, are called *scale-free models.*

We've discussed how traits like obesity, recycling, and caring about world poverty can spread through social networks, so that when one person changes their behavior they make others more likely to do the same. We've also discussed how some people—connectors—are linked to many more people than others. Putting these two facts together, we can see that connectors are much more influential than the average person. When they change a behavior, it will have much more of a ripple effect because they're within three degrees of separation of many more people than the average individual. Connectors are often the ones who help push trends forward, and they can make or break the success of a new idea.

Connectors who bridge different groups of people also play a vital role in the spread of ideas. Think of a randomly selected friend of yours. Now think of another randomly selected friend. Do those two friends know one another? Chances are they do. Most of us have social networks filled with friends who know one another and who share similar attitudes. An analysis of social networks on Facebook found that both altruistic and non-altruistic people had similar numbers of friends, but that they were embedded in separate networks of like-minded people (Christakis and Fowler *Connected* 300). The altruists stuck mostly with other altruists, and the non-altruists stuck mostly with other non-altruists. Tightly clustered groups are good for enforcing group behavior; if a lot of your friends are commenting to one another that a new health care bill is good, chances are that you'll agree with them. What tightly clustered groups aren't good at is adopting new ideas. This is where connectors come in.

Though some connectors sit at the center of a dense cluster of friends, others are linked to a number of different clusters. For example, a group of environmental activists in a small town might include one activist who's also a Republican committee-member and a prominent congregant at a local church. That activist is particularly important because he or she can help transmit the behaviors of the environmental activists to other social circles via links of close friendship.

Some activists, particularly those who perceive themselves as holding very progressive views, only want to collaborate with people who have virtually identical beliefs to theirs. Some will even refuse to work with anyone who doesn't agree with them on an entire list of social issues—feminism, gay rights, animal rights, capitalism, etc. This attitude will create a tiny group with very similar views, but won't help spread any of those views to the wider public. Instead of rejecting those who inhabit different social circles or possess different viewpoints on other issues, we should embrace these connectors as particularly important for spreading our message to new audiences. A college social justice organization might be taken aback when a hard-partying fraternity brother shows up for a meeting, and be tempted not to take him seriously. But that person could help spread new behaviors to those in his own social circle, and might also provide the organization with access to a new pool of volunteers.

In trying to create social change, activists should focus on changing the behaviors of connectors. Because connectors are linked to so many people, or provide bridges between very different groups of people, getting a connector to make a change will have a much larger ripple effect than getting an average person to make a change. For example, getting five connectors to spay or neuter their companion animal will lead to many more animals ultimately being spayed or neutered (as the effect filters to their many friends, their friends' friends, and to their friends' friends' friends) than getting five average people to do the same. Connectors spread new behaviors far (reaching a large number of people) and wide (reaching new social clusters), speeding up the spread of social change.

But how can we activists find these powerful connectors? The rise of online social networking sites like Facebook, Twitter, and MySpace means that we now have access to detailed maps of who's linked to whom and who the major connectors are—those with the largest number of friends or followers. A small portion of these people may be friend collectors who don't personally know as many people as their profile suggests. But for the most part, those who have more online friends really are more connected to others. This doesn't mean that someone with one thousand Facebook friends has one thousand meaningful links through which new behaviors can be spread. As was discussed earlier, changes spread only through deep social connections. But users with a large number of friends on Facebook usually have a larger number of meaningful online connections than users with a small number of friends. Research published in *The Economist* found that Facebook users with 150 friends maintained a relationship with 19 to 22 other users on average, whereas Facebook users with 500 friends maintained a relationship with 39 to 47 other users (the range in each answer represents the difference between men and women, with women being more communicative) (*The Economist* 2009; Byron *et al.*). If you're going to be promoting your cause online, finding the major connectors and focusing some of your outreach efforts on them can create a major ripple effect.

For example, imagine that a college environmental club has started a Facebook group called "We Want Ohio State to Switch to Wind Power!" In trying to get as many group members as possible (which would show student support for the initiative), naturally those in the environmental club will first approach their friends about joining the Facebook group. But the outreach needn't end there. By browsing through friends' profiles and the profiles of friends of friends, club members should be able to identify twenty of the most well-connected students at the school. Club members can then befriend those individuals, and after chatting them up for a few days can tell the connectors about the wind-power campaign and ask them to invite their many friends to join the group.

Mapping out networks of our friends and our friends' friends on these sites has been made a little easier by the development of applications that automatically create such maps. The Twitter Mention Map Application (Mention Map) shows which other users a tweeter is talking about. The Facebook Social Graph application (Social Graph) plots a graph of all of your Facebook friends and their connections to one another. One major limitation of this and similar applications for Facebook and MySpace is that those currently in existence only allow you to look at users with one degree of separation from you. So you can find which of your friends are the most well-connected to other friends of yours, but you can't see which of your friends are the most well-connected to the wider world. Furthermore, you can only look up your own social-network map, and not anyone else's. Perhaps more advanced applications will be developed in the future to allow mapping to at least two degrees of separation.

Despite their limitations, the graphing applications currently available can still be useful in helping increase your influence as an activist. For example, let's say you're holding a major conference and you want as many people from your social network as possible to attend. Naturally, you're going to invite all of your Facebook friends to come to the event and post about it repeatedly on your wall. However, after mapping which of your friends are the biggest connectors in your social circle, you can contact the five or ten most connected individuals and ask them to also post about the event to their wall. That way, many of the people in your social circle will be hearing about the event not only from you, but from several other of their Facebook friends—making it more likely they'll attend.

Other ways doubtless exist to locate and use connectors to promote your activist cause. Think about the people you know and pick out those couple of friends who seem to know everyone. Make a mental (or written) note of who these people are, and be sure to put special emphasis on talking to them when promoting an event, a behavioral change, a fundraising drive, or anything else.

Moving on from our immediate friends, there are other very visible connectors in society. Politicians, prominent businesspeople, and civic leaders are major connectors, interacting with and befriending a wide variety of people. Whatever behavior an activist organization is promoting, it would make sense to put special emphasis on getting campaign materials in the hands of connectors like these. If an average person decides to go vegetarian, several dozen of that person's friends will find out and maybe think about doing the same themselves. If a city council–member goes vegetarian, the many hundreds of people that the council member interacts with will find out about it, creating much larger ripples.

Some activist organizations aren't trying to spread a particular behavior; they're trying to prevent a behavior from spreading or reduce its prevalence in society. Examples include efforts to stop the spread of AIDS, and to reduce the numbers of smokers and obese Americans. Here too, targeting the connectors in a network will lead to much greater success than targeting the general population. AIDS-prevention efforts should focus first on providing condoms and scheduling regular HIV testing of the biggest connectors: prostitutes and others with large numbers of sexual partners. By working with the most-connected one percent of the population, a non-profit can do as much to stop the spread of AIDS as they would have by working with a much larger percentage of the general population (Barabasi 139–142).

Christakis and Fowler conducted some theoretical research on how to deal with the spread of new diseases when widespread immunization takes a lot of time and a lot of money, and when there may not be enough supply to go around. For example, the 2009 swine flu pandemic continued for months before vaccines became available for the general population. Until enough supply existed to vaccinate everyone, what should federal health agencies have done? Reserved vaccines for those most susceptible to the illness, such as young children? Reserved them for those who had money to pay for them? Or distributed them on a first-come, first-served basis until they ran out?

Christakis and Fowler looked at what would happen if, instead of immunizing everyone against a disease, the government focused on immunizing those who were most connected. The pair found that immunizing the thirty percent of the population most connected would do just as much to prevent the spread of the disease as immunizing ninety-nine percent of the population at random (Christakis and Fowler *Connected* 133).

Researcher David Bahr and colleagues wondered if they could create a model to replicate the way that obesity spread through the Framingham Heart Study participants. They created a computer simulation with several hundred thousand fictitious people, inserted a small percentage of obese individuals into the mix, and let the simulation begin. Slowly, obesity began to spread through the "population" in a similar way to how it had happened among the Framingham participants. Now that Bahr and his team had created a valid model for the spread of obesity, they turned to their main question: How could the spread of obesity be stopped, or reversed?

One solution that worked extremely well in the model was to encourage people to diet not with friends but with friends of friends. That way, the social norm of dieting was spread further through the social network and its influence reached more widely. This strategy also put particular social pressure on the mutual friend (the person who knows both dieters) to make a similar change. When Bahr and his colleagues plugged this technique into their virtual society, the obesity epidemic began to reverse itself. In fact, the researchers found that obesity could be reversed quickly with only one percent of the population initially going on a diet, as long as the dieters were placed in the right spots throughout the social network (Bahr *et al.* 2009). Of course, such precision isn't possible in the real world. But the fact remains that focusing on friends of friends can have more of an impact at spreading change than focusing on friends; and it doesn't take a large percentage of people to initiate social transformation.

What appears to be most effective stands in contrast to the initial impulse most of us have upon changing our own behavior, which is to talk about the change with those close to us. When a person learns about the environmental impact of plastic bottles, they'll typically want to let their co-workers, friends, and family members know about what they've learned, and encourage them to stop buying bottled water. The same is true for a person who's just donated to the victims of a natural disaster or bought a hybrid car. The research, however, indicates that instead of focusing on these people, if we really want to spread that behavior we should focus on their friends.

Online social networks make connecting with friends of friends extremely easy. For example, if you post the following update on your Facebook page or Twitter feed, a couple of hundred people might see it: "Undercover investigation: male chicks are ground up alive by egg industry! Video at http://tinyurl.com/mzamns. Please don't eat eggs!" On the other hand, if you ask ten friends to post it on their Facebook pages or Twitter feeds, then several thousand people (friends of friends) will see the posting, and your ten friends will be very likely to watch the video as well. If both you and a friends' friend stop eating eggs, not only will that behavior ripple out across a much wider set of networks, but your mutual friend becomes more likely to stop eating eggs as well.

Alternatively, activists could contact friends of friends directly via social networking websites: "Hi, my name is Nick, we're both friends of Michael Brown. I wanted to let you know the non-profit I work for is having a walkathon to help animals next month; if you're interested in taking part here's the website. . . ." Not only do you reach a wider audience, but you also make it more likely that your immediate friends will join the walkathon as well. Even if you don't use social networking sites, you can employ this technique the old-fashioned way by asking your friends to put you in touch with friends of theirs who might be interested in your cause.

We might also set up situations where we introduce to one another two friends of ours who are making a similar change, but who don't know one another. For example, an environmental activist might have two acquaintances who are both in the process of trying to reduce their home energy use. By introducing these two acquaintances to one another the activist provides them with additional social support, which makes them more likely to succeed. This in turn helps the ripple effect of their changes spread over a wide social network. It's also possible that the two budding environmentalists have other mutual friends who could be influenced to reduce energy usage as well.

In working for social change, we as activists need to recognize that connections matter when it comes to spreading new behaviors through society. By focusing outreach efforts on connectors, befriending new connectors, and involving friends of friends in our efforts, we can create large ripple effects that lead to more change more quickly.

DIFFUSION

So far, we've discussed how one person's decision (to smoke, to eat healthily, to volunteer, etc.) increases the likelihood of many other people doing the same thing. We also discussed some of the reasons why this happens and ways that activists can use social networks to spread their ideas. But several questions remain as to how ideas diffuse through a society. For example, why did some people in the nineteenth century begin supporting women's rights and why did it take many decades to get the majority of the American public to accept the idea? Why do some beliefs grow and spread until nearly everyone has adopted them, and why do others stagnate at low levels of acceptance? Though our concern as activists is usually on the spread of new behaviors, these questions could be posed about any innovation, including new consumer products. The fundamental principles of diffusion apply in both cases, and research in this area can shed light on how social change happens and how we can help it along.

Diffusion is the process by which something new is spread through society over time. Diffusion can be caused by activists, salesmen, and others whose goal is to disseminate a new idea or product. This is referred to as *centralized diffusion*, because the push for change is coming from a central source. Diffusion can also be decentralized, spreading through social networks in the ways we discussed earlier.

Successful diffusion usually follows what's called an *s-shaped curve*: at first, a tiny number of people change, and very gradually that number increases. At a certain point, when ten to twenty-five percent of a society has adopted the change, acceptance suddenly and dramatically increases, as most of those who hadn't yet made the change now decide to do so. In a relatively short period of time, acceptance leaps to eighty to ninety percent, after which it levels off. Over time, most of the remainder of society gradually adopts the innovation (Rogers 5–11).

Of course, not all diffusion is successful. Some innovations will plateau at a certain level of acceptance and not increase. For example, the number of vegetarians in a particular country might gradually rise until it reaches say, fifteen percent, and then plateau for years or even decades without much growth beyond that point. Other innovations may fail completely, either never gaining much acceptance or enjoying a short increase in popularity and then falling out of fashion. Gas-guzzling Hummers seem at this point to be an example of the latter; with production of new Hummers ended, these vehicles seem destined to decline in use until they're nearly gone from U.S. roads.

Since every innovation is different, there's no easy answer as to why some succeed and others fail. But looking at the steps successful innovations take on their way to becoming accepted might provide some insight into how we can be more successful in spreading our own ideas.

As we discussed earlier, most people don't decide which behaviors to choose or which attitudes to hold based on careful analysis. Instead, they look to their peers to hear their judgments and see what they're doing. However, a small percentage of people are trailblazers, willing to try out new ideas and behaviors when virtually no one else has done so. These *early adopters* can assume many forms. Ethical early adopters might take up novel philosophical positions, like the belief in animal rights or (a few hundred years ago) the notion that slavery and racism are wrong, despite public ridicule for their stance. Technological early adopters are those people first in line to buy the new gadgets launched each year by Apple regardless of the price tag.

Salesmen, activists, and others who actively push for a change play the key role in persuading innovators and early adopters. Researchers Bryce Ryan and Neal Gross conducted one of the pioneering studies on diffusion, tracking the spread of hybrid corn seed–usage among farmers in the Midwest. Ryan and Gross were the first to find that agents of change like salesmen and advertisers were important sources of persuasion for early adopters (Ryan and Gross 1943).

For the remaining adopters, what caused most farmers to switch over was hearing about the new seeds from neighbors—even though they'd first heard about hybrid corn through a salesman. Additional research has confirmed that while innovators and early adopters can be persuaded by salesmen or the media, interpersonal channels of communication usually play the key role for everyone else (Beal and Rogers 1960; Rogers 200). Data suggest that, once an attitude has spread to more than half of a population, community norms begin to play a more important role than individual attitudinal change from any source (Hornik and Romer 1992). For example, once racism is seen as wrong by the majority of the public then society will begin to police itself against racism. After that, while still important, non-profits that fight racism aren't as vital in spreading that norm as they were when racism was still socially acceptable.

Late adopters and laggards—those last to adopt a new belief—are more likely than early adopters to subsequently abandon the belief. This result may be because they were pressured by social norms to accept it and they never really believed in it themselves (Rogers 188).

MAKING DIFFUSION SUCCESSFUL

Are there particular characteristics that can help us distinguish between who the early adopters of an innovation will be and who will lag behind? Knowing the answer to this could be a great help for activists promoting a cause that isn't yet widely accepted. Studies indicate that early adopters can be motivated to change by activists, and that only after a critical number of them have changed will the rest of society follow suit as interpersonal networks become activated. So the key question for activists is: How can we identify early adopters? By focusing most of our efforts on them, we should be able to speed up the diffusion process.

A meta-analysis of nine hundred studies on diffusion found that certain traits were often correlated to innovativeness, meaning that people who possessed these traits were more likely to be early adopters. Personality traits of innovative people include: greater empathy (this was shown to be correlated with innovativeness in 64 percent of the studies analyzed); greater ability to deal with abstractions (63 percent); greater rationality (79 percent); more favorable attitude to change (75 percent); more able to cope with risk and uncertainty (73 percent); more favorable attitude on education (81 percent) and science (74 percent); feeling more in control of their own life (82 percent); more motivated to achieve (61 percent); higher aspirations for themselves (74 percent); and greater intelligence (100 percent). Confirming the importance of intelligence as a key trait of innovators, researchers Christakis and Fowler found that when they analyzed the decline of smoking among members of the Framingham Heart Study, well-educated people who quit were more influential in getting others to do the same than less well-educated people who quit (Christakis and Fowler *Connected* 118).

Other traits that were found to correlate to innovativeness include: more social participation (73 percent); more highly connected with others (100 percent); more cosmopolitan (interacting with people outside their local social circle) (76 percent); more contact with agents of change (87 percent); greater exposure to mass media (69 percent); greater exposure to interpersonal communication (77 percent); more actively seeking information on innovations (86 percent); and greater knowledge of innovations (76 percent) (Rogers 352–76).

This may seem like an overwhelming list of characteristics, but for ease of use it can be boiled down to a few primary qualities: early adopters are more likely to be intelligent, socially active, progressive/open to change, and living in a metropolitan area. Later adopters and laggards typically have the opposite qualities: they're less educated, not as cosmopolitan, and possess fewer channels of interpersonal communication (Rogers 107).

You may have noticed one trait that could distinguish innovators from late adopters that's missing from the list: wealth. While economic status is somewhat correlated to innovativeness, with those of higher income generally being more innovative, the relationship is not perfectly linear. The meta-analysis found that in half of the studies analyzed, the lower-middle class was more innovative than the upper-middle class. This phenomenon is called the *Cancian Dip* (Rogers 352–376). Its existence means that while those lowest on the economic ladder are less likely to be innovators and those at the top more, for the rest of society economic status can't predict how innovative a person will be.

Given the traits that correlate to innovativeness, it's not surprising that as a general rule of thumb metropolitan areas of the U.S. lean heavily Democratic (a party whose buzzwords focus on change and progress), whereas rural areas lean heavily Republican (a party that emphasizes traditional values). Clearly, that isn't the only factor at play, but it's an important one. The traits also explain why those in rural areas—especially those with low incomes and limited social circles—are often the last to adopt moderately new ideas, like racial or gender equality, and the acceptance of homosexuality. This pattern is not unique to the U.S. For example, the main support base of fundamentalist Iranian President Mahmoud Ahmadinejad is those who live in the country's rural villages. Residents in the capital city of Tehran favor a number of democratic reforms, and the majority of them want Ahmadinejad out of office.

Activists working to spread a relatively new idea through society will be more successful if they target people who are likely to be innovative. This means that activists should generally focus their outreach on metropolitan areas, and in particular on the more intelligent and socially active residents of those areas. Most activist organizations do this already because they find metro area residents to be more receptive and because such areas allow them to reach more people.

Focusing on innovators first can help build up the number of supporters for an idea until it reaches the critical growth stage, where the power of social networks kicks in and the majority of the public begins to accept the idea because they're hearing about it from friends and neighbors. Once this critical growth period has set in, activists may be more effective by switching their focus to exploiting social networks in the ways described earlier. This situation occurs because most adopters (everyone other than the early adopters) are influenced to do so primarily by friends and colleagues, not by activists. Once more than half the population has been persuaded, social norms are activated as well and start providing their own source of influence on the remainder of the population.

The diffusion process indicates that for activists who are trying to move a behavior from the margin to the mainstream, the central task is to persuade a critical number of early adopters to make a change. Once this tipping point (to borrow another phrase popularized by writer Malcolm Gladwell) has been reached, the acceptance of the idea is likely to spread fairly rapidly on its own from the ripple effects of social networks, and later through the persuasive power of community norms. But aside from just generating as numerically many supporters as possible, is there anything else that activists can do in the early stages to push their issue past the tipping point, to begin reaching more than just the early adopters?

Research suggests that the s-shaped diffusion curves of successful innovations often take off around the time that opinion leaders in a society begin adopting the new idea. Separate studies conducted by John Stone (Stone 1952) and Frank Petrini (Petrini 1968) show that salespeople and activists will get the greatest response to their efforts when opinion leaders are adopting them, which usually occurs when between three and sixteen percent of the public has adopted the idea. The meta-analysis of diffusion studies also indicates that activists' success will be linked to how much they work through opinion leaders (Rogers and Shoemaker 1971).

Who are opinion leaders in a society? Members of the media are, because they take in stories and attitudes from other people and transmit them to a huge audience. The "media" include both the mainstream news outlets and those running popular online content like blogs and podcasts. People in the entertainment industry, creating music or movies or television for public consumption, are also opinion leaders. They imbue what they produce with the attitudes they've adopted, transmitting social norms to a wide audience. Celebrities of any sort become opinion leaders as a result of the public attention paid to their behaviors and beliefs. Political, religious, and civic leaders are also opinion shapers to the extent they operate in the public eye: writing op-ed pieces for newspapers, giving public interviews, making speeches to a congregation or community group, etc.

For the most part, the influence that opinion leaders have on others is different from the influence that friends have on friends through social networks. Opinion leaders may be directly linked to a large number of people, and that in and of itself will have influence; but their biggest impact is in transmitting social norms through the media, the culture, and public-policy decisions.

Because getting opinion leaders to support a new idea has been shown to be a critical step in the diffusion process, activist groups should emphasize reaching out to them as an important part of their efforts. Persuading an average person to spay or neuter their companion animal can help prevent a number of animals from being killed in shelters due to the lack of good homes. But whoever it was that persuaded longtime *The Price Is Right* game-show host Bob Barker that spaying and neutering are important probably prevented tens of thousands of animals from being euthanized. Barker spent decades signing off on his show with a reminder to "have your pets spayed and neutered." This is why organizations like the Gay and Lesbian Alliance Against Defamation, the Humane Society of the U.S., the World Wildlife Fund, and many other major non-profits devote personnel and sometimes entire offices to influencing the attitudes of Hollywood actors, writers, and producers.

Though opinion leaders are not early adopters *per se* (if they were too quick to change, they'd become too marginal to be viewed as authorities) they frequently possess similar traits to innovators and are more innovative than the average person (Rogers 308–309). Indeed, though they sit in positions of influence, they themselves are susceptible to influence by activists and are often quicker to change than the average person. Every opinion leader has friends who have influence over them, and sometimes just learning about an issue through an article or video is enough to turn them (like anyone else) into supporters of a cause. Small activist organizations might not be able to tackle Hollywood, but they can influence opinion leaders at the local level: members of the media, politicians, business and civic leaders, block captains, pastors and rabbis, and others whose opinion the public (or segments of it) look to for guidance. Because people do tend to be homophilic, clustering in social circles with like-minded people, activists should target different sets of opinion leaders in society. Focusing only on religious leaders may lead to influence among communities of regular worshippers, but the message might not make its way into other social circles.

Research into social networks and the diffusion of innovations teaches us that focusing our outreach on key individuals at key times can help our ideas spread much faster than conducting indiscriminate outreach. Though we won't always see the beneficial results in the short term, extensive research on this subject makes clear that targeting connectors and early adopters can put us on a faster track to success in changing society.

chapter nine

SOCIAL MARKETING

THE BIRTH OF SOCIAL MARKETING

In 1952, psychologist G. D. Weibe posed the now-famous question: "Can brother-hood be sold like soap?" (Weibe 1952). Weibe wondered whether traditional market-ing techniques—the kind used to sell Tide detergent or Nike shoes—could also be used to promote socially beneficial behaviors. Could the same methods that succeeded in promoting fast food and helped spread the obesity epidemic be used to shrink fast-food's popularity if put in the hands of public-health agencies? If traditional marketing techniques could be used to combat social problems, non-profits would have a wealth of information available to them. As of 2005, U.S. companies were spending nearly seven billion dollars per year on marketing research (Inside Research 2010). A lot of the information gathered by for-profit companies is kept private; but many fundamental principles have filtered down to fill the pages of college marketing textbooks, marketing research journals, and other publications.

A decade after Weibe posed his question, public-health organizations began using marketing techniques to promote family planning in India. Their efforts were success-ful, and in the years that followed similar programs sprang up in other countries. These early efforts were often supported by private companies like condom manufacturers that stood to benefit from the success of family-planning campaigns. In 1971, the term *social marketing* was coined to describe the application of marketing techniques to solving societal problems. The field of social marketing has been growing ever since, with many books and an academic journal devoted to the technique. Government entities like the Office of National Drug Control Policy and the Centers for Disease Control, as well as a number of non-profits, use social marketing to try to create behavioral change, primarily on public-health issues (Andreasen *Social Marketing in the 21st Century* 88–92).

The answer to Weibe's question is, generally speaking: "No, brotherhood cannot be sold like soap." The techniques that succeed in social marketing are different from those used in traditional advertising. The main reason for this is that in trying to create social change, we're often dealing with high-involvement behaviors for which the public has very ambivalent or negative feelings (Andreasen *Marketing Social Change* 38). Getting someone to install solar panels on their roof requires generating a huge amount of motivation in that person, showing them companies that can do the installation, getting them to understand the benefits, and ensuring they have the ability to spend thousands to tens of thousands of dollars on the installation. Even before any of that, non-profits usually have to create a change in values so the person begins to believe strongly in the importance of environmental protection. On the other hand, getting someone to choose a Wendy's hamburger over other dinner selections or the Hair Cuttery over another hair salon is much simpler because there are far fewer barriers to action. People have to eat and they want to get their hair cut. All that traditional advertisers need to do is convince the public that their product is superior or easier to access.

Furthermore, traditional advertisers succeed by appealing to the public's self-interest: "You'll benefit from our product by looking wonderful/smelling great/having more free time/being entertained." When it comes to social marketing, often what we're encouraging people to do has no direct benefits. Buying fair-trade coffee benefits coffee growers but mildly inconveniences the coffee drinker (it costs more and is harder to find). Reducing consumption is good for the environment, but might make the person who does it feel deprived when they compare themselves with their friends. When the social change we're advocating does benefit the targeted person, it's often a long-term benefit that comes at the expense of short-term pleasure. Convincing someone to quit smoking will be in their interests in the long run, but in the short term they'll feel stressed, agitated, and constantly crave the pleasure of a cigarette. Getting an individual to eat healthily is good for them in the long run, but it comes at the expense of the immediate gratification that fatty, salty, and sugary foods provide.

Traditional advertising methods can be used to increase awareness of a societal issue in the same way they can increase awareness of a brand name, so that people learn about the dangers of smoking or the threat of global warming. But when it comes to creating behavioral change, mimicking practices common in the advertising industry will often fail.

While the specific practices used by traditional advertisers aren't too useful, the methods they use to create and test their practices are very useful. Think back to Malcolm Gladwell's comment: "We have an innate belief that a dogged and indiscriminate application of effort is best and will work—it is not, and will not, and often is not even possible." When it comes to promoting their cause, activists typically assume that all that matters is getting information out to the public. How the message should be crafted and which audience it should be presented to aren't always taken into consideration. And rarely is any follow-up work done to see if and how much behavioral change was created. If traditional advertisers approached their work with such a lack of rigor, they'd be fired on the spot.

Social marketing takes a page from the playbook of traditional advertising by implementing a system to design and test different methods of creating behavioral change. It begins by figuring out a way to quantify success (think back to our discussion of a bottom line in Chapter One); if we can't measure our success, chances are we're not having any. Once you figure out your bottom line and how you will measure your success, it's time for the first step of social marketing: targeting your audience.

TARGETING YOUR AUDIENCE

Every behavioral change, like every consumer product, is more appealing to certain groups of people than others. Titleist, which manufactures golf clubs, is not likely to advertise in *Time* magazine or any other general-interest publication. An advertisement in *Time* could increase sales, but Titleist will get much more bang for their advertising buck by targeting golf enthusiasts through ads in *Golf Digest* magazine and commercials during televised golf competitions. Nike doesn't design their ads to appeal to the elderly, who are less active and less interested in Nike's products. Retirement condos in Florida aren't promoted with ads featuring BMX bikers or scantily clad models.

The same principle holds true when promoting a behavioral change: some audiences will be more receptive to our message than others. For example, when it comes to vegetarian advocacy, polls have found that teenagers and college students are more likely to go vegetarian than adults. Therefore, animal advocacy organizations that target people in their teens and early twenties will likely create more vegetarians than organizations that don't target their advocacy efforts. Some segments of the public would probably not be worth targeting at all—for example, people in rural areas where farming is the primary occupation. In a world of infinite resources, everyone would be targeted because everyone has the potential for change; but given our limited time and resources, activists should focus on the low-hanging fruit—the audience most likely to be receptive to the message.

Often, activists will need to target a number of different segments of society, each in a different way. A campaign to prevent the construction of new factory farms in a particular county might target four types of townspeople to enlist their support. For those sympathetic toward animals, messages could center on factory farming's cruel treatment of animals. For those who are environmentally minded, the focus could be on the impact to the local ecology of such farms. For those who live nearby, public-health concerns like asthma and air pollution might be the most prominent message. And for older residents, emphasis might be placed on how a factory farm would dramatically change the long-standing quality of life in the town, bringing in heavy truck traffic and crowding out small farmers. Using separate messages for separate target audiences is much more effective than employing a single message for the entire public. Research also suggests that segmenting your audience and providing the one message most compelling to each segment is more effective than providing multiple messages to all people (Ginsberg 2007).

(On a cautionary note, we do need to keep in mind the issue of spillover. As discussed in an earlier chapter, encouraging opposition to factory farms on the grounds that they harm public health will not cause your audience to later care more about the environment. This may be acceptable and necessary for winning the campaign against factory farms in a county. But for other issues, getting people to change for the right reasons may be important. This thorny issue is why social marketing is more complicated than traditional advertising, and why appealing to people's current concerns is sometimes a bad idea.)

Today, the Internet has made micro-targeting extremely easy. Anyone can easily purchase Facebook ads targeting a very narrowly defined segment of society—for example, men aged eighteen to twenty-one who attend the University of California-San Diego and enjoy surfing. Google AdWords and some other services also allow for targeted online outreach, and some firms offer targeted postal mailing lists. Because self-identity is so important in shaping people's behavioral decisions, formal or informal membership communities can provide excellent dotted lines on which to segment and then target messages. If I love a particular band and an advertisement informs me that the band's singer supports Greenpeace, that provides great modeling for me to do the same. The 2008 Obama Presidential campaign put this same principle to work: supporters could purchase bumper stickers reading "Catholics for Obama," "Hispanics for Obama," "Teachers for Obama," and many other variations on the theme, each of which modeled the idea that others in that group should also vote for Obama.

An environmental organization encouraging a reduction in driving might target groups like bird watchers, backpackers, fans of eco-conscious actor Leonardo DiCaprio, global poverty activists, and other segments of society—with a different message for each group but with the same behavioral change being promoted. An outreach campaign targeting thirty audience segments with thirty unique messages would take longer to set up, but could be much more effective in promoting the same behavioral change. A national organization like Amnesty International could use micro-targeted ads to recruit volunteers from Ivy League universities who'd be interested in setting up chapters at their schools. A union seeking to recruit members from a large non-union company could use micro-targeted Facebook ads to reach employees of that company.

ADDRESSING THE BCOS

Once you've chosen an audience (or audiences), the next issue is deciding which message will most appeal to them. This might seem counterintuitive. After all, we're often trying to create attitudinal and behavioral change at the same time ("Wow, I didn't know how many plastic water bottles are discarded every year; I'd better stop buying bottled water"). Shouldn't we give the audience the message that we want them to hear? Isn't that the whole point of being an activist?

It shouldn't be. If we just want to make our opinion known, like we would in a blog or in conversation with friends, we don't have to be concerned with audience reaction. But if we want to create behavioral change—which should be the goal of all activists—we need to pay attention to what does and doesn't motivate our audience. Activists should spend as much time listening to feedback as they spend designing flyers, websites, and other outreach materials.

Because we activists really believe in the change we're promoting, we assume that if others aren't swayed to our side (or are only partially swayed) it's because of their character flaws: they're ignorant, lazy, selfish, or have no self-control! Having that attitude doesn't give us any insight into how to more effectively persuade people. In fact, it can lead us to a number of mistakes, one of which is an overreliance on communications: if we think ignorance is to blame, we conclude that disseminating more information in a catchier format will get our audience to do what we want. As we discussed earlier, however, awareness alone doesn't always lead to behavioral change, so creating slicker brochures or distributing more of them may not make us any more successful (Coffman).

A second mistake we make by blaming our audience is that we ignore the importance of testing different messages. After all, we think we know the problem—people are lazy, selfish, etc.—and we conclude that there's nothing we can do to change that. Instead, we should be doing the hard work of testing different messages to see which ones are most effective.

Lastly, a dismissive attitude toward the audience leads us to ignore competition. We need to keep in mind that we're not the only ones trying to sway people on the issue. Social norms, personal circumstances, advertising, past habits, inertia, and other forces provide competing and sometimes insurmountable forces inhibiting change (Andreasen *Social Marketing in the 21st Century* 94–99). A key aspect of social marketing is learning more about the target audience in order to understand where our competition is coming from and how to respond to it.

One common framework used by social marketers in developing campaign messages is BCOS. BCOS stands for the different factors that will influence a person to make or not make a behavioral change: **b**enefits, **c**osts, **o**thers (social norms), and **s**elf-assurance (that one is able to make the change) (Andreasen *Social Marketing in the 21st Century* 102).

People will naturally gravitate toward behaviors that have significant benefits and few costs. Costs and benefits can be physical (whether it's easy or hard to physically make the change). For example, buying one hundred percent–recycled paper products requires overcoming the barrier of finding stores that sell these products. The challenge might be mental: change may seem impossible, too complex, or requiring too much of a time commitment (Weinstein 1998). Or it could be social (would family members be happy or angry with the person for openly supporting gay marriage?). Or financial (McKenzie-Mohr, Smith and Smith 1999). Identifying the costs to change and minimizing them is essential for getting people to adopt a new behavior.

More important than actual benefits and costs are what your audience perceives the costs and benefits to be. A local foods activist who buys all their produce from a farmers' market may feel it's easy to eat locally, but their audience will probably have the perception that it's very hard to do so, because they've never visited a farmers' market. We shouldn't assume that we already know the perceived costs to the behavioral change we're promoting; we need to find out by asking our audience. They should be our primary source of information about what the barriers and costs are. Similarly, we shouldn't assume that we know their perceptions of what others think about the issue, or their perceptions of whether they have the ability to make the change.

A person who feels there are major costs to changing will not likely be persuadable; but a more mild perception of costs may be overcome by using the tools of influence discussed earlier (McKenzie-Mohr 119). People usually perceive behavior as more convenient after they've begun doing it, so getting them started is a key step. Research on diffusion found that innovations that allowed for a trial use or provided free samples were usually adopted more quickly (Rogers 172). Giving out coupons for cups of fair-trade coffee might spark people's interest and lead them to begin purchasing fair-trade coffee on a regular basis. Bringing a friend along to volunteer with you for one day at Habitat for Humanity is a good way to get that friend to become a regular volunteer. Environmental organizations might challenge the public to try leaving their car at home for two days during Earth Week. Getting people to take this trial step may lead some of them to continue leaving their car at home for two days every week after they see how easy it is to use public transportation or bike to work.

Most of the behavioral changes activists promote don't provide direct benefits to their audience. Instead, the benefits are to animals, the environment, or other people. However, we can link behavioral changes to values like social responsibility, compassion, and self-respect so that people who change their behavior gain emotionally, by feeling like they're living out their values and helping others. If the change we're promoting does benefit our audience (like quitting smoking or eating healthily), in addition to the long-term positive outcomes we should emphasize immediate benefits: increased energy, the support of our loved ones, and breathing more easily (Andreasen *Marketing Social Change* 229, 232).

Promoting benefits and minimizing costs are the main focus of traditional advertising. But concern about what others will think is also crucial to individuals considering a behavioral change. Studies on the use of birth control have repeatedly found that what people think their partners want them to do significantly alters their choices in this area (Jaccard and Davidson 1972). The easiest way to find out who influences your audience is to ask them. Aside from friends and family members, there may be organizations, public figures, or others whose opinions influence your audience's decisions. We should ask them what they think these influential others believe about the issue we're promoting.

Self-assurance is also critical for those considering a new behavior. People who feel that they don't have the ability to make a change will rarely try to do so, even if they want to and even if others would support them. For these people, promoting benefits, reducing costs, and invoking social norms won't help. Instead, social marketers need to provide them with the information, skills, or support mechanisms that will lead them to believe they can succeed. Groups promoting spaying and neutering are most effective when they present detailed lists of facilities that offer low-cost services and a description of how to set up an appointment. Environmental organizations that offer directories of where to buy recycled paper, compact fluorescent light bulbs, and other green products will be much more successful than those that just encourage the public to make a switch.

Surveying your audience on any of the BCOS issues can help shape the materials you create, the messages you use, and the approach you take in promoting social change. Whether we're trying out a new leaflet, launching a new website, giving lectures on a topic, conducting an advertisement campaign, or in any other way disseminating information and encouraging the public to do something, the only way to see how well we're succeeding is by tracking data and by polling our audience.

Is the target audience being reached? How is our audience responding to different program elements: the design of materials, the particular messages used, the way those messages reach the public? Are there important barriers that we've failed to address? Is our audience understanding the important benefits of making the switch? Surveying our audience to get answers to these questions can help us revise our outreach efforts and continually improve our effectiveness. Surveying should be done with the intent to find answers to specific questions that affect how we'll proceed with our outreach campaign. For example, would flyers that encourage biking to work be more persuasive if they focused on the personal benefits of biking (greater health, more energy) or on the negative impacts of driving (carbon emissions, air pollution)? Research that is biased in any way (for example, by not getting a representative sample of people or through interviewer influence) must be avoided because it can steer our outreach in an ineffective direction.

The true test of the effectiveness of our campaign is how many members of our audience have adopted the behavioral change we're promoting. When possible, these data should be gathered directly instead of through our audience reporting the data themselves. This is because people will often misreport whether and how much they're doing something. Researchers studying the impact of some pro-recycling campaigns weighed the amount of material being recycled by households to see if their campaigns produced an increase, a far more accurate measurement than they would have gotten by asking households if they were recycling more. An animal welfare organization conducting a spay-and-neuter drive can keep track of the number of surgeries performed to see if that number has risen as a result of their efforts. In many instances, this direct gathering of data is not possible, and we have to rely on self-reports from our audience. When this is the case, it's best to keep questions as specific as possible. For example, polls that have asked the public, "Are you a vegetarian," generate much higher percentages saying "yes" than polls that ask the more specific question: "Do you ever eat red meat, poultry, or fish?"

While polling audiences and gathering data might seem too complicated to undertake, or might seem like they'd take up valuable time that activist organizations don't have to spare, they're nonetheless vital to success. For-profit companies do both types of testing religiously, and social-marketing professionals stress that lack of testing (and the consequent failure to refine a campaign) is the leading cause for the failure of non-profits' outreach efforts (Andreasen *Social Marketing in the 21st Century* 97).

Testing will almost surely reveal that certain campaigns are more effective than others, and that these deserve the majority of a group's time and money. In surveying their audience and gathering data, non-profits may also find that fairly small changes make a big difference in effectiveness. In the Humane Society of the United States' Proposition 2 initiative in California to ban intensive factory farming practices, focus-group testing of TV ads led the HSUS to completely change their ad strategy. They found that voters didn't react favorably to clever or humorous ads; they just wanted to know the facts about the problem, what Prop 2 entailed, and who supported it. Changing the ads to give the public what they wanted made HSUS's extensive television ad campaign an important part of their winning strategy (Humane Spot 2009).

STAGES OF CHANGE

It's obvious that creating social change is a gradual process. Diffusion research examines the distinct stages in that process and what factors help an innovation to spread.

Just as change on the societal level happens in stages, so too does behavioral change by individuals.

From the late 1970s through the present, researcher James Prochaska and colleagues created and developed what they call the *Transtheoretical Model*, a system that analyzes how ready a person is to adopt a healthy new behavior and that provides suggestions on how to direct that person from one stage to the next. The Transtheoretical Model (TM) is used by many public-health organizations in the U.S. and abroad, particularly for providing guidance in getting patients to stop smoking, drinking, using drugs, or having unsafe sex. Despite TM's widespread popularity, meta-analytic studies of its research have shown it to be of little use in creating behavioral change (Riemsma *et al.* 2003; Horowitz 2003; Bridle *et al.* 2005; Aveyard *et al.* 2006; 2009). Unfortunately, many books and non-profits continue to promote TM as an effective approach for changing behavior.

Although the Model itself seems to be of no use, the specific stages that Prochaska identified are worth looking at as a reminder of the stages most people go through in adopting new behaviors. The first stage is the *pre-contemplation* stage, in which a person either has never thought about the behavior or isn't interested in it. Next comes the *contemplation* stage, where the person begins to think about the behavior and its costs and benefits. Then follow *preparation and action*, where the person is ready to act but may not have done so yet; they may have doubts about their ability to make the change, or may need a final push. The final stage is *maintenance*, in which the person continues to stick with the new behavior. Depending on the particular behavioral change, maintenance might be helped along by prompts (to access a yearly health screening, for example) or may require greater personal commitment and changes in self-identity (for major changes such as quitting smoking or stopping driving) (Andreasen *Social Marketing in the 21st Century* 74).

Most public outreach by non-profits is focused on the contemplation stage: getting individuals to consider an issue and see the benefits of a change in behavior. Animal protection groups distribute pamphlets about vegetarianism, public-health organizations run TV advertisements pointing out the dangers of smoking, and environmental organizations screen movies like *An Inconvenient Truth* to educate the public about the dangers of global warming. However, as has been discussed, educating the public about an issue and even changing their attitudes will often fail to create behavioral change. Activists need to pay particular attention to the preparation and action stage, providing the how-to's of behavioral change and minimizing perceived costs to help the person put their new attitudes into action.

The maintenance stage is another area often overlooked by activists. Once someone decides to stop buying clothing in sweatshops or start eating only locally grown produce, how can we help that person maintain their commitment? While the solutions will vary on an issue-by-issue basis, a general rule of thumb is to continue to make the costs of the behavior as low as possible and consistently reiterate the benefits. Many non-profits already use this strategy to help their members maintain behavioral changes. Groups supporting the local foods movement distribute guides to farmers' markets and Community Supported Agriculture (CSA) programs. At the same time, they continue to educate their members about the environmental impact of the modern food system. Major environmental organizations' newsletters are often a mixture of advice on how to live more sustainably and updates on the terrible environmental impacts of various industries.

In addition to striving to educate new audiences about our issue, we activists should also make it as easy as possible for those who've made a change to maintain their new behavior. Getting a person to continue to use public transportation (when that person wouldn't do so otherwise) does just as much good for the environment as persuading someone else to start using public transportation. The same holds true for most other activist issues.

UPSTREAM APPROACHES

A great deal of activists' effort is focused "downstream": the goal is to change the behaviors of individuals without necessarily addressing the broader social forces that steer individuals toward the undesirable behaviors. Unfortunately, those social forces can often cause downstream efforts to be ineffective. For example, a campaign to get children to eat healthily is likely to fail if their school cafeteria is filled with junk food and their parents are too busy to prepare healthy meals (Andreasen *Social Marketing in the 21st Century* 74). Encouraging people to bike to work can be a very tough sell in a sprawling city that lacks sufficient bike lanes. Convincing people to buy sweatshop-free clothing can be very difficult when few stores carry ethically produced clothing lines.

Upstream approaches to social change concentrate not on changing individuals but on changing systems and social forces. A major benefit of this type of approach is that a single change upstream can create significant changes downstream without having to rely on the willingness and commitment of individuals (who, as we know, are often slow to change, even when they believe in that change). For example, banning unhealthy foods in school cafeterias leads kids to eat more healthily without them having to make any special effort. Laws banning the most intensive factory-farm confinement practices lead consumers to cause less suffering with their food choices, without any effort required on their part. Trying to convince everyone to make these choices on their own (a downstream approach) would be an impossible task. When the speed limit was lowered to fifty-five miles per hour in 1973, highway deaths from motor-vehicle accidents dropped by sixteen percent. That one system change did more to reduce roadway fatalities than public-education efforts encouraging motorists to drive safely and wear seat-belts (Rogers 107).

Dr. Martin Balluch, director of the Austrian animal advocacy organization VGT (Verein Gegen Tierfabriken), proposes what he terms the *stability hypothesis*: that the social environment will determine how most people live their lives, and that on any particular issue people will generally adopt the default position. Balluch likens humans to balls resting in the trough of a check mark. For any particular social issue, it takes sustained energy for a person to move up and away from the default position toward a more compassionate lifestyle. As a result, only a minority of people will have the energy to make and maintain such switches. Social norms, the existence bias, and the attitude/behavior gap lead most people to stay resting in the default position on each issue (Abolitionism Vs. Reformism).

While this analysis paints a bleak picture of the likelihood of downstream approaches influencing more than a small portion of the population, this situation can be used to the activists' advantage. By changing laws and policies, activists can change behavior without having to change individual attitudes. With each new law, the trough moves a little bit in the direction we wish it to go. Furthermore, within one or two generations, this position will become the new norm and the issue will be a settled one, in which an old wrong from the past was corrected. Such an attitudinal shift is apparent in the U.S. on the issue of civil rights; fewer than sixty years ago (about two generations) racial integration was a hotly contested social question and segregation was the norm throughout much of the country. Today, anyone who openly supports segregation will be rightly characterized as racist and ignorant.

Balluch suggests: "While trying to change people's minds has very limited success and even less influence on behavior, system change leads to 100 percent success in behavioral change.... [W]e have to conclude that ... activists should primarily try to change the system and not people's minds. The latter is simply hopeless as a strategy to change society" (Abolitionism Vs. Reformism).

Activists trying to create upstream changes can push for new laws or policy changes that circumvent the need to sway individual members of the public. Upstream efforts can also include changing systems in ways that seem minor yet have a significant impact on behavior, while still leaving individuals the freedom to make their own choices.

Choice architecture refers to the process of setting up or altering systems in a way that nudges people toward better behaviors (Thaler and Sunstein). For example, cafeterias that wish to promote healthy eating might stock their impulse-buy counters with fresh fruits, and place vegetable and whole-grain dishes in the most visible locations. A USDA study found that giving college students pre-paid debit cards that could be used only for healthy food (they had to use cash for other food) led students to choose more meals that were healthy. The debit cards also encouraged students to purchase lower-calorie meals. Students given the pre-paid debit cards consumed less sugar, fat, and caffeine. Students who had to use cash for all food purchases ate less healthily, and students who were able to use a prepaid debit card for all food purchases consumed the least healthful food (Just *et al.* 2009). Unfortunately, most college dining services use the latter system for students with meal plans. If student health was their primary concern, an alternate payment system would be more effective.

In another study, a company wanted to encourage its employees to opt into a savings plan whereby a portion of their paycheck was transferred directly to their 401(k) account each month. Promoting a plan that began immediately and stayed at the same rate led to an average savings rate of only 3.5 percent among employees. When the company promoted an alternate savings system called Give More Tomorrow, in which the savings plan didn't begin for a few months but then gradually increased its savings rate after that, employees' average savings rate quadrupled to 13.6 percent (Lehrer 92). Other studies have found that requiring restaurants to publicize their hygiene rating to customers significantly reduced subsequent hygiene violations—more so than the citations and fines that had previously been used as deterrents to bad behavior (Thaler and Sunstein 239).

One hotly debated topic in the U.S. is whether organ donation should be an opt-in or opt-out system. In other words, when people die should they automatically be considered organ donors unless they've specified that they don't wish to be? Or (as is currently the case) should people who die be assumed not to be organ donors unless they've specified that they wish to be? The first policy would result in many more donations and consequently save many lives, but some people see it as a violation of individual rights. The organ donation issue makes clear the major role that choice architecture plays in shaping society.

Choice architecture can be a useful tool for many activist organizations. Right now, some electric companies offer customers the option of paying more money to source their energy from renewable sources such as wind power. An environmental non-profit might work with a sustainability-minded energy company to change this from an opt-in system to an opt-out one, so that customers are automatically signed up for renewable energy unless they choose to opt out. Customers would retain their freedom of choice, but human nature being what it is, many more people would be signed up for renewable energy sources than would have been the case with an opt-in system. Health-focused groups could try to work with high school and college cafeterias to adjust the placement of different foods to promote healthier food choices. Non-profits of any type might set up a fundraising initiative similar to the Give More Tomorrow plan, where donors provide credit-card information and agree to have a donation be deducted at some point in the future, possibly on a monthly basis or at an increasing rate.

chapter ten

FRONTIERS OF INFLUENCE

MOST OF THE RESEARCH DISCUSSED SO FAR PROVIDES DIRECT guidance on how to be more effective in our activism. There are several research tools that could also be useful but that can't provide immediate advice. Transition Matrices and Game Theory are two such tools, and employing them could greatly benefit activists who are willing to gather the data required to use them. There are also a few bodies of knowledge that can help activists increase their influence, but about which little empirical research has been undertaken.

THE TRANSITION MATRIX

For many issues, behavioral change is not an all-or-nothing proposition. Consider, for example, environmental activists' attempts to encourage people to drive less. In an ideal world, people would drive rarely, if ever, with public transportation and biking being the norm. In the real world, though, few people are willing to reduce their driving, and those that are are often only interested in small reductions, at least initially. Yet the fact remains that even small reductions in driving (especially when undertaken by a number of people) can have a significant positive impact on the environment. In promoting alternative means of transportation, environmental activists have a range of requests they could make to the public: buy a more fuel-efficient car, leave your car home one day each week, leave your car home three days a week, take public transit to work five days a week, sell your car and rely on public transit and car-share programs; etc.

Earlier, we discussed the foot-in-the-door technique—how small requests often make people more likely to agree to subsequent similar but larger requests. Foot-in-the-door research strongly suggests that if we can get people to leave their car home one day a week, we'll increase the likelihood of later getting them to leave their car home three or even five days a week. Of course, what we really want to do is create as much change as possible—moving people further and further along a path of reduced driving.

For situations where we're trying to move people to greater or lower levels of a particular behavior, a very useful mathematical model can be used to track how people move up and down the ladder of behavioral change. It's called a *transition matrix*, and while there's little indication of this tool ever having been used for advocacy purposes, it could prove quite helpful. A transition matrix is a chart showing the probability that members of your target audience will move from one position to another (Andreasen *Social Marketing in the 21st Century* 124). An example of a transition matrix from the non-advocacy world is a chart researchers compiled on the likelihood that jury members will change their opinion after further deliberation. For example, if a jury is currently split 7–2 in favor of a guilty verdict, what is the likelihood that after further deliberation they'll switch to a 9–0 guilty verdict? What is the probability they'll switch to a 5–4 vote of not guilty? This information is extremely valuable to the courts in understanding how long juries should continue deliberating before the process is ended and a hung jury is declared (Neilson and Winter 2008).

Creating a transition matrix could be useful in analyzing certain advocacy issues. For example, what is the probability that someone who always drives will begin using public transportation occasionally? What is the probability that someone who currently takes public transportation to work each day will get rid of their car entirely? And if a person does that, what is the probability that they will later revert to driving to work each day?

Before discussing why that data would be useful, let's turn to a clearer example: vegetarian advocacy. Animal activists hope to move people as far as possible along a continuum that starts with average or high meat consumption and continues to reduced meat consumption, then to vegetarianism, and then to veganism. What is the probability that a typical meat eater will go vegetarian? If they first reduce their meat consumption, are such individuals more or less likely to become vegetarians? And how likely is it that a vegetarian will go vegan?

Having this data would be a huge help for animal activists trying to reduce the number of animals raised and killed for food each year. The data might reveal a bottleneck in the process that's particularly hard for the public to get past and that therefore deserves special attention from advocacy groups. It might reveal that the process gets easier or harder as the public moves from one stage to the next. It might also suggest which request should be made of the public (reducing meat consumption, vegetarianism, or veganism).

For example, the data might show that the best way to get people to go vegan is to advocate vegetarianism to the general public, and then once people are vegetarian begin promoting veganism to them. The data could also indicate whether people who reduce their meat consumption become more or less likely to go vegetarian. (Based on the extensive research regarding the foot-in-the-door technique, it's likely that "meat reducers" would be more likely to go vegetarian than average meat eaters).

This data would be very helpful in providing solid answers to the question of what message to promote and to whom. Right now, that question generates considerable disagreement in the animal protection community, and is perceived as an opinion that cannot be proven either way. Data gathering would take some time and expense but could provide solid answers on this issue and make advocates of vegetarianism much more effective in their work.

To return to the issue of driving, creating a transition matrix on that issue would have similar benefits to environmental activists. The data might show that once people reduce slightly the amount they drive, they become much more likely to take further steps—meaning activists should focus on promoting the first step. Conversely, it might illustrate that while it's easy to get people to make small reductions, moving from these to moderate-sized reductions is very difficult—a bottleneck that needs to be addressed. Compiling data could demonstrate to environmental activists which requests they should make of the public and which stages they should focus on.

GAME THEORY

If you've seen the popular film *A Beautiful Mind* then you've already learned about the pioneer of modern *game theory*, Nobel Prize–winning professor John Nash. Game theory is the study of how two or more people interact when each has their own agenda that they're pursuing. It operates under the presumption that people are rational in the sense that they possess a set of preferences and personal interests and they generally act toward those preferences when they're able to. For example, if a person greatly prefers chocolate to hard candies, when purchasing snack food at a stand that only sells those two items the person will usually choose chocolate. A person who prefers to have unsafe sex despite the risks of HIV and other diseases will generally have unsafe sex unless other factors prevent them from doing so.

Game theorists try to understand how people interact and whether it's possible to predict the outcome of a complicated situation by understanding the motives of each player. Bruce Bueno de Mesquita, a prominent game theorist who's been lauded by the CIA for his success in predicting the outcome of complex political situations using mathematical models, offers a basic formula for at-home *predictioneering*, as he calls it. Bueno de Mesquita believes that "it is possible for us to anticipate actions, to predict the future, and, by looking for ways to change incentives, to engineer the future across a stunning range of considerations that involve human decision-making" (De Mesquita).

Activists thinking about starting a campaign might use Bueno de Mesquita's formula or another game theory formula to try to predict whether their campaign is likely to succeed, and therefore worth undertaking. Furthermore, in analyzing the key individuals who would play a role in the success or failure of a campaign, activists might find that by changing the beliefs of a few seemingly less-important people they can affect the outcome of the campaign. Like a chess game, activists can consider what actions their opponents are likely to take in response to the campaign and make decisions accordingly to stave off any problems. They can also make decisions about when to bluff, when to talk tough or use a soft sell, and who to focus persuasive efforts on.

Bueno de Mesquita's formula for at-home predictioneering is to consider all of the important actors in a given situation and then think about what each person wants on a numeric scale of options from zero to one hundred. For example, in a campaign regarding environmental regulations, a scale can be constructed of how strict the different parties want new environmental laws to be. Industry groups might desire a zero on the scale: no new regulations (they may even want a reduction in regulation). Environmental groups would likely want a one hundred on the scale, meaning very stringent regulations. A senator from a liberal state might want a seventy on the scale: tighter regulations, but not so tight as to create a public backlash.

Next, make an educated guess as to the salience of the issue for each individual—how important the issue is to them—on a scale of zero to one hundred, with one hundred meaning the issue is extremely important. Lastly, decide how influential each person is in creating the outcome they want to see, also on a scale of zero to one hundred. A small grassroots environmental group would be much lower on the scale of influence than a well-funded lobbying group.

We'll call a party's position on the scale of desired outcomes to be P, the salience of the issue to be S, and their amount of influence to be I. Using the following formula, we can find the weighted mean position, the average of what key individuals—given their varying levels of concern and power—want to happen: (the sum of I x S x P of each player)/(the sum of I x S of each player). The result will tell you where the outcome is likely to fall on the scale of possible outcomes.

There's a second and complimentary way to predict outcome. Using the following formula, you can find the relative power of each key individual: $[S$ x $I]/[(S$ x I of Individual 1) + $(S$ x I of Individual 2) + $(S$ x I of Individual 3), etc]. At each individual's position on the scale of desired outcomes, write down the amount of relative power that person holds. This is the amount of power that will be brought to bear in support of that outcome on the scale of possible outcomes. The actual outcome is likely to be the position on the scale for which less than fifty percent of the power is to the left and less than fifty percent of power is to the right. This is called the *majority power approximation*.

According to Bueno de Mesquita, students in his classes who glean information about international political issues from newspaper articles and who use the two formulas above in tandem make correct predictions seventy to seventy-five percent of the time (De Mesquita 53–59). (As an aside, it should be noted that the formula Bueno de Mesquita uses for his personal predictions is much more complicated and is a proprietary secret.)

Using game theory to advise non-profits on how and whether to conduct campaigns appears to hold potential promise. However, its use would be limited to situations where information is known about most of the key individuals. Some non-profits considering a campaign and wanting to use a game theory model to predict the outcome will encounter the significant problem of not knowing the preference or salience of key individuals, especially for smaller campaigns where these individuals aren't public figures. It's also important to keep in mind that the actual efficacy of Bueno De Mesquita's formula or other similar game theory formulas haven't been empirically tested.

NEGOTIATING, SOCIAL ENGINEERING, AND OTHER AREAS OF INFLUENCE

There are other areas of influence that could play a role in the success of activist efforts, but for which the current research record is extremely limited or not applicable.

Negotiating is a skill that could be very useful for certain activists. While a number of books have been written on the art of negotiating, most research on the topic is focused on highly specific negotiation situations not relevant to activism. Activists who anticipate being in negotiations would do well to learn more about the skill of negotiating, but the scientific record can't provide much guidance at this time.

Another skill that could come in handy is the art of *social engineering*—using subterfuge to gain access to private information. Social engineers are essentially low-tech hackers, using a playbook of techniques to trick security guards, company employees, and others into giving them access to desirable information. Environmental activists trying to find out the future plans of a mountaintop coal-removal company might use social engineering to gain access to that information so they can use it for campaign purposes. A study conducted on social engineering found that employees with certain personality traits were much more likely to turn over confidential information: these included those who experienced a strong need to reciprocate favors, those who were more trusting of authority figures, and those who felt it was important to follow through on commitments (Workman 315–31). Aside from that study, however, no other empirical research has been published on the issue. Activists interested in learning the basic techniques of social engineering can consult books specific to the field.

In addition to negotiating and social engineering, there are other areas of influence that are a matter of skill and that at this point have not been well-examined by scientific research. For example, while we discussed a few techniques for developing rapport with someone, by and large the ability to make friends is an art that can't or at least hasn't yet been dissected into specific elements by empirical research. Similarly, leadership skills are quite useful but aren't easy to research. These talents and others like them represent important areas of influence, and activists wishing to improve their effectiveness should search for the best advice that books and experienced individuals in these fields can offer.

CONCLUSION

While the vast majority of my work is now focused on animal advocacy, I also volunteer with Books Through Bars, a non-profit that packs and ships free books to prison inmates. One evening several years ago, in the midst of reading letters from inmates and picking out books to send them, I found that by doing my job in a slightly more streamlined manner I could get an extra package or two of books out each night that I volunteered. I realized then that a very small change in what I was doing would mean the difference between an inmate getting something interesting to read to help pass the day, and that inmate spending the day with only the numbing boredom of prison life. The happiness of a real person was at stake, and the outcome would be determined by how intelligent I was in my volunteer efforts.

Examining the scientific record to find ways that we as activists can be more influential in reshaping society is not a merely academic pursuit. Its purpose is not to satisfy curiosity about how behavior can be changed, or to prove any specific point. Its purpose is utilitarian. At the root of each of our activist causes is the reality that people and animals are suffering and the environment is being destroyed. The deciding factor in how much these things will continue happening is how intelligent we are with our advocacy work. Learning how behaviors can be changed, how ideas diffuse through society, and how to measure our effectiveness can and will mean the difference between lives saved and lives lost. It will mean the difference between suffering and happiness for real people and real animals, and the preservation or destruction of real areas of lands.

With that much on the line, we can't afford to be any less diligent in our self-education than medical students, investment bankers, or any other professionals whose success depends on their learning the body of knowledge relevant to their field. As activists we must be psychologists at heart, determined to understand how people operate so that we can be more effective at changing behaviors and changing society. We also need to examine how we ourselves operate, so that we can put our time and energy into areas of advocacy that will reduce the most suffering and create the most happiness and preservation of life.

If we are truly altruistic—which I hope all activists are—then we should push ourselves to be as intelligent as possible in our efforts to create a better world. Research can play a central role in that process, cutting through competing opinions and anecdotal evidence to give clear guidance on what is most effective. The research has been done and the lessons are waiting to be learned. Putting them into practice is up to you.

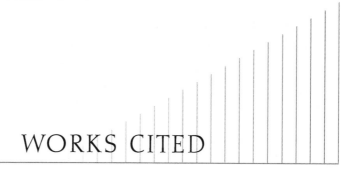

WORKS CITED

"AARP—Heath Action Now! Myths Vs. Facts." *AARP,*. 2010. 3 Mar 2010. <http://aarp. convio.net/site/pagenavigator/myths_vs_facts>.

Aarts, H., and A. Dijksterhuis. " How Often Did I Do It? Experienced Ease of Retrieval and Frequency Estimates of Past Behavior." *Acta Psychologica* 103.1–2 (1999):77–89.

"Abolitionism Vs. Reformism." Association against Animal Factories. 1996–2010 Verein Gegen Tierfabriken. 4 May 2010. <www.vgt.at/publikationen/texte/ artikel/20080325abolitionism/index_en.php>

"Abortion Information You Can Use." *Heritage House 77, Inc.* 2006. 9 June 2010. <www. abortionfacts.com/bible/pastor_cole.asp>

Aderman, D. "Elation, Depression, and Helping Behavior." *Journal of Personality and Social Psychology* 24 (1972):91–101.

Aderman, D., Brehm, S. S., and L. B. Katz. "Empathic Observation of an Innocent Victim: The Just World Revisited." *Journal of Personality and Social Psychology* 29.3 (1974):342–347.

"Adventist Health Studies." Wikipedia. 2010. Wikimedia Foundation, Inc. 20 Feb 2010. <http://en.wikipedia.org/aiki/adventist_health_studies>.

"Advocating Meat Reduction and Vegetarianism to Adults in the U.S." Humane Research Council, 2007. 1 Mar 2010. <www.humanespot.org/node/1956>.

Allyn, J., and L. Festinger. "The Effectiveness of Unanticipated Persuasive Communications." *The Journal of Abnormal and Social Psychology* 62.1 (1961):35–40.

Alter, A. L., and D. M. Oppenheimer. "Predicting Short-Term Stock Fluctuations by Using Processing Fluency." *Proceedings of The National Academy of Sciences* 103 (2006):9369–9372.

Altheide, D., and J. Johnson. "Counting Souls: A Study of Counseling at Evangelical Crusades." *The Pacific Sociological Review* 20.3 (1977):323–348.

"An Arbitrary Coherence Problem: Novices and Experts at a Wine-Tasting Experiment." Eds. Brouard, J., and A. Sutan. 2009. 2 Mar 2010. <www.wine-economics.org/meetings/reims2009/programinfo/abstracts/brouard_sutan.pdf>.

Anderson, C. J. "The Psychology of Doing Nothing: Forms of Decision Avoidance Result from Reason and Emotion." *Psychological Bulletin* 129.1 (2003):139–166.

Anderson, N. H. "Integration Theory and Attitude Change." *Psychological Review* 78.3 (1971):171–206.

———. *Methods of Information Integration Theory.* New York: Academic Press, 1982.

Andreasen, A. R. *Marketing Social Change: Changing Behavior to Promote Health, Social Development, and the Environment.* Washington, D.C.: Jossey-Bass, 1995.

———. *Social Marketing in the 21st Century.* Thousand Oaks, Calif.: Sage Publications, 2005.

Archer, D., et al. "Energy Conservation and Public Policy: The Mediation of Individual Behavior." *Energy Efficiency: Perspectives On Individual Behavior* (1987):69–92.

Ariely, D. *Predictably Irrational: The Hidden Forces That Shape Our Decisions.* New York: Harper Collins, 2008.

Aronson, E., and M. O'Leary. "The Relative Effectiveness of Models and Prompts on Energy Conservation: A Field Experiment in a Shower Room." *Journal of Environmental Systems* 12 (1983):219–224.

Aronson, E., Turner, J., and J. Carlsmith. "Communicator Credibility and Communication Discrepancy as Determinants of Opinion Change." *The Journal of Abnormal and Social Psychology* 67.1 (1963):31–36.

Ashmore, R. D., Ramchandra, V., and R. A. Jones. *Censorship as an Attitude Change Induction.* Paper Presented at the Meeting of the Eastern Psychological Association, New York. April 1971.

Aveyard, P, Massey, L., Parsons, A., Manaseki, S., and C. Griffin. "The Effect of Transtheoretical Model Based Interventions on Smoking Cessation." *Social Science and Medicine* 68.3 (2009):397–403.

Aveyard, P., Lawrence, T., Cheng, K. K., Griffin, C., Croghan, E., and C. Johnson. "A Randomized Controlled Trial of Smoking Cessation for Pregnant Women to Test the Effect of a Transtheoretical Model-Based Intervention on Movement in Stage and Interaction with Baseline Stage." *British Journal of Health Psychology* (2006):263–378.

Bahr, D. B., Raymond, C., Wyatt, H., and J. Hill. "Exploiting Social Networks to Mitigate the Obesity Epidemic." *Obesity* 17.4 (2009):723–728.

Baker, S., and R. Petty. "Majority and Minority Influence: Source-Position Imbalance as a Determinant of Message Scrutiny." *Journal of Personality and Social Psychology* 67.1 (1994):5–19.

Bamberg, Moser. "How Does Environmental Concern Influence Specific Environmentally Related Behaviors? A New Answer to an Old Question." *Journal of Environmental Psychology* 23.1 (2003):21–32.

———. "Twenty Years After Hines, Hungerford, and Tomera: A New Meta-Analysis of Psycho-Social Determinants of Pro-Environmental Behaviour." *Journal of Environmental Psychology* 27.1 (2007):14–25.

Bamberg, S. "Effects of Implementation Intentions on the Actual Performance of New Environmentally Friendly Behaviours—Results of Two Field Experiments." *Journal of Environmental Psychology* 22 (2002):399–411.

Bandura, A., Grusec, J., Menlove, F. "Vicarious Extension of Avoidance Behavior through Symbolic Modeling." *Journal of Personality and Social Psychology* 5 (1967):16–23.

Barabási, Albert-László. *Linked: The New Science of Networks.* New York: Basic Books, 2002.

Bateson, M., Nettle, D., and G. Roberts. "Cues of Being Watched Enhance Cooperation in a Real-World Setting." *Biology Letters* 2.3 (2006):412–414.

Batson, C. D. *The Altruism Question.* Hillsdale, N.J.: Lawrence Erlbaum, 1991.

———. "Addressing the Altruism Question Experimentally." In *Altruism and Altruistic Love: Science, Philosophy, and Religion in Dialogue.* Eds. Post, S. G., and L. G. Underwood. London: Oxford University Press, 2002, 89–105.

———. "Rational Processing or Rationalization? The Effect of Disconfirming Information on a Stated Religious Belief." *Journal of Personality and Social Psychology* 32.1 (1975):176–184.

Batson, C. D., Early, S., and G. Salvarani. "Perspective Taking: Imagining How Another Feels Versus Imagining How You Would Feel." *Personality and Social Psychology Bulletin* 23 (1997):751–758.

Batson, C. D., Sager, K., Garst, E., Kang, M., Rubchinsky, K., and K. Dawson. "Is Empathy-Induced Helping Due to Self-Other Merging?" *Journal of Personlaity and Social Psychology* 73 (1997):495–509.

Batson, C. D., and J. L. Weeks. "Mood Effects of Unsuccessful Helping: Another Test of the Empathy-Altruism Hypothesis." *Personality and Social Psychology Bulletin* 22 (1996):148–157.

Batson, D., Ahmad, N., and D. Lishner. "Empathy and Altruism." *Oxford Handbook of Positive Psychology*. Eds. C. Snyder and S. Lopez. New York: Oxford Press, 2002, 417–424.

Baumeister, Roy F., Stillwell, Arlene M., and Todd F. Heatherton. "Guilt: An Interpersonal Approach." *Psychological Bulletin* 115.2 (1994):243–267.

Beal, G. M., and E. M. Rogers. "The Adoption of Two Farm Practices in a Central Iowa Community: Ames, Iowa Agricultural and Home Economics Experiment Station." *Special Report* 26 (1960).

Beaman, A., *et al.* "Self-Awareness and Transgression in Children: Two Field Studies." *Journal of Personality and Social Psychology* 37.10 (1979):1835–1846.

Bem, D. J. "Self-Perception Theory." In *Advances in Experimental Social Psychology* 6. Ed. L. Berkowitz. New York: Academic Press, 1972. 1–62.

Benson, P., Karabenick, S., and R. Lerner. "Pretty Pleases: The Effects of Physical Attractiveness, Race, and Sex on Receiving Help." *Journal of Experimental Social Psychology* 12.5 (1976):409–15.

Benton, A., Kelley, H., and B. Liebling. "Effects of Extremity of Offers and Concession Rate on the Outcomes of Bargaining." *Journal of Personality and Social Psychology* 24.1 (1972):73–83.

Bickman, L. "Environmental Attitudes and Actions." *Journal of Social Psychology* 87 (1972):323–324.

———. "The Social Power of a Uniform." *Journal of Applied Social Psychology* 4 (1974):47–61.

Block, L., and P. Keller. "When to Accentuate the Negative: The Effects of Perceived Efficacy and Message Framing on Intentions to Perform a Health-Related Behavior." *Journal of Marketing Research* 32.2 (1995):192–203.

Bochner, S., and C. Insko. "Communicator Discrepancy, Source Credibility, and Opinion Change." *Journal of Personality and Social Psychology* 4.6 (1996):614–621.

Bornstein, R. F. "Exposure and Affect: Overview and Meta-Analysis of Research, 1968–1987." *Psychological Bulletin* 106 (1989):265–289.

Bornstein, R. F., Leone, D. R., and D. J. Galley. "The Generalizability of Subliminal Mere Exposure Effects." *Journal of Personality and Social Psychology* 53 (1987):1070–1079.

Brehm, J. W. *A Theory of Psychological Reactance.* New York: Academic Press, 1966.

Brehm, S. S., and J. W. Brehm. *Psychological Reactance.* New York: Academic Press, 1981.

Brehm, S., Kassin, S., and S. Fein. *Social Psychology.* New York: Houghton Mifflin Company, 2005.

Bridle, C., Riemsma, R. P., Pattenden, J., Sowden, A. J., Mather, L., Watt, I. S., and A. Walker. "Systematic Review of the Effectiveness of Health Behavior Interventions Based on the Transtheoretical Model." *Psychology and Health* (2005):283–301.

Brock, T., and J. Balloud. "Behavioral Reciprocity to Dissonant Information." *Journal of Personality and Social Psychology* 6.4 (1967):413–428.

Broeder, D. "The University of Chicago Jury Project." *Nebraska Law Review* 38 (1959):744–760.

Brown, K. W., and T. Kasser. "Are Psychological and Ecological Well-Being Compatible? The Role of Values, Mindfulness, and Lifestyle." *Social Indicators Research* 74.2 (2005):349–368.

Bryne, D., Rasche, L., and K. Kelley. "When 'I Like You' Indicates Disagreement: An Experimental Differentiation of Information and Affect." *Journal of Research In Personality* 8.3 (1974):207–217.

Burger, J. "The Foot-in-the-Door Compliance Procedure: A Multiple-Process Analysis and Review." *Personality and Social Psychology Review* 3.4 (1999):303–325.

Burgess, T., and S. Sales. "Attitudinal Effects of 'Mere Exposure': A Reevaluation." *Journal of Experimental Social Psychology* 7 (1971):461–472.

Burns, S. "Social Psychology and the Stimulation of Recycling Behaviors: The Block Leader Approach." *Journal of Applied Social Psychology* 21 (1991):611–629.

Burt, C., and K. Strongman. "Use of Images in Charity Advertising; Improving Donations and Compliance Rates." *International Journal of Organisational Behavior.* 8.8 (2004):571–580.

Byron, L., Lento, T., Marlow, C., and I. Rosenn. "Maintained Relationships on Facebook." 11 Mar 2010 <www.facebook.com/#!/notes/facebook-data-team/maintained-relationships-on-facebook/55257228858>.

Cacioppo, J. T., and R. E. Petty. "Stalking Rudimentary Processes of Social Influence: A Psychophysiological Approach." In *Social Influence: The Ontario Symposium* 5. Ed: M. Zanna, *et al.* Hillsdale, N.J.: Lawrence Erlbaum, 1987.

Camerer, C. F., and R. Hogarth. "The Effects of Financial Incentives in Experiments: A Review and Capital-Labor-Production Framework." *Journal of Risk and Uncertainty* 19.1 (1999):7–42.

Caprara, G., Schwartz, S., Capanna, C., Vecchione, M., and C. Barbaranelli. "Personality and Politics: Values, Traits, and Political Choice." *International Society of Political Psychology* 27.1 (2006):1–28.

Castellow, W., Wuencsh, K., and C. Moore. "Effects of Physical Attractiveness on the Plaintiff and Defendant in Sexual Harassment Judgments." *Journal of Social Behavior and Personality* 5 (1990):547–562.

Chaiken, A. L., and J. M. Darley. "Victim or Perpetrator: Defensive Attribution of Responsibility and the Need for Order and Justice." *Journal of Personality and Social Psychology* 25 (1973):268–275.

Chaiken, S. "Communicator Physical Attractiveness and Persuasion." *Journal of Personality and Social Psychology* 37.8 (1979):1387–1397.

———. "The Heuristic Model of Persuasion." In *Social Influence: The Ontario Symposium* 5. Ed: M. Zanna, *et al.* Hillsdale, N.J.: Lawrence Erlbaum, 1987.

Chaiken, S., and M. Baldwin. "Affective-Cognitive Consistency and The Effect of Salient Behavioral Information On The Self-Perception of Attitudes." *Journal of Personality and Social Psychology* 41.1 (1981):1–12.

Chartrand, T. L., and J. A. Bargh. "The Chameleon Effect: The Perception-Behavior Link and Social Interaction." *Journal of Personality and Social Psychology* 76 (1999):893–910.

Christakis, N., and J. H. Fowler. "The Spread of Obesity in a Large Social Network over 32 Years." *New England Journal of Medicine* 357.4 (2007):370–379.

Christakis, Nicholas, and James Fowler. *Connected: The Surprising Power of Our Social Networks and How They Shape Our Lives.* New York: Little Brown & Company, 2009.

Christensen, A., Moran, P., and J. Wiebe. "Assessment of Irrational Health Beliefs: Relation to Health Practices and Medical Regimen Adherence." *Health Psychology* 18.2 (1999):169–176.

Cialdini, R. B. "Crafting Normative Messages to Protect the Environment." *Current Directions in Psychological Science* 12.4 (2003):105–109.

———. *Influence: The Psychology of Persuasion.* New York: Harper Collins, 1998.

Cialdini, R. B., Vincent, J. E., Lewis, S. K., Catalan, J., Wheeler, D., and B. K. Darby. "Reciprocal Concessions Procedure for Inducing Compliance: The Door-in-the-Face Technique." *Journal of Personality and Social Psychology* 31 (1975):206–215.

Cialdini, R., and D. Schroeder. "Increasing Compliance by Legitimizing Paltry Contributions: When Even a Penny Helps." *Journal of Personality and Social Psychology* 34.4 (1976):599–604.

Cialdini, R., and K. Ascani. "Test of a Concession Procedure for Inducing Verbal, Behavioral, and Further Compliance with a Request to Give Blood." *Journal of Applied Psychology* 61.3 (1976):295–300.

Cialdini, R., Green, B., and A. Rusch. "When Tactical Pronouncement of Change Becomes Real Change: The Case of Reciprocal Persuasion." *Journal of Personality and Social Psychology* 6 (1992).

Cialdini, R., Reno, R., and C. Kallgren. "A Focus Theory of Normative Conduct: Recycling the Concept of Norms to Reduce Littering in Public Places." *Journal of Personality and Social Psychology* 58 (1990):1015–1026.

Clark, R. D. "Effects of Majority Defection and Multiple Minority Sources on Minority Influence." *Group Dynamics* 5 (2001):57–62.

Coffman, J. *Public Communication Campaign Evaluation: An Environmental Scan of Challenges, Criticisms, Practice, and Opportunities.* Harvard Family Research Project, May

2002. Retrieved May 1, 2010, <www.hfrp.org/publications-resources/browse-our-publications/public-communication-campaign-evaluation-an-environmental-scan-of-challenges-criticisms-practice-and-opportunities>.

Coulter, R. H., and M. B. Pinto. "Guilt appeals in Advertising: What Are Their Effects?" *Journal of Applied Psychology* 80.6 (1995):697–705.

Craig, K. D., and K. M. Prkachin. "Social Modeling Influences on Sensory Decision Theory and Psychophysiological Indexes of Pain." *Journal of Personality and Social Psychology* 36.8 (1978):805–815.

Crano, W. D. "Milestones in the Psychological Analysis of Social Influence." *Group Dynamics: Theory, Research, and Practice* 4 (2000):68–80.

Crano, W., and E. Alvaro. "The Context/Comparison Model of Social Influence: Mechanisms, Structure, and Linkages that Underlie Indirect Attitude Change." *European Review of Social Psychology* 8 (1997).

Crompton, T. "Weathercocks and Signposts: The Environmental Movement at a Crossroads." 2008. 1 Mar 2010. <www.wwf.org.uk/Filelibrary/Pdf/Weathercocks_Report2.pdf>.

Crompton, T., and T. Kasser. *Meeting Environmental Challenges: The Role of Human Identity.* WWF: Distributed By Green Books, 2009.

Das, D., Kerkhof, P., and J. Kuiper. "Improving the Effectiveness of Fundraising Messages: The Impact of Charity Goal Attainment, Message Framing, and Evidence on Persuasion." *Journal of Applied Communication Research* 36.2 (2008):161–175.

Davis, B., and E. Knowles. "A Disrupt-Then-Reframe Technique of Social Influence." *Journal of Personality and Social Psychology* 76.2 (1999):192–199.

De Dreu, C. W., and N. K. De Vries. *Group Consensus and Minority Influence: Implications For Innovation.* Malden, Mass.: Wiley-Blackwell, 2001.

De Mesquita, B. *The Predictioneer's Game: Using the Logic of Brazen Self-Interest to See and Shape the Future.* New York: Random House, 2009.

"Deaths: Final Statistics for 2006." Centers for Disease Control and Prevention. 2006. 9 June 2010. <www.cdc.gov/nchs/data/nvsr/nvsr57/nvsr57_14.pdf>

Deleon, I., and R. Fuqua. "The Effects of Public Commitment and Group Feedback on Curbside Recycling." *Special Issue: Litter Control and Recycling. Environmental Behavior* 27 (1995):233–250.

Deyoung, R. "Exploring the Difference between Recyclers and Non-Recyclers: The Role of Information." *Journal of Environmental Systems* 18 (1989):341–335.

Diekmann, A., and P. Preisendorfer. "Environmental Behavior: Discrepancies between Aspirations and Reality." *Rationality and Society* 10 (1998):79.

"Diesel Idling Facts and Myths." *Indiana Department of Environmental Management.* 2009. 1 Mar 2010. <www.in.gov/idem/4459.htm>.

Dillard, J. P., Kinney, T. A., and M. G. Cruz. "Influence, Appraisals, and Emotions in Close Relationships." *Communication Monographs* 63.2 (1996):105–130.

Dillard, J., and M. Pfau. *The Persuasion Handbook: Developments In Theory and Practice.* Thousand Oaks, Calif.: Sage Publications, 2002.

Dolliver, Mark. "It's Getting More Difficult to 'Buy American.'" *AdWeek*, 7 July 2009.

Doob, A., and A. Gross. "Status of Frustrator as an Inhibitor of Horn-Honking Responses." *Journal of Social Psychology* (1968):481–486.

Dovidio, J. F. "Helping Behavior and Altruism: An Empirical and Conceptual Overview." In *Advances in Experimental Social Psychology.* Ed. L. Berkowitz. New York: Academic Press, 1984. Vol. 17, 361–427.

Downs, A. C., and P. M. Lyons. "Natural Observations of the Links between Attractiveness and Initial Legal Judgments." *Personality and Social Psychology Bulletin* 17 (1990):541–547.

Drachman, D., Decarufel, A., and C. Insko. "The Extra Credit Effect in Interpersonal Attraction." *Journal of Experimental Social Psychology* 14.5 (1978):458–465.

Driskell, J. E., Copper, C., and A. Moran. "Does Mental Practice Enhance Performance?" *Journal of Applied Psychology* 79.4 (1994):481–492.

Eagly, A. H., Wood, W., and S. Chaiken. "Causal Inferences aAbout Communicators and Their Effect on Opinion Change." *Journal of Personality and Social Psychology* 36.4 (1978):424–435.

Eagly, A., Ashmore, R., Makhijani, M., and L. Longo. "What Is Beautiful Is Good, But .. . : A Meta-Analytic Review of Research on the Physical Attractiveness Stereotype." *Psychological Bulletin* 110.1 (1991):109–128.

Eagly, A., Wood, W., and S. Chaiken. "Causal Inferences about Communicators and

Their Effect on Opinion Change." *Journal of Personality and Social Psychology* 36.4 (1978):424–435.

Eayrs, Ellis. "Charity Advertising: For or against People with a Mental Handicap?" *British Journal For Social Psychology* 4 (1990):349–66.

Efran, M. G., and E. W. Patterson. *The Politics of Appearance*. Unpublished Manuscript. University of Toronto, 1976.

Eidelman, S., Crandall, C. S., and J. Pattershall. "The Existence Bias." *Journal of Personality and Social Psychology* 97.5 (2009):765–775.

Elliott, M., and C. Armitage. "Effects of Implementation Intentions on the Self-Reported Frequency of Drivers' Compliance with Speed Limits." *Journal of Experimental Psychology: Applied* 12.2 (2006):108–117.

Emswiller, T., Deaux, K., and J. E. Willits. "Similarity, Sex, and Requests for Small Favors." *Journal of Applied Social Psychology* 1 (1971):284–291.

Erb, H., Bohner, G., Schmilzle, K., and S. Rank. "Beyond Conflict and Discrepancy: Cognitive Bias and Majority Influence." *Personality and Social Psychology Bulletin* 24.6 (1998):620–633.

Eriksson, L., Garvill, J., and A. M. Nordlund. "Interrupting Habitual Car Use: The Importance of Car Habit Strength and Moral Motivation for Personal Car Use Reduction." *Transportation Research Part F: Traffic Psychology and Behaviour* 11 (2008):10–23.

Esses, V., and J. Dovidio. "The Role of Emotions in Determining Willingness to Engage in Intergroup Contact." *Personality and Social Psychology Bulletin* 28.9 (2002):1202–1214.

Evans, F. B. "Selling as a Dyadic Relationship: A New Approach." *American Behavioral Scientists* 6 (May) (1963):76–79.

"Facts and Myths about Generic Drugs." *U.S. Food and Drug Administration.* 2009. 1 Mar 2010. <www.fda.gov/drugs/resourcesforyou/consumers/buyingusingmedicine-safely/understandinggenericdrugs/ucm167991.htm>.

Fazio, R. H. "Self-Perception Theory: A Current Perspective." In *Social Influence: The Ontario Symposium* 5. Ed. M. Zanna, *et al.* Hillsdale, N.J.: Lawrence Erlbaum, 1987. 129–150.

Feinberg, R. A. "Credit Cards as Spending Facilitating Stimuli." *Journal of Consumer Research* 13 (1986):348–356.

Festinger, L. "Informal Social Communication." *Psychological Review* 57.5 (1950):271–282.

Finger, M. "From Knowledge to Action? Exploring the Relationship between Environmental Experiences, Learning and Behavior." *Journal of Social Issues* 50 (1994):141–160.

Fink, E., Kaplowitz, S., and C. Bauer. "Positional Discrepancy, Psychological Discrepancy, and Attitude Change: Experimental Tests of Some Mathematical Models." *Communication Monographs* 50.4 (1983):413–430.

Flynn, F. "What Have You Done for Me Lately? Temporal Adjustments to Favor Evaluations." *Organizational Behavior and Human Decision Processes* 91.1 (2003):38–50.

"Fox News—Home of Outrageous Smears, Falsehoods—Promotes 'Tea Parties' Protesting 'Journalistic Malpractice.'" *Media Matters for America.* 2009. 1 Mar 2010. <http://mediamatters.org/research/200910170002>.

Fragale, A., and C. Heath. "Evolving Informational Credentials: The (Mis)Attribution of Believable Facts to Credible Sources." *Personality and Social Psychology Bulletin* 30.2 (2004):225–236.

Fransson, Garling. "Environmental Concern: Conceptual Definitions, Measurement Methods, and Research Findings." *Journal of Environmental Psychology* 19.4 (1999):369–382.

Freedman, J. L. "Long-Term Behavioral Effects of Cognitive Dissonance." *Journal of Experimental Social Psychology* 1 (1965):145–155.

Freedman, J., and D. Sears. "Warning, Distraction, and Resistance to Influence." *Journal of Personality and Social Psychology* 1 (1965):262–266.

Freedman, J. L., and S. C. Fraser. "Compliance without Pressure: The Foot-in-the-Door Technique." *Journal of Personality and Social Psychology* 4 (1966):195–203.

Friedrich, B., and M. Ball. *The Animal Activist's Handbook: Maximizing Our Positive Impact In Today's World.* New York: Lantern Books, 2009.

Gaertner, S., and J. Dovidio. *Reducing Intergroup Bias: The Common Ingroup Identity Model.* Philadelphia: Psychology Press, 2000.

Galinsky, A. D., and G. Ku. "The Effects of Perspective-Taking on Prejudice: The

Moderating Role of Self-Evaluation." *Personality and Social Psychology Bulletin* 30.5 (2004):594–604.

Garcia, S. M., Weaver, K., Moskowitz, G. B, and J. M. Darley. "Crowded Minds: The Implicit Bystander Effect." *Journal of Personality and Social Psychology* 83 (2002):843–853.

Garner, R. "Post-It Note Persuasion: A Sticky Influence." *Journal of Consumer Psychology* 15.3 (2005):230–237.

———. "What's in a Name? Persuasion Perhaps?" *Journal of Consumer Psychology* 15.2 (2005):108–116.

Garrow, David. *Bearing the Cross; Martin Luther King, Jr. and the Southern Christian Leadership Conference.* New York: William Morrow, 1986, 246.

Gatersleben, B., et. al. *Materialistic and Environmental Values of Young Volunteers in Nature Conservation Projects.* University of Surrey, U.K.: Resolve Working Paper, 2008.

Geller, E. S., Erickson, J. B, and B. A. Buttram. "Attempts to Promote Residential Water Conservation with Educational, Behavioral, and Engineering Strategies." *Population and Environment* 6 (1983):96–112.

Geller, E. S. "Evaluating Energy Conservation Programs: Is Verbal Report Enough?" *Journal of Consumer Research* 8 (1981):331–335.

"George Carlin: Back in Town." Dir. Rocco Urbisci. MPI Home Video, 1996.

Gerard, H., and G. Mathewson. "The Effects of Severity of Initiation on Liking for a Group: A Replication." *Journal of Experimental Social Psychology* 2.3 (1966):278–287.

Gigerenzer, G., and D. Goldstein. "Reasoning the Fast and Frugal Way: Models of Bounded Rationality." *Psychological Review* 103.4 (1996):650–669.

Ginsberg, Carolyn. "Helping People Want to Change." Taking Action For Animals Conference, Humane Society of The United States. Washington, D.C. 28 July 2007.

"Giving USA 2008, The Annual Report on Philanthropy." *Charity Navigator.* Aafrc Trust For Philanthropy, 2010. Web. 1 Mar 2010. <www.charitynavigator.org/index.cfm?bay=content.view&cpid=42>.

Gladwell, Malcom. *The Tipping Point.* New York: Little, Brown and Company, 2000.

"Global Warming Myths and Facts." *Environmental Defense Fund.* 2010. 20 Feb 2010. <www.fightglobalwarming.com/page.cfm?tagid=274>.

Goldstein, N., Cialdini, R., and V. Griskevicius. "A Room With a Viewpoint: Using Social Norms to Motivate Environmental Conservation in Hotels." *Journal of Consumer Research* 35.3 (2008).

———. "Maximizing Motivation to Cooperate toward the Fulfillment of a Shared Goal: Initiation Is Everything." 2008. Awaiting Publication.

Good, J. "Shop 'Til We Drop? Television, Materialism and Attitudes about the Natural Environment." *Mass Communication and Society* 10 (2007):365–383.

Greenwald, A. G., Carnot, C. G., Beach, R., and B. Young. "Increasing Voting Behavior by Asking People if They Expect to Vote." *Journal of Applied Psychology* 72 (1987):315–318.

Grosmick, H., *et al.* "Shame and Embarrassment as Deterrents to Non-Compliance with the Law: The Case of the Anti-Littering Campaign." *Environment and Behavior* 23 (1991):233–251.

Haddock, G., Rothman, A. J., Reber, R., and N. Schwarz. "Forming Judgments of Attitude Certainty, Intensity, and Importance: The Role of Subjective Experiences." *Personality and Social Psychology Bulletin.* 25.7 (1999):771–782.

Hamermesh, D., and J. Biddle. "Beauty and the Labor Market." *The American Economic Review* 84.5 (1994):1174–1194.

Harrison, A. A. "Mere Exposure." In *Advances in Experimental Social Psychology (Vol. 10).* Ed. L. Berkowitz. New York: Academic Press, 1977. 39–83.

Hertz, E. E. "Myths and Facts." *Myths and Facts, Inc.* 2010. 1 Mar 2010. <http://mythsandfacts.com/>.

Higgins, E. T., Rholes, W., and C. Jones. "Category Accessibility and Impression Formation." *Journal of Experimental Social Psychology* 13.2 (1977):141–154.

Higham, P., and D. Carment. "The Rise and Fall of Politicians: The Judged Heights of Broadbent, Mulroney and Turner Before and After the 1988 Canadian Federal Election." *Canadian Journal of Behavioural Science* 24.3 (1992):404–409.

Hinsz, V., Tindale, R., and D. Vollrath. "The Emerging Conceptualization of Groups as Information Processes." *Psychological Bulletin* (1997).

Homburg, A., Stolberg, A., and W. Wagner. "Coping with Global Environmental Problems: Development and First Validation of Scales." *Environment and Behaviour* 39 (2007):754–778.

Hopper, J., and J. Nielsen. "Recycling as Altruistic Behavior: Normative and Behavioral Strategies to Expand Participation in a Community Recycling Program." *Environment and Behavior* 23 (1991):195–220.

Hornik, R., and D. Romer. "HIV Education for Youth: The Importance of Social Consensus in Behaviour Change." *Aids Care* 4.3 (1992):285–303.

Horowitz, S. M. "Applying the Transtheoretical Model to Pregnancy and STS Prevention: A Review of the Literature." *American Journal of Health Promotion* 17.5 (2003):304–328.

"How Many Vegetarians Are There?" McStay, J., and J. Cunningham. 2009. 2 Mar 2010. <www.vrg.org/press/2009poll.htm>.

Howard, D. J. "The Influence of Verbal Responses to Common Greetings on Compliance Behavior: The Foot-in-the-Mouth Effect." *Journal of Applied Social Psychology* 20 (1990a):1185–1196.

"HSUS's Mike Markarian on Research and the "Shelter Pet Project." Green, C. Humane Spot.org, 2009. 26 October 2009. <www.humanespot.org/node/3494>.

Hunt, J., Domzal, T., and J. Kernan. "Causal Attribution and Persuasion: The Case of Disconfirmed Expectancies." In *Advances in Consumer Research (Vol. 9)*. Ed. A. Mitchell. Ann Arbor, Mich.: Association for Consumer Research, 1981.

Hunter, J., Danes, J., and S. Cohen. *Mathematical Models of Attitude Change (Volume 1)*. New York: Academic Press, 1984.

Hutton, R. R. "Advertising and the Department of Energy's Campaign for Energy Conservation." *Journal of Advertising* 11 (1982):27–39.

Inside Research: Trend and Industry Growth Indexes and Reports. Inside Research Co. 2010. 4 Mar 2010. <www.insideresearch.com/trend.htm>.

Isen, A. M. "Success, Failure, Attention, and Reaction to Others: The Warm Glow of Success." *Journal of Personality and Social Psychology* 15 (1970):294–301.

Isen, A. M., and P. A. Levin. "Effect of Feeling Good on Helping: Cookies and Kindness." *Journal of Personality and Social Psychology* 21 (1972):384–388.

Iyengar, S., Huberman, G., and W. Jiang. "How Much Choice Is Too Much? Contributions to 401(K) Retirement Plans." In *Pension Design and Structure: New Lessons From Behavioral Finance*. Eds. O. Mitchell and S. Utkus. New York: Oxford University Press, 2004, 83–96.

Jaccard, J. J., and A. R. Davidson. "Toward an Understanding of Family Planning Behaviors: An Initial Investigation." *Journal of Applied Social Psychology* 2 (1972):228–235.

Janis, I. L. "Attitude Change Via Role Playing." *Theories of Cognitive Consistency: A Sourcebook*. Eds. R. Ableson, E. Aronson, W. Mcguire, T. Newcomb, M. Rosenberg, and P. Tennenbaum. Chicago: Rand Mcnally, 1968, 810–818.

Janis, I. L., Kaye, D., and P. Kirschner. "Facilitating Effects of 'Eating While Reading' on Responsiveness to Persuasive Communications." *Journal of Personality and Social Psychology* 1 (1965):181–186.

Jones, C., and E. Aronson. "Attribution of Fault to a Rape Victim as a Function of Respectability of the Victim." *Journal of Personality and Social Psychology* 26.3 (1973):415–419.

Jones, E., and K. Davis. "From Acts to Dispositions: The Attribution Process in Person Perception." *Advances In Experimental Psychology* 2 (1965):219–266.

Jones, J., Pelham, B., Carvallo, M., and M. Mirenberg. "How Do I Love Thee? Let Me Count the Js: Implicit Egotism and Interpersonal Attraction." *Journal of Personality and Social Psychology* 87.5 (2004):665–683.

Jordan, J., Hungerford, H. R., and A. N. Tomera. "Effects of 2 Residential Environmental Workshops on High School Students." *Journal of Environmental Education* 18 (1986):15–22.

Joy, Melanie. *Why We Love Dogs, Eat Pigs, and Wear Cows: An Introduction To Carnism*. San Francisco: Conari Press, 2009, 121.

Just, D., Wansink, B., Mancino, L., and J. Guthrie. "Behavioral Economic Concepts to Encourage Healthy Eating in School Cafeterias." *USDA*, 2008. <www.ers.usda.Gov/publications/err68/err68_reportsummary.pdf>.

Kahneman, D., and A. Tversky. "Choices, Values, and Frames." *American Psychologist* 39.4 (1984):341–350.

Kallgren, C., Reno, R., and R. Cialdini. "A Focus Theory of Normative Conduct: When

Norms Do and Do Not Affect Behavior." *Personality and Social Psychology Bulletin* 26.8 (2000):1002–1012.

Kanfer, F., and A. Goldstein. *Helping People Change.* New York: Pergamon Press, 1975.

Kasser, T., et al. *Materialistic Values: Their Causes and Consequences. Psychology and Consumer Culture: The Struggle for a Good Life in a Materialistic World.* Eds. T. Kasser and A. D. Kanner. Washington, D.C.: American Psychological Association, 2004.

Keller, P. A. "Converting the Unconverted: The Effect of Inclination and Opportunity to Discount Health-Related Fear appeals." *Journal of Applied Psychology* 84 (1999):403–415.

Kelley, H. "The Warm-Cold Variable in First Impressions of Persons." *Journal of Personality* 18 (1950):431–439.

Kempf, A., and S. Ruenzi. "Status Quo Bias and the Number of Alternatives: An Empirical Illustration from the Mutual Fund Industry." *Journal of Public Finance* 7.4. (2006):204–213.

Kennedy, E., Beckley, T., Mcfarlane, B., and S. Nadeau. "Why We Don't 'Walk the Talk': Understanding the Environmental Values/Behavior Gap in Canada." *Humane Ecology Review* 16.2 (2009).

Kenrick, D. T., Reich, J. W., and R. B. Cialdini. "Justification and Compensation: Rosier Skies for the Devalued Victim." *Journal of Personality and Social Psychology* 34.4 (1976):654–657.

Koerth-Barker, M. "Swine Flu Facts, Swine Flu Myths." *National Geographic Society.* 2009. 3 Mar 2010. <http://news.nationalgeographic.com/news/2009/04/090427–swine flu-facts.html>.

Kraut, R. E. "Effects of Social Labeling on Giving to Charity." *Journal of Experimental Social Psychology* 9 (1973):551–562.

Kruglanski, A. W., and D. M. Mackie. "Majority and Minority Influence: A Judgmental Process Analysis." *European Review of Social Psychology* 1 (1990).

Larson, M. et al. "Brief Report: Effects of Informational Feedback on Aluminum Can Recycling." *Behavioral Interventions* 10 (1995):111–117.

Lefkowitz, M., Mouton, R., and J. Srygley. "Status Factors in Pedestrian Violation of Traffic Signals." *The Journal of Abnormal and Social Psychology* 51.3 (1955):704–706.

Lehrer, J. *How We Decide.* New York: Houghton Mifflin, 2009.

Lerner, M. J. "Evaluation of Performance as a Function of Performer's Reward and Attractiveness." *Journal of Personality and Social Psychology* 1.4 (1965):355–360.

Lerner, M. J., and C. H. Simmons. "The Observer's Reaction to the 'Innocent Victim': Compassion or Rejection?" *Journal of Personality and Social Psychology* 4 (1966):203–210.

Lerner, M., and D. Miller. "Just World Research and Attribution Process: Looking Back and Ahead." *Psychological Bulletin* 85.5 (1978):1030–1051.

Levav, J., and G. Fitzsimons. "When Questions Change Behavior: The Role of Ease of Representation." *Association For Psychological Science* 17.3 (2006):207–213.

Leventhal, H. *et al.* "Effects of Fear and Instructions on How to Cope with Danger." *Journal of Personality and Social Psychology* 6 (1967):313–321.

Leventhal, H. "Findings and Theory in the Study of Fear Communications." In *Advances in Experimental Social Psychology* 5. Ed. L. Berkowitz. New York: Academic Press, 1970, 119–186.

Leventhal, H., Singer, R., and S. Jones. "Effects of Fear and Specificity of Recommendation upon Attitudes and Behavior." *Journal of Personality and Social Psychology* 2.1 (1965):20–29.

Levine, J. "Reaction to Opinion Deviance in Small Groups." *Psychology of Group Influence*. Ed. P. Paulus. Hillsdale, N.J.: Lawrence Erlbaum Associates, 1989.

Lincoln, A., and G. Levenger. "Observers' Evaluations of the Victim and the Attacker in an Aggressive Incident." *Journal of Personality and Social Psychology* 22.2 (1972):202–210.

Lipsitz, A., Kallmeyer, K., Ferguson, M., and A. Abas. "Counting on Blood Donors: Increasing the Impact of Reminder Calls." *Journal of Applied Social Psychology* 19 (1989).

Locke, K. S., and L. M. Horowitz. "Satisfaction in Interpersonal Interactions as a Function of Similarity in Level of Dysphoria." *Journal of Personality and Social Psychology* 58 (1990):823–831.

Loke, E., Bryan, J., and L. Kendall. "Goals and Intentions as Mediators of the Effects of Monetary Incentives on Behavior." *Journal of Applied Psychology* 52.2 (1968):104–121.

Lott, A. J., and B. E. Lott. "Group Cohesiveness as Interpersonal Attraction: A Review of Relationships with Antecedent and Consequent Variables." *Psychological Bulletin* 64 (1965):259–309.

Lynn, M., and B. Shurgot. "Responses to Lonely Hearts Advertisements: Effects of Reported Physical Attractiveness, Physique, and Coloration." *Personality and Social Psychology Bulletin* 10.3 (1984):349–357.

MacDonald, A. P. "More on the Protestant Ethic." *Journal of Consulting and Clinical Psychology* 39.1 (1972):116–122.

Maddux, W. W., Mullen, E., and A. D. Galinsky. "Chameleons Bake Bigger Pies and Take Bigger Pieces: Strategic Behavioral Mimicry Facilitates Negotiation Outcomes." *Journal of Experimental Social Psychology* 44.2 (2008):461–468.

Maheswaran, D., and J. Meyers-Levy. "The Influence of Message Framing and Issue Involvement." *Journal of Marketing Research* 27.3 (1990):361–367.

Manis, M., Cornell, S. D., and J. C. Moore. "Transmission of Attitude Relevant Information through a Communication Chain." *Journal of Personality and Social Psychology* 30 (1974):81–94.

Masiz, M. B., Settle, R. B., and D. C. Leslie. "Elimination of Phosphate Detergents and Psychological Reactance." *Journal of Marketing Research* 10 (1973):390–395.

Mauro, R. "The Constable's New Clothes: Effects of Uniforms on Perceptions and Problems of Police Officers." *Journal of Applied Social Psychology* 14 (1984):42–56.

Mayo, R., Schul, Y., and E. Burnstein. "I Am Not Guilty Versus 'I Am Innocent': The Associative Structure Activated in Processing Negations." *Journal of Experimental Social Psychology* 40 (2004):433–449.

Mazis, M. B. "Antipollution Measures and Psychological Reactance Theory: A Field Experiment." *Journal of Personality and Social Psychology* 31 (1975):654–666.

McCall, M., and H. J. Belmont. "Credit Card Insignia and Restaurant Tipping: Evidence for an Associative Link." *Journal of Applied Psychology* 81.5 (1996):609–613.

McGlone, M. S., and J. Tofighbakhsh. "Birds of A Feather Flock Conjointly (?): Rhyme As Reason In Aphorisms." *Psychological Science* 11 (2000):424–428.

McKenzie-Mohr, D., and S. Oskamp. "Psychology and Sustainability: An Introduction." *Journal of Social Issues* 51.4 (1995):1–14.

McKenzie-Mohr, D., Smith, W., and W. A. Smith. *Fostering Sustainable Behavior: Community-Based Social Marketing.* Gabriola Island, B.C.: New Society Publishers, 1999, 51–52.

Meeus, W. H., and Q. A. Raaijmakers. "Administrative Obedience." *European Journal of Social Psychology* (1986):16.

Melamed, B. F., Yurcheson, E., Fleece L., Hutcherson, S., and R. Hawes. "Effects of Film Modeling on the Reduction of Anxiety-Related Behaviors in Individuals Varying in Level of Previous Experience in the Stress Situation." *Journal of Consulting and Clinical Psychology* 46 (1978):1357–1374.

"Mention Map." 5 Mar 2010. <http://apps.asterisq.com/mentionmap/#>.

Milden, G. J., *et al.* "Using Feedback, Reinforcement, and Information to Reduce Energy Consumption in Households." *Journal of Economic Psychology* 3 (1983):65–86.

Milgram, S. *Obedience to Authority: An Experimental View.* New York: Harper and Row, 1974.

Miller, R. L., Seligman, C., Clark, N. T., and M. Bush. "Perceptual Contrast Versus Reciprocal Concession as Mediators of Induced Compliance." *Canadian Journal of Behavioral Science* 8.4 (1976):401–409.

Milne, S., Sheeran, P., and S. Orbell. "Prediction and Intervention in Health-Related Behavior: A Meta-Analytic Review of Protection Motivation Theory." *Journal of Applied Social Psychology* 30 (2000):106–143.

Moore, D. A., Kurtzberg, T. R., Thompson, L., and M. W. Morris. "Long and Short Routes to Success in Electronically-Mediated Negotiations: Group Affiliations and Good Vibrations." *Organizational Behavior and Human Decision Processes* 77 (1999):22–43.

Morris, M., Nadler, J., Kurtzberg, T., and L. Thompson. "Schmooze or Lose: Social Friction and Lubrication in Email Negotiations." *Group Dynamics: Theory, Research and Practice* 6.1 (2002):89–100.

Morwitz, V., Johnson, E., and D. Schmittlein. "Does Measuring Intent Change Behavior?" *Journal of Consumer Research* 20.1 (1993).

Moscovici, S., and M. Zavalloni. "The Group as a Polarizer of Attitudes." *Journal of Personality and Social Psychology* 12 (1969):125–135.

Moscovici, S., and P. Neve. "Studies in Social Influence: Those Absent Are in the Right:

Convergence and Polarization of Answers in the Course of a Social Interaction." *European Journal of Social Psychology* 1.2 (1971):201–214.

Moscovici, S., Mugny, G., Van Avermaet, E. (Eds.) *Perspectives On Minority Influence.* New York: Cambridge University Press, 1985.

Moskowitz, G. B. "The Mediational Effects of Attributions and Information Processing iIn Minority Social Influence." *British Journal of Social Psychology* 35 (1996):47–66.

"Myths and Facts about Marijuana." *Drug Policy Alliance.* 2010. 6 Mar 2010. <www.drug-policy.org/marijuana/factsmyths/>.

Nabi, Robin. "The Effect of Disgust-Eliciting Visuals on Attitudes toward Animal Experimentation." *Communication Quarterly* 46 (1998):472–484.

Neilson, W., and H. Winter. "Votes Based on Protracted Deliberations." *Journal of Economic Behavior and Organization* 67.1 (2008):308–321.

Nelkin, Dorothy. *Selling Science: How the Press Covers Science and Technology.* New York: Freeman, 1987.

Nemeth, C. J., and J. L. Kwan. "Minority Influence, Divergent Thinking and Detection of Correct Solutions." *Journal of Applied Social Psychology* 17 (1987):788–799.

Nolan, J., Schultz, W., Cialdini, R., Goldstein, N., and V. Griskevicius. "Normative Social Influence Is Underdetected." *Personality and Social Psychology Bulletin* 34 (2008):913–924.

"NRA-ILA: Fables, Myths and Other Tall Tales." *National Rifle Association of America, Institute for Legislative Action.* 2003 1 Mar 2010. <www.nraila.org/media/misc/fables.htm>.

O'Keefe, D. J. "Guilt and Social Influence." *Communication Yearbook* 23 (2000):67–102.

O'Keefe, D. J., and J. D. Jensen. "The Advantages of Compliance or the Disadvantages of Noncompliance? A Meta-Analytic Review of the Relative Persuasive Effectiveness of Gain-Framed and Loss-Framed Messages." *Communication Yearbook* 30 (2006):1–43.

O'Connor, R. "Relative Efficacy of Modeling, Shaping, and the Combined Procedures for Modification of Social Withdrawal." *Journal of Abnormal Psychology* 79.3 (1972):327–334.

Omoto, A., and M. Snyder. "Sustained Helping without Obligation: Motivation, Longevity of Service, and Perceived Attitude Change among Aids Volunteers." *Journal of Personality and Social Psychology* 68.4 (1995):671–686.

Oskamp, S., and P. W. Schultz. *Attitudes and Opinions.* Mahwah, N.J.: Lawrence Erlbaum Associates, 2005.

Pallak, M., Cook, D., and J. J. Sullivan. "Commitment and Energy Conservation" *Applied Social Psychology Annual.* Ed. L. Bickman. Beverly Hills: Sage, Publications, 1980, 235–253.

Pardini, A., and R. D. Katzev. "The Effects of Strength of Commitment on Newspaper Recycling." *Journal of Environmental Systems* 13 (1983–84):245–254.

Parker, Ian. "The Poverty Lab." *The New Yorker.* 17 May 2010.

Pelham, B. W., Mirenberg, M. C., and J. T. Jones. "Why Susie Sells Seashells by the Seashore: Implicit Egotism and Major Life Decisions." *Journal of Personality and Social Psychology* 82 (2002):469–487.

Peters, D. P., and S. J. Ceci. "Peer-Review Practices of the Psychological Journals: The Fate of Published Articles, Submitted Again." *The Behavioral and Brain Sciences* 5 (1982):187–195.

Petrini, F., et al. *The Information Problem of an Agricultural College.* Uppsala, Sweden: Nordisk Jordbrukforkning, 1968, 50.

Pickett, G. M., Kangun, N., and S. J. Grove. "Is There a General Conserving Consumer? A Public Policy Concern." *Journal of Public Policy and Marketing* 12 (1993):234–243.

Piliavin, J. A., Grube, J. A., and P. L. Callero. "Role as a Resource for Action in Public Service." *Journal of Social Issues* 58 (2002):469–485.

Pliner, P., et al. "Compliance without Pressure: Some Further Data on the Foot-in-the-Door Technique." *Journal of Experimental Social Psychology* 10 (1974):17–22.

"Power in America: Wealth, Income, and Power." *Who Rules America?* 2010. 21 Feb 2010. <http://sociology.ucsc.edu/whorulesamerica/power/wealth.html>.

"Prevalence of Overweight, Obesity and Extreme Obesity among Adults: United States, Trends 1960–62 through 2005–2006." Centers for Disease Control and Prevention: NCHS Health E-Stat. 2006. 1 Mar 2010. <www.cdc.gov/nchs/data/hestat/overweight/overweight_adult.htm>.

Pruitt, D., and D. Johnson. "Mediation as an Aid to Face Saving in Negotiation." *Journal of Personality and Social Psychology* 14.3 (1970):239–246.

"Public Lukewarm on Animal Rights." David W. Moore. 2003. 2 Mar 2010. <www.Gallup.Com/Poll/8461/Public-Lukewarm-Animal rights.aspx>.

"Rank-Size Distribution." *Wikipedia.* 2010. Wikimedia Foundation, Inc. 20 Feb 2010. <http://en.wikipedia.org/wiki/rank-size_distribution>.

Razran, G. H. "Conditioning Away Social Bias by the Luncheon Technique." *Psychology Bulletin* 35 (1938):693.

———. "Conditional Response Changes in Rating and Appraising Sociopolitical Slogans." *Psychological Bulletin* 37 (1940):481.

Redelmeier, D., and E. Shafir. "Medical Decision-making in Situations that Offer Multiple Alternatives." *Journal of the American Medical Association* 273.4 (1995).

Regan, D. "Effects of a Favor and Liking on Compliance." *Journal of Experimental Social Psychology* 7.6 (1971):627–639.

Reinhart, Amber, and T. Feeley. "Comparing the Persuasive Effects of Narrative Versus Statistical Messages: A Meta-Analytic Review." Paper Presented at the Annual Meeting of the NCA 93rd Annual Convention, Chicago, Nov 15, 2007.

"Residential Sprinkler Myths and Facts: The Arguments against Sprinklers." *U.S. Fire Administration.* 2009. 1 Mar 2010. <www.usfa.dhs.gov/citizens/all_citizens/home_fire_prev/sprinklers/facts.shtm>.

Rhodewalt, F., and S. Agustsdottir. "Effects of Self-Presentation on the Phenomenal Self." *Journal of Personality and Social Psychology* 50.1 (1986):47–55.

Richins M. L., and S. Dawson. "Materialism as a Consumer Value: Measure Development and Validation." *Journal of Consumer Research* 19 (1992):303–316.

Riemsma, R., Pattenden, J., Bridle, C., Sowden, A., Mather, L., Watt, I., and A. Walker. "Systematic Review of the Effectiveness of Stage Based Interventions to Promote Smoking Cessation." *British Medical Journal* 326 (2003):1175–1181.

Ritov, I., Baron, J. "Status-Quo and Omission Biases." *Journal of Risk and Uncertainty* 5.1 (1992):49–61.

"Robocop." *Wikipedia.* 2010. 30 May 2010. <http://en.wikipedia.org/wiki/robocop_%28character%29>

Rogers, E. M. *Diffusion of Innovations.* New York: Simon and Schuster Inc., 1983.

Rogers, E. M., and F. Shoemaker. *Communication of Innovations: A Cross-Cultural Approach.* New York: Free Press, 1971.

Rogers, R. W., and R. C. Mewborn. "Fear appeals and Attitude Change: Effects of a Threat's Noxiousness, Probability of Occurrence, and the Efficacy of Coping Responses." *Journal of Personality and Social Psychology* 34 (1976):54–61.

Rosenhan, D. K., Salovey, P., and K. Hargis. "The Joys of Helping: Focus of Attention Mediates the Impact of Positive Affect on Altruism." *Journal of Personality and Social Psychology* 40 (1981):899–905.

Ross, C. "Rejected." *New West.* (1979, February 12):39–43.

Rothman, A. J., Salovey, P., Antone, C., Keough, K., and C. D. Martin. "The Influence of Message Framing on Intentions to Perform Health Behaviors." *Journal of Experimental Social Psychology* 29 (1993):408–433.

Ryan, Bryce, and N. C. Gross. "The Diffusion of Hybrid Seed Corn in Two Iowa Communities." *Rural Sociology* 8 (1943):15–24.

Samuelson, W., and R. Zeckhauser. "Status Quo Bias in Decision-making." *Journal of Risk and Uncertainty* 1.1 (1988):7–59.

Sarason, I. G., Sarason, B. R., Pierce, G. R., Shearin, E. N., and M. H. Sayers. "A Social Learning Approach to Increasing Blood Donations." *Journal of Applied Social Psychology* 21 (1991).

Saunders, S., and D. Munro. "The Construction and Validation of a Consumer Orientation Questionnaire (SCOI) Designed to Measure Fromm's (1995) 'Marketing Character' in Australia." *Social Behavior and Personality: An International Journal* 28.3 (2000):219–240.

Schindler, R. "Consequences of Perceiving Oneself as Responsible for Obtaining a Discount: Evidence for Smart-Shopper Feelings." *Journal of Consumer Psychology* 7.4 (1998):371–392.

Schlenker, B., and J. Trudeau. "Impact of Self-Presentations on Private Self-Beliefs: Effects of Prior Self-Beliefs and Misattribution." *Journal of Personality and Social Psychology* 58.1 (1990):22–32.

Schultz, P., Nolan, J., Cialdini, R., Goldstein, N., and V. Griskevicius. "The Constructive, Destructive, and Reconstructive Power of Social Norms." *Psychological Science* 18 (2007):429–434.

Schultz, P. W., Gouveia, V. V., Cameron, L. D., Tankha, G., Schmuck, P., and M. Franek. "Values and Their Relationship to Environmental Concern and Conservation Behaviour." *Journal of Cross-Cultural Psychology* 36 (2005):457–475.

Schwartz, S. H. "Universals in the Content and Structure of Values: Theoretical Advances and Empirical Tests in 20 Countries." *Advances In Experimental Social Psychology* 25 (1992):1–62.

Schwarz, N., Sanna, L., Skurnik, I., and C. Yoon. "Metacognitive Experiences and the Intricacies of Setting People Straight: Implications for Debiasing and Public Information Campaigns." *Advances in Experimental Social Psychology* 39 (2007):127–161.

Schwarzwald, J., Raz, M., and M. Zvibel. "The Efficacy of the Door in the Face Technique When Established Behavioral Customs Exist." *Journal of Applied Social Psychology* 9 (1979):576–586.

Schweitzer, M. "Disentangling Status Quo and Omission Effects: An Experimental Analysis." *Organizational Behavior and Human Decision Process* 58 (1994):457–476.

"Security and Prosperity Partnership Myths Vs. Facts." *Security and Prosperity Partnership of North America.* 2005. 1 Mar 2010. <www.spp.gov/myths_vs_facts.asp>.

Seligman, C., and J. Darley. "Feedback as a Means of Decreasing Residential Energy Consumption." *Journal of Applied Psychology* 62 (1977):363–368.

Settle, R. B., and L. L. Godon. "Attribution Theory and Advertiser Credibility." *Journal of Marketing Research* 11 (1974):181–185.

Shafir, E., and R. Leboeuf. "Rationality." *Annual Review of Psychology* 53 (2002):491–517.

Shaw, L. L., Batson, C. D., and R. M. Todd. "Empathy Avoidance: Forestalling Feeling for Another in Order to Escape the Motivational Consequences." *Journal of Personality and Social Psychology* 67.5 (1994):879–887.

Sherif, C. W., Sherif, M., and R. E. Nebergall. *Attitude and Attitude Change.* Philadelphia: W. B. Saunders Company, 1965.

Sherif, M. "An Experimental Approach to the Study of Attitudes." *Sociometry* 1.1 (1937):90–98.

Sherman, S. J. "On the Self-Erasing Nature of Errors of Prediction." *Journal of Personality and Social Psychology* 39 (1980):211–221.

Simons, C. W., and J. A. Piliavin. "Effect of Deception on Reactions to a Victim." *Journal of Personality and Social Psychology* 21.1 (1972):56–60.

Skrunik, I., Yoon, C., Park, D., and N. Schwarz. "How Warnings about False Claims Become Recommendations." *Journal of Consumer Research* 31.4 (2005).

Small, D., Loewenstein, G., and P. Slovic. "Can Insight Breed Callousness? The Impact of Learning about the Identifiable Victim Effect on Sympathy." Working Paper. University of Pennsylvania, 2005.

Smith, G. H., and S. D. Hunt. "Attributional Processes in Promotional Situations." *Journal of Consumer Research* 5 (1978):149–158.

"Social Graph." Facebook Inc., 2010. <http://apps.facebook.com/socgraph/>.

Sorrentino, R. M., and J. E. Hardy. "Religiousness and Derogation of an Innocent Victim." *Journal of Personality*. 42.3. (2006):372–382.

Stangor, C., Sechrist, G., and J. Jost. "Changing Racial Beliefs by Providing Consensus Information." *Personality and Social Psychology Bulletin* 27.4 (2001):486–496.

Stangor, Charles, and Diane Ruble. "Strength of Expectancies and Memory for Social Information: What We Remember Depends on How Much We Know." *Journal of Experimental Social Psychology* 25.1 (1989) 18–35.

"Statement of Commander's Intent, Vision and Philosophy." *United States Marine Corps.* 2010. 9 June 2010. <www.usmc.mil/unit/2ndmaw/mag29/hmla269/pages/documents/269commandphilosophyhackett.pdf>.

Stewart, J. E., II. "Defendant's Attractiveness as a Factor in the Outcome of Trials." *Journal of Applied Social Psychology* 10 (1980):348–361.

Stone, J. T. *How Country Agricultural Agents Teach.* Mimeo Bulletin. East Lansing: Michigan State University, Agricultural Extension Service, 1952.

Stone, J., Aronson, E., Crain, A. L., Winslow, M. P., and C. B. Fried. "Inducing Hypocrisy as a Means of Encouraging Young Adults to Use Condoms." *Personality and Social Psychology Bulletin* 20 (1994):116–128.

Stotland, E. "Exploratory Investigations of Empathy." In *Advances in Experimental Social Psychology*. Ed. L. Berkowitz. New York: Academic Press, 1969. Vol. 4, 271–313.

Strohmetz, D., Rind, B., Fisher, R., and M. Lynn. "Sweetening the Till: The Use of

Candy to Increase Restaurant Tipping." *Journal of Applied Social Psychology* 32.2 (2002):300–309.

"Survey: Foundations Often Rely on Anecdotes to Assess Impact." *Mass Nonprofit.* N.P., 24 Dec 2009. Web. 1 May 2010. <www.massnonprofit.org/news. php?artid=1763&catid=13>.

Swap, W. C. "Interpersonal Attraction and Repeated Exposure to Rewards and Punishers." *Personality and Social Psychology Bulletin* 3 (1977):248–251.

Thaler, R. H., and C. R. Sunstein. *Nudge: Improving Decisions about Health, Wealth, and Happiness.* New Haven: Yale University Press, 2008.

"The Size of Social Networks." *The Economist.* 26 Feb. 2009.

"The Stanford Prison Experiment." Philip G. Zimbardo. 1999–2000. 1 Mar. 2010. <www.prisonexp.org>.

"The Vaccine-Autism Link: Facts and Myths." ABC News Internet Ventures. 2007. 1 Mar 2010. <http://abcnews.go.com/health/story?id=3266085&page=1>.

Thøgersen, J. "Spillover Process in the Development of a Sustainable Consumption Pattern." *Journal of Economic Psychology* 20 (1999):53–81.

Thøgersen, J., and F. Olander. "Spillover of Environment-Friendly Consumer Behavior." *Journal of Environmental Psychology* 23 (2003):225–236.

Thøgersen, J., and T. Crompton. "Simple and Painless? The Limitations of Spillover in Environmental Campaigning." *Journal of Consumer Policy* 13.2 (2009):24.

Thompson, C. "Are Your Friends Making You Fat?" *The New York Times Magazine.* 10 Sept. 2009.

Tormata, Z., Petty, R., and P. Briñol. "Ease of Retrieval Effects in Persuasion: A Self-Validation Analysis." *Personality and Social Psychology Bulletin* 28.2 (2002):1700–1712.

Travers, J., and S. Milgram. "An Experimental Study of the Small World Problem." *Sociometry* 32.4. (1969):425–443.

Tversky, A., and D. Kahneman. "Loss-aversion in Riskless Choice: A Reference-Dependent Model." *Quarterly Journal of Economics* 106.4 (1991):1039–1061.

Tybout, A., and R. Yalch. "The Effect of Experience: A Matter of Salience?" *Journal of Consumer Research* 6.4 (1980):406–413.

Vallacher, R. R., and D. M. Wegner. *A Theory of Action.* Hillsdale, N.J.: Lawrence Erlbaum, 1985.

Van Baaren, R., Holland, R., Steenaert, B., and A. Van Knippenberg. "Mimicry for Money: Behavioral Consequences of Imitation." *Journal of Experimental Social Psychology* 39.4 (2003):393–398.

Vangelisti, A. L., Daly, J. A., and J. R. Rudnick. "Making People Feel Guilty in Conversations: Techniques and Correlates." *Human Communication Research* 18 (1991):3–39.

"Vegetarianism in America." 2010. 20 Feb. 2010. *Vegetarian Times.* Cruz Bay Publishing, Inc. <www.vegetariantimes.com/features/archive_of_editorial/667>.

Walster, E. "Assignment of Responsibility for an Accident." *Journal of Personality and Social Psychology* 3.1 (1966):73–79.

Wang, T., and R. Katzev. "Group Commitment and Resource Conservation: Two Field Experiments on Promoting Recycling." *Journal of Applied Social Psychology* 20 (1990):265–275.

Watts, W., and L. E. Holt. "Persistence of Opinion Change Induced Under Conditions of Forewarning and Distraction." *Journal of Personality and Social Psychology* 37.5 (1979):778–789.

Weaver, K., Garcia, S. M., Schwarz, N., and D. T. Miller. "Inferring the Popularity of an Opinion from Its Familiarity: A Repetitive Voice Can Sound Like a Chorus." *Journal of Personality and Social Psychology* 92.5 (2007):821–833.

Webley, P., Burgoyne, C. B., Lea, S. E. G., and B. M. Young. *The Economic Psychology of Everyday Life.* New York: Psychology Press, 2001.

Weibe, G. D. "Merchandising Commodities and Citizenship on Television." *Public Opinion Quarterly* 15 (1952):679–91.

Weinstein, N. D. "The Precaution Adoption Process." *Health Psychology* 7.4 (1988):355–386.

Wells, G., and R. Petty. "The Effect of Over Head Movements on Persuasion: Compatibility and Incompatibility of Responses." *Basic and Applied Social Psychology* 1.3 (1980):219–230.

Werner, C. M. *et al.* "Commitment, Behavior, and Attitude Change: An Analysis of Voluntary Recycling." *Journal of Environmental Psychology* 15 (1995):197–208.

Werner, C., Rhodes, M., and K. Partain. "Designing Effective Instructional Signs With Schema Theory: Case Studies of Polystyrene Recycling." *Environment and Behavior* 30 (1998) 709.

Whitley, B., and M. Kite. *The Psychology of Prejudice and Discrimination.* Wadsworth Publishing, 2005.

Whittaker, J. "Social Pressure in the Modification and Distortion of Judgment: A Cross-Cultural Study." *International Journal of Psychology* 2.2 (1967):109–113.

Wicklund, R. A., *Freedom and Reactance.* Hillsdale, N.J.: Lawrence Erlbaum, 1974.

Wilson, D. W. "Is Helping a Laughing Matter?" *Psychology* 18 (1981):6–9.

Wilson, P. "Perceptual Distortion of Height as a Function of Ascribed Academic Status." *The Journal of Social Psychology* 74.1 (1968):97–102.

Winett, R., *et al.* "Effects of Television Modeling on Residential Energy Conservation." *Journal of Applied Behavior Analysis* 18 (1985):33–44.

Wood, W., and J. Quinn. "Forewarned and Forearmed? Two Meta-Analysis Syntheses of Forewarnings of Influence Appeals." *Psychological Bulletin* 129.1 (2003):119–138.

Wood, W., Lundgren, S., Ouellette, J. A., Busceme, S., and T. Blackstone. "Minority Influence: A Meta-Analytical Review of Social Influence Processes." *Psychological Bulletin* 115 (1994):323–345.

Woodside, A. G., and J. W. Davenport. "Effects of Salesman Similarity and Expertise on Consumer Purchasing Behavior." *Journal of Marketing Research* 11 (1974) 198–202.

Worchel, S., and S. E. Arnold. "The Effects of Censorship and the Attractiveness of the Censor on Attitude Change." *Journal of Experimental Social Psychology* 9 (1973):365–377.

Worchel, S., Arnold, S. E., and M. Baker. "The Effect of Censorship on Attitude Change: The Influence of Censor and Communicator Characteristics." *Journal of Applied Social Psychology* 5 (1975):222–239.

Workman, M. "Gaining Access with Social Engineering: An Empirical Study of the Threat." *Information Systems Security* 16 (2007):315–331.

Young, F. W. *Initiation Ceremonies.* New York: Bobbs-Merrill, 1965.

Zajonc, R. B. "The Attitudinal Effects of Mere Exposure." *Journal of Personality and Social Psychology Monographs* 9.2 (1968).

NOTES

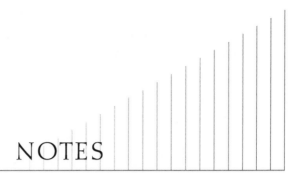

1 Just kidding!

2 This dead zone was created by waste runoff from animal agriculture in the central U.S. The waste drains from water tables into the Mississippi River and is carried downstream into the Gulf of Mexico. According to the U.S. Environmental Protection Agency, animal agriculture is the leading cause of water pollution in America.

3 For the record, those people and places are fictitious but the statement is true.

4 Here's the math if you're curious, and we'll call the new vegetarian John Doe. Our sample size is 1,110 people. These are John's 10 friends, each of their ten friends (100 people), and each of their ten friends (1,000 people). 10 plus 100 plus 1000 gives us 1,110 people within three degrees of separation from the new vegetarian. (Though this certainly wouldn't exist in the real world, for the sake of the exercise we'll assume that John's friends—like everyone else's friends—don't know one another, so there's no overlap in friend circles.) If John had not gone vegetarian, the likelihood that those 1110 others would go vegetarian would be a uniform 3 percent. 1,110 people x .03 = 33.3, so about 33 of the people in that group would probably go vegetarian at some point in their lives. Now, let's see what happens when the person at the center of this social network does go vegetarian. The first 10 people (John's immediate friends) now have a 4 percent chance of going vegetarian, meaning .4 of them will go veg. The next 100 people (John's friends' friends) have a 3.5 percent chance of going vegetarian, meaning 3.5 of them will. And the next 1,000 people (John's friends' friends' friends) have a 3.2 percent chance of going vegetarian, meaning 32 of them will make the switch. Add up the .4, 3.5, and 32 people, and

you have 35.9 new vegetarians. That's about 2.6 more vegetarians than if John had not made the switch, meaning that in choosing to go vegetarian he led about two- and-a- half others to do the same. Of course, in the real world friends overlap, so the actual number of people who would go vegetarian (whether John does or doesn't) would be reduced. But it's clear that John's decision to go vegetarian makes it more likely that others will go vegetarian as well.

ABOUT THE AUTHOR

NICK COONEY is the founder and director of The Humane League, an animal advocacy organization based in Philadelphia, Pennsylvania, that focuses on farm animal-protection issues. Nick has written for publications including *The Philadelphia Inquirer* and *Z Magazine*, and his advocacy work has been featured in hundreds of media outlets including *Time Magazine*, the *Wall Street Journal*, and National Public Radio. Nick holds a degree in Non-Violence Studies from Hofstra University and formerly worked conducting nutrition-education programs with the University of Pennsylvania's Urban Nutrition Initiative.

Of Related Interest from Lantern Books

The Lifelong Activist
How to Change the World without Losing Your Way
Hillary Rettig
9781590560907

The Animal Activist's Handbook
Maximizing Our Positive Impact in Today's World
Matt Ball and Bruce Friedrich
9781590561201

Move the Message
Your Guide to Making a Difference and Changing the World
Josephine Bellaccomo
9781590560297

www.lanternbooks.com